WILEY PLUS

for *Accounting Principles,* Fourth Canadian Edition

Check with your instructor to find out if you have access to *WileyPLUS*!

Study More Effectively with a Multimedia Text

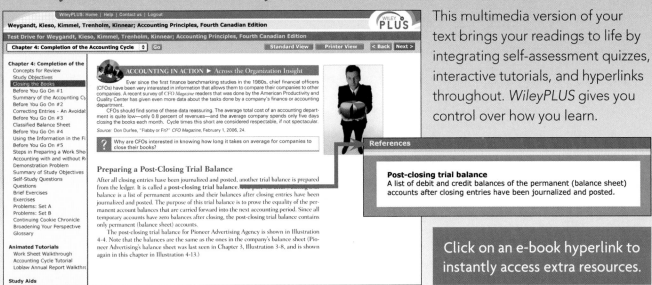

This multimedia version of your text brings your readings to life by integrating self-assessment quizzes, interactive tutorials, and hyperlinks throughout. *WileyPLUS* gives you control over how you learn.

Click on an e-book hyperlink to instantly access extra resources.

Grasp key concepts by exploring the various interactive tools in Read, Study & Practice.

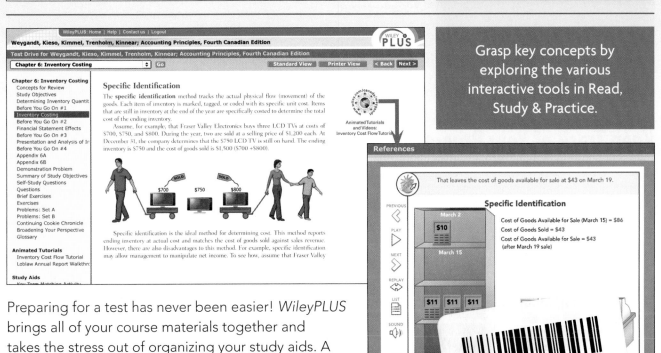

Preparing for a test has never been easier! *WileyPLUS* brings all of your course materials together and takes the stress out of organizing your study aids. A streamlined study routine saves you time and lets you focus on learning.

for *Accounting Principles,* Fourth Canadian Edition

Complete and Submit Assignments On-line Efficiently

Your homework questions contain links to the relevant section of the multimedia text, so you know exactly where to go to get help solving each problem. In addition, use the Assignment area of *WileyPLUS* to monitor all of your assignments and their due dates.

Your instructor can assign homework online for automatic grading and you can keep up-to-date on your assignments with your assignment list.

Keep Track of Your Progress

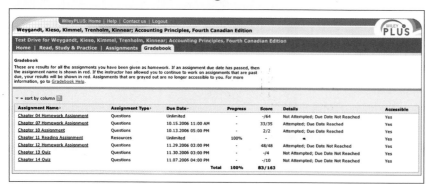

Your personal Gradebook lets you review your answers and results from past assignments as well as any feedback your instructor may have for you.

Keep track of your progress and review your completed questions at any time.

Technical Support: http://higheredwiley.custhelp.com
Student Resource Centre: http://www.wileyplus.com

For further information regarding *WileyPLUS* and other Wiley products, please visit www.wiley.ca.

ACCOUNTING PRINCIPLES

FOURTH CANADIAN EDITION

ACCOUNTING

PRINCIPLES

▶ **Jerry J. Weygandt** *Ph.D., C.P.A.*

Arthur Andersen Alumni Professor of Accounting
University of Wisconsin – Madison

▶ **Donald E. Kieso** *Ph.D., C.P.A.*

KPMG Peat Marwick Emeritus Professor of Accounting
Northern Illinois University

▶ **Paul D. Kimmel** *Ph.D., C.P.A.*

University of Wisconsin – Milwaukee

▶ **Barbara Trenholm** *M.B.A., F.C.A.*

University of New Brunswick – Fredericton

▶ **Valerie A. Kinnear** *M.Sc. (Bus. Admin.), C.A.*

Mount Royal College

John Wiley & Sons Canada, Ltd.

To our students – past, present, and future

Library and Archives Canada Cataloguing in Publication

Accounting principles / Jerry J. Weygandt ... [et al.].

4th Canadian ed.

Includes index.

ISBN 978-0-470-83858-7 (pt. 1)
ISBN 978-0-470-83860-0 (pt. 2)
ISBN 978-0-470-83861-7 (pt. 3)

1. Accounting--Textbooks. I. Weygandt, Jerry J.

HF5635.A3778 2006   657'.044   C2006-906471-7

Production Credits

Editorial Manager: Karen Staudinger
Publishing Services Director: Karen Bryan
Media Editor: Elsa Passera Berardi
Editorial Assistant: Sheri Coombs
Director of Marketing: Isabelle Moreau
Design & Typesetting: OrangeSprocket Communications
Cover Design: Interrobang Graphic Design
Bicentennial Logo Design: Richard J. Pacifico
Printing & Binding: Quebecor World Inc.

Printed and bound in the United States
1 2 3 4 5 QW 11 10 09 08 07

John Wiley & Sons Canada, Ltd.
6045 Freemont Blvd.
Mississauga, Ontario L5R 4J3
Visit our website at: www.wiley.ca

CONTENTS—PART TWO

concepts for review >>

Before studying this chapter, you should understand or, if necessary, review:

a. How to record revenue. (Ch. 3, pp. 106–107 and Ch. 5, pp. 231–234)

b. Why adjusting entries are made. (Ch. 3, pp. 108–109)

c. How to calculate interest. (Ch. 3, p. 117)

Personal Touch Helps Keep Receivables Healthy

Whitehill Technologies: www.whitehilltech.com

MONCTON, N.B.—Since its founding in 1997, Whitehill Technologies has grown from just two employees to a staff of more than 100 and annual sales of more than $11 million. Today, the company's software—which enables companies in the financial services, legal, and insurance sectors to create business documents from data stored on older systems—is used by nearly 700 clients in 45 countries.

Whitehill's revenue comes from software licence sales, services such as installation, training, and template customization, and ongoing maintenance. The company usually has about $2.5 million in accounts receivable at any time.

"We bill for licence fees up front—they're due upon receipt—and our regular terms for services and maintenance are n/30," explains Paul Gunn, Whitehill's VP of Finance and Administration. "With our resellers, it's a little different—we have some that settle quarterly and others that settle monthly."

Contrary to some large companies, Whitehill does not charge interest for amounts past due; nor does it offer discounts for early payment. As Mr. Gunn points out, the fact that the company has "the ability to cut off support" is usually enough to encourage payment on time.

The company uses a weekly aging report to keep track of its receivables. "When an invoice is nearing 30 days, we will initiate contact with the client, usually by telephone or e-mail to make sure it's in their system," explains Mr. Gunn. "If it gets on to 45 days, we would talk with our project manager and look for an additional contact in the organization."

An account over 90 days goes on a red flag list. "At that point, senior management would likely get involved," says Mr. Gunn. But by keeping personal contact every step of the way, he adds, the company usually gets customers to pay long before that happens. Still, the company records an estimate for bad debts every year.

"When Whitehill was starting out and growing, accounts receivable collections provided our lifeblood (cash)," says Mr. Gunn. "As we have grown and become stronger financially, we've continued to manage our receivables with the same level of diligence and attention." With receivables, the key is to stay on top of them at all times by having a process for dealing with them at whatever stage they're at.

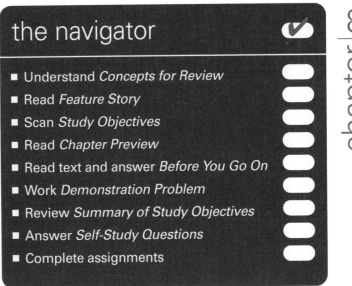

the navigator

■ Understand *Concepts for Review*
■ Read *Feature Story*
■ Scan *Study Objectives*
■ Read *Chapter Preview*
■ Read text and answer *Before You Go On*
■ Work *Demonstration Problem*
■ Review *Summary of Study Objectives*
■ Answer *Self-Study Questions*
■ Complete assignments

chapter 8

Accounting for Receivables

study objectives >>

After studying this chapter, you should be able to:

1. Record accounts receivable transactions.
2. Calculate the net realizable value of accounts receivable and account for bad debts.
3. Account for notes receivable.
4. Demonstrate the presentation, analysis, and management of receivables.

As indicated in our feature story, management of receivables is important for any company that sells on credit, as Whitehill Technologies does. In this chapter, we will first review the journal entries that companies make when goods and services are sold on account and when cash is collected from those sales. Next, we will learn how companies estimate, record, and then, in some cases, collect their uncollectible accounts. We will also learn about notes receivable.

The chapter is organized as follows:

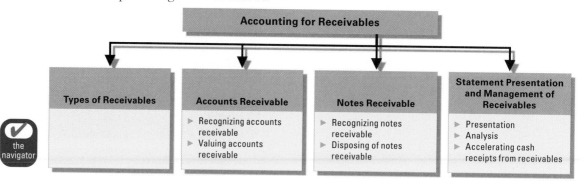

Types of Receivables

The term "receivables" refers to amounts due from individuals and other companies. They are claims that are expected to be collected in cash. The two most common types of receivables are accounts receivable and notes receivable.

Accounts receivable are amounts owed by customers on account. They result from the sale of goods and services. These receivables are generally expected to be collected within 30 days or so, and are classified as current assets. They are usually the most significant type of claim held by a company.

Notes receivable are claims for which formal instruments of credit are issued as proof of the debt. A note normally requires the debtor to pay interest and extends for periods of 30 days or longer. Notes receivable may be either current assets or long-term assets, depending on their due dates. Notes and accounts receivable that result from sale transactions are often called **trade receivables**.

Other receivables include interest receivable, loans or advances to employees, and recoverable sales and income taxes. These receivables are generally classified and reported as separate items in the current or noncurrent sections of the balance sheet, according to their due dates.

Accounts Receivable

Two important accounting issues for accounts receivable—recognizing accounts receivable and valuing accounts receivable—will be discussed in this section. A third issue—accelerating cash receipts from receivables—is discussed later in the chapter.

Recognizing Accounts Receivable

study objective 1

Record accounts receivable transactions.

Recognizing accounts receivable is relatively straightforward. For a service company, a receivable is recorded when the service is provided on account. For a merchandising company, a receivable is recorded at the point of sale of merchandise on account. Recall that in Chapter 5 we also saw how accounts receivable are reduced by sales returns and allowances and sales discounts.

To review, assume that Adorable Junior Garment sells merchandise on account to Zellers on July 1 for $1,000 with payment terms of 2/10, n/30. On July 4, Zellers returns merchandise worth $100 to Adorable Junior Garment. On July 10, Adorable Junior Garment receives payment from Zellers for the balance due. Assume Adorable Junior Garment uses a periodic inventory system. The journal entries to record these transactions on the books of Adorable Junior Garment are as follows:

July 1	Accounts Receivable—Zellers	1,000	
	Sales		1,000
	To record sale of merchandise on account.		
4	Sales Returns and Allowances	100	
	Accounts Receivable—Zellers		100
	To record merchandise returned.		
10	Cash [($1,000 − $100) × 98%]	882	
	Sales Discounts [($1,000 − $100) × 2%]	18	
	Accounts Receivable—Zellers		900
	To record collection of accounts receivable.		

A	=	L	+	OE
+1,000				+1,000

Cash flows: no effect

A	=	L	+	OE
−100				−100

Cash flows: no effect

A	=	L	+	OE
+882				−18
−900				

↑ Cash flows: +882

If Adorable Junior Garment used a perpetual inventory system, a second journal entry to record the cost of the goods sold (and the cost of the goods returned) would be required for the July 1 and July 4 transactions.

Subsidiary Accounts Receivable Ledger

Adorable Junior Garment does not have only Zellers as a customer. It has hundreds of customers. If it recorded the accounts receivable for each of these customers in only one general ledger account, as we did above in Accounts Receivable, it would be hard to determine the balance owed by a specific customer, such as Zellers, at a specific point in time.

Instead, most companies that sell on account use a subsidiary ledger to keep track of individual customer accounts. As we learned in Chapter 5, a subsidiary ledger gives supporting detail to the general ledger. Illustration 8-1 on the next page shows an accounts receivable control account and subsidiary ledger, using assumed data.

Each entry that affects accounts receivable is basically posted twice—once to the subsidiary ledger and once to the general ledger. Normally entries to the subsidiary ledger are posted daily, while entries to the general ledger are summarized and posted monthly. For example, the $1,000 sale to Zellers was posted to Zellers' account in the subsidiary ledger on July 1. It was also summarized with other sales entries (Kids Online $6,000 + Snazzy Kids $3,000 + Zellers $1,000 = $10,000) in a special sales journal and posted to the accounts receivable control account in the general ledger at the end of the month, on July 31.

Collections on account (Kids Online $4,000 + Snazzy Kids $1,000 + Zellers $900 = $5,900) were also posted individually to the subsidiary ledger accounts and summarized and posted in total to the general ledger account. Non-recurring entries, such as the sales return of $100, are posted to both the subsidiary and general ledgers individually.

Note that the balance of $4,000 in the control account agrees with the total of the balances in the individual accounts receivable accounts in the subsidiary ledger (Kids Online $2,000 + Snazzy Kids $2,000 + Zellers $0). There is more information about how subsidiary ledgers work in Appendix C at the end of this textbook.

| | GENERAL LEDGER | | | | | |

Accounts Receivable is a control account.

Accounts Receivable   No. 112

Date	Explanation	Ref.	Debit	Credit	Balance
2007					
July 4				100	(100)
31			10,000		9,900
31				5,900	4,000 ◀

| | ACCOUNTS RECEIVABLE SUBSIDIARY LEDGER | | | | |

The subsidiary ledger is separate from the general ledger.

Kids Online   No. 112-203

Date	Explanation	Ref.	Debit	Credit	Balance
2007					
July 11	Invoice 1310		6,000		6,000
19	Payment			4,000	2,000 ◀

Snazzy Kids Co.   No. 112-413

Date	Explanation	Ref.	Debit	Credit	Balance
2007					
July 12	Invoice 1318		3,000		3,000
21	Payment			1,000	2,000 ◀

Zellers Inc.   No. 112-581

Date	Explanation	Ref.	Debit	Credit	Balance
2007					
July 1	Invoice 1215		1,000		1,000
4	Credit memo 1222			100	900
10	Payment			900	0 ◀

Interest Revenue

At the end of each month, the company can use the subsidiary ledger to easily determine the transactions that occurred in each customer's account during the month and then send the customer a statement of transactions for the month. If the customer does not pay in full within a specified period (usually 30 days), most retailers add an interest (financing) charge to the balance due. Interest rates vary from company to company, but rates for retailers can be as high as 28.8 percent per year.

When financing charges are added, the seller recognizes interest revenue. If Kids Online still owes $2,000 at the end of the next month, August 31, and Adorable Junior Garment charges 18 percent on the balance due, the entry that Adorable Junior Garment will make to record interest revenue of $30 ($2,000 × 18% × $\frac{1}{12}$) is as follows:

A	=	L	+	OE
+30				+30

Cash flows: no effect

Aug. 31	Accounts Receivable—Kids Online	30	
	Interest Revenue		30
	To record interest on amount due.		

Although Whitehill Technologies in our feature story does not charge interest on its overdue accounts, interest revenue is often a significant amount for service and merchandising companies. As discussed in Chapter 5, interest revenue is included in other revenues in the non-operating section of the income statement.

Nonbank Credit Card Sales

In Chapter 7, we learned that debit and bank credit card sales are cash sales. Sales on credit cards that are not directly associated with a bank are reported as credit sales, not cash sales. Nonbank credit card sales result in an account receivable until the credit card company pays the amount owing to the seller.

To illustrate, assume that Kerr Music accepts a nonbank credit card on October 24 for a $500 bill. The entry for the sale by Kerr Music (assuming a 4% service fee) is:

Oct. 24	Accounts Receivable—Credit Card Company	480	
	Credit Card Expense ($500 × 4%)	20	
	Sales		500
	To record nonbank credit card sale.		

A	=	L	+	OE
+480				−20
				+500

Cash flows: no effect

When cash is received from the credit card company, Kerr Music will record this entry:

Nov. 7	Cash	480	
	Accounts Receivable––Credit Card Company		480
	To record redemption of credit card billing.		

A	=	L	+	OE
+480				
−480				

↑ Cash flows: +480

Advances in technology have created a rapidly changing credit card environment. Transactions and payments can be processed much more quickly, and often electronically, which reduces the time to collect cash from the credit card company. As collection time becomes shorter, credit card transactions are becoming more like cash transactions to the business.

How does a business know if it should debit Cash or Accounts Receivable when it processes a credit card transaction? Basically, it should consider how long it takes to collect the cash. If it takes longer than a few days to process the transaction and collect the cash, it should be treated as a credit sale as shown above.

Company credit cards, such as Petro-Canada and Canadian Tire, are always recorded as credit sales. When the credit card transaction results in an account receivable from the customer—as opposed to from the credit card company as shown above—the accounting treatment is the same as we have previously seen for accounts receivable.

Credit card expenses, along with debit cards expenses discussed in Chapter 7, are reported as an operating expense in the income statement.

ACCOUNTING IN ACTION ▶ Business Insight

The average interest rate on a bank credit card in Canada is 18 percent. Interest on non-bank cards, such as Petro-Canada, can be as high as 28.8 percent. The Bank of Canada interest rate is 4.5 percent. Why are credit card rates so much higher than other interest rates?

The Bank of Canada interest rate is called the "risk-free" rate. This means that, theoretically, money can be borrowed at 4.5 percent if there is no other credit risk. The difference between the Bank of Canada rate and credit card rates is called a "risk premium." Banks justify this higher interest rate by saying that credit cards are a greater risk. They argue that they have to cover their losses from fraud as well as their administrative costs.

? Since the interest rates on company credit cards are so high, why don't all companies have their own credit cards?

BEFORE YOU GO ON . . .

▶Review It

1. The stores that form the Forzani Group do not have their own company credit cards. Customers use cash, debit cards, or bank credit cards to pay for merchandise. Why then does the company report accounts receivable on its balance sheet? (*Hint:* See Note 2(h) on Revenue Recognition.) The answer to this question is at the end of the chapter.
2. What are the similarities and differences between a general ledger and a subsidiary ledger?
3. How is interest revenue calculated and recorded on late accounts receivable?
4. What are the differences between bank credit cards and nonbank credit cards?

▶Do It

Information for Kinholm Company follows for its first month of operations:

Credit Sales			Cash Collections		
Jan. 5	Sych Co.	$12,000	Jan. 16	Sych Co.	$9,000
9	Downey Inc.	5,000	22	Downey Inc.	3,500
13	Pawlak Co.	6,000	28	Pawlak Co.	6,000

Calculate (a) the balances that appear in the accounts receivable subsidiary ledger for each customer, and (b) the accounts receivable balance that appears in the general ledger at the end of January.

Action Plan

- Use T accounts as a simple method of calculating account balances.
- Create separate accounts for each customer and post their transactions to their accounts.
- Create one account for the Accounts Receivable control account.
- Post the total credit sales and the total cash collections to the general ledger.

Solution

ACCOUNTS RECEIVABLE SUBSIDIARY LEDGER

Sych Co.

Jan. 5	12,000	Jan. 16	9,000
Bal.	3,000		

Downey Inc.

Jan. 9	5,000	Jan. 22	3,500
Bal.	1,500		

Pawlak Co.

Jan. 13	6,000	Jan. 28	6,000
Bal.	0		

GENERAL LEDGER

Accounts Receivable

Jan. 31	23,000[a]	Jan. 31	18,500[b]
Bal.	4,500		

[a] $12,000 + $5,000 + $6,000 = $23,000
[b] $9,000 + $3,500 + $6,000 = $18,500

Related exercise material: BE8–1, BE8–2, BE8–3, BE8–4, E8–1, E8–2, and E8–3.

Valuing Accounts Receivable

study objective 2

Calculate the net realizable value of accounts receivable and account for bad debts.

After receivables are recorded in the accounts, the next question is how these receivables should be reported on the balance sheet. Receivables are assets, but determining the amount to report as an asset is sometimes difficult because some receivables will become uncollectible. A receivable can only be reported as an asset if it will give a future benefit. This means that only collectible receivables can be reported as assets in the financial statements. This collectible amount is called the **net realizable value** of the receivables.

Whitehill Technologies in our feature story works closely with customers to collect its receivables. But even if each of Whitehill's customers satisfied Whitehill's credit requirements before the credit sale was approved, inevitably, some accounts receivable become uncollectible. For example, a usually reliable customer may suddenly not be able to pay because of an unexpected decrease in its revenues or because it is faced with unexpected bills.

You might be wondering why a company would sell goods or services on credit if there is a risk of not collecting the receivable. These companies are expecting that the increase in revenues and profit from selling on credit will be greater than any uncollectible accounts or credit losses. Such losses are considered a normal and necessary risk of doing business on a credit basis.

When receivables are written down to their net realizable value because of credit losses, owner's equity must also be reduced. This is done by recording an expense, known as **bad debts expense**, for the credit losses. The key issue in valuing accounts receivable is when to record these credit losses. If the company waits until it knows for sure that the specific account will not be collected, it could end up recording the bad debts expense in a different period than when the revenue is recorded.

Helpful hint Bad debts expense is also sometimes called *uncollectible account expense.*

Consider the following example. Assume that in 2007 Quick Buck Computer Company decides it could increase its revenues by offering computers to students without requiring any money down and with no credit approval process. On campuses across the country, it sells one million computers with a selling price of $700 each. This increases Quick Buck's revenues and receivables by $700 million. The promotion is a huge success! The 2007 balance sheet and income statement look great. Unfortunately, in 2008, nearly 40 percent of the student customers default on their accounts. This makes the year 2008 income statement and balance sheet look terrible. Illustration 8-2 shows that the promotion in 2007 was not such a great success after all.

Year 2007	**Year 2008**
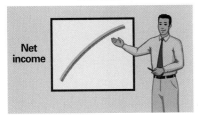	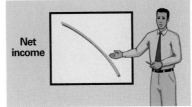
Huge sales promotion. Sales increase dramatically. Accounts receivable increase dramatically.	Customers default on loans. Bad debts expense increases dramatically. Accounts receivable drop dramatically.

Illustration 8-2 ◀

Effects of mismatching bad debts

If credit losses are not recorded until they occur, bad debts expense is not matched to sales revenues in the income statement. Recall that the matching principle requires expenses to be recorded in the same period as the sales they helped generate. Quick Buck Computer Company's income was overstated in 2007 and understated in 2008 because we did not match the bad debts expense with sales revenue.

In addition, the accounts receivable in the balance sheet are not reported at the amount that is actually expected to be received. Consequently, Quick Buck Computer's receivables are overstated at the end of 2007, which misrepresents the amount that should have been reported as an asset.

To avoid this mismatch, we therefore cannot wait until we know exactly which receivables are uncollectible. Instead, in the accounting period where the sales occur, we must estimate the uncollectible accounts receivable. Because we do not know which specific accounts receivable will need to be written off, we use what is known as the allowance method.

The **allowance method** of accounting for bad debts estimates uncollectible accounts at the end of each accounting period. This gives better matching of expenses with revenues on the income statement because credit losses that are expected to happen from sales or service revenue in that accounting period are recorded in the same accounting period as when the revenue was earned. It also ensures that receivables are stated at their net realizable value on the balance sheet. It removes the amounts that the company estimates it will not collect.

The allowance method is required for financial reporting purposes when bad debts are material (significant) in amount. It has three essential features:

1. Recording estimated uncollectibles: The amount of uncollectible accounts receivable is estimated at the end of the accounting period. This estimate is treated as bad debts expense and is matched against revenues in the accounting period where the revenues are recorded.
2. Recording the write-off of an uncollectible account: Actual uncollectibles are written off when the specific account is determined to be uncollectible.
3. Recovery of an uncollectible account: When an account that was previously written off is later collected, the original write-off is reversed and the collection is recorded.

We will see that neither the write-off nor the later recovery affect the income statement, and matching is therefore not affected by the timing of these entries.

1. Recording Estimated Uncollectibles

To illustrate the allowance method, assume that Adorable Junior Garment has net credit sales of $1.2 million in 2007. Of this amount, $200,000 remains uncollected at December 31. The credit manager estimates (using techniques we will discuss in the next section) that $24,000 of these receivables will be uncollectible. The adjusting entry to record the estimated uncollectible accounts is:

A	=	L	+	OE			
−24,000				−24,000			

Cash flows: no effect

Dec. 31	Bad Debts Expense	24,000	
	Allowance for Doubtful Accounts		24,000
	To record estimate of uncollectible accounts.		

Note that Bad Debts Expense is used, instead of debiting a contra sales account, as we did for sales returns and allowances. An expense account is used because the responsibilities for granting credit and collecting accounts are normally separated from sales and marketing. Bad Debts Expense is reported in the income statement as an operating expense. The estimated uncollectibles are matched with sales in 2007 because the expense is recorded in the year when the sales are made.

Also note that Allowance for Doubtful Accounts—a contra asset account—is used instead of a direct credit to Accounts Receivable. As mentioned earlier, this is mainly because we do not know which individual customers will not pay. We do not know which specific accounts to credit in the subsidiary ledger. Recall that subsidiary ledger accounts must balance with Accounts Receivable, the control account. This would not happen if the control account was credited and the subsidiary ledger accounts were not. Also, the estimate for uncollectibles is just an estimate. A contra account helps to separate estimates from actual amounts, such as those found in Accounts Receivable.

The account balance in Allowance for Doubtful Accounts is deducted from Accounts Receivable in the current assets section of the balance sheet. Assuming that Adorable Junior Garment has an unadjusted balance of $1,000 in Allowance for Doubtful Accounts, its ending balance of $25,000 ($1,000 + $24,000) would be reported as follows:

ADORABLE JUNIOR GARMENT
Balance Sheet (partial)
December 31, 2007

Current assets		
Cash		$ 14,800
Accounts receivable	$200,000	
Less: Allowance for doubtful accounts	25,000	175,000
Merchandise inventory		310,000
Prepaid expenses		25,000
Total current assets		524,800

The $25,000 in Allowance for Doubtful Accounts shows the receivables that are expected to become uncollectible in the future. The amount $175,000 is the expected net realizable value of the accounts receivable at the statement date. The $175,000 is added to cash, merchandise inventory, and prepaid expenses to calculate total current assets, and not the total accounts receivable.

The net realizable value can be presented by the formula shown in Illustration 8-3.

Accounts Receivable	−	Allowance for Doubtful Accounts	=	Net Realizable Value
$200,000	−	$25,000	=	$175,000

Illustration 8-3 ◀

Formula for calculating net realizable value

Estimating the Allowance. For Adorable Junior Garment, the amount of the expected bad debts expense in the journal entry on the previous page ($24,000) was given. But how was this estimate calculated? There are two approaches that most companies use to determine this amount: (1) percentage of sales, and (2) percentage of receivables.

Percentage of Sales Approach. The **percentage of sales approach** calculates bad debts expense as a percentage of net credit sales. Management determines the percentage based on past experience and the company's credit policy.

To illustrate, assume that Adorable Junior Garment decides to use the percentage of sales approach. It concludes that 2 percent of net credit sales will become uncollectible. Recall that net credit sales for the calendar year 2007 are $1.2 million. The estimated bad debts expense is $24,000 (2% × $1,200,000). The adjusting entry is:

Dec. 31	Bad Debts Expense	24,000	
	Allowance for Doubtful Accounts		24,000
	To record estimate of bad debts expense.		

A	=	L	+	OE
−24,000				−24,000

Cash flows: no effect

Recall that Allowance for Doubtful Accounts had a credit balance of $1,000 before the adjustment. After the adjusting entry is posted, the accounts will show the following:

Bad Debts Expense		Allowance for Doubtful Accounts	
Dec. 31 Adj. 24,000		Dec. 31 Bal. 1,000	
		31 Adj. 24,000	
		Dec. 31 Bal. 25,000	

Helpful hint Because the income statement is emphasized in the percentage of sales approach, the balance in the allowance account is not involved in calculating the bad debts expense in the adjusting entry.

When calculating the amount in the adjusting entry ($24,000), the existing balance in Allowance for Doubtful Accounts is ignored. But after posting the adjusting entry, the balance in Allowance for Doubtful Accounts should be a reasonable approximation of the uncollectible accounts receivable. If actual write-offs in the next year are very different from the amount that was estimated, a different percentage should be used in calculating the adjusting entry in future years.

This approach to estimating uncollectibles results in an excellent matching of expenses with revenues because the bad debts expense is related to the sales recorded in the same period. Because an income statement account (Sales) is used to calculate another income statement account (Bad Debts Expense), and any balance in the balance sheet account (Allowance for Doubtful Accounts) is ignored, this approach is often called the **income statement approach**.

The percentage of sales approach is quick and easy to use. This is why it is often used to update bad debts for interim reports.

Percentage of Receivables Approach. Under the **percentage of receivables approach**, management uses past experience to estimate the percentage of receivables that will become uncollectible accounts. The easiest way to do this is to multiply the total amount of accounts receivable by a percentage based on an overall estimate of the total uncollectible accounts.

Another way to calculate uncollectible accounts is to use different percentages depending on how long the accounts receivable have been outstanding. This way is more sensitive to the actual status of the accounts receivable. A schedule must be prepared, called an **aging schedule**, which shows the age of each account receivable. The longer a receivable is past due or outstanding, the less likely it is to be collected. The estimated percentage of uncollectible accounts therefore increases as the number of days outstanding increases.

After the ages of the different accounts receivable are determined, the loss from uncollectible accounts is estimated. This is done by applying percentages, based on past experience, to the totals in each category. An aging schedule for Adorable Junior Garment is shown in Illustration 8-4.

Illustration 8-4 ▶

Aging schedule

Customer	Total	Number of Days Outstanding				
		0–30	31–60	61–90	91–120	Over 120
Bansal Garments	$ 6,000		$ 3,000	$ 3,000		
Bortz Clothing	3,000	$ 3,000				
Kids Online	4,500				$ 2,000	$ 2,500
Snazzy Kids Co.	17,000	2,000	5,000	5,000	5,000	
Tykes n' Tots	26,500	10,000	10,000	6,000	500	
Zellers	42,000	32,000	10,000			
Wal-Mart	61,000	48,000	12,000	1,000		
Others	40,000	5,000	10,000	10,000	5,000	10,000
	$200,000	$100,000	$50,000	$25,000	$12,500	$12,500
Estimated percentage uncollectible		5%	10%	20%	30%	50%
Estimated uncollectible accounts	$ 25,000	$ 5,000	$ 5,000	$ 5,000	$ 3,750	$ 6,250

Note the increasing percentages from 5 percent to 50 percent. This percentage increase shows that there is more concern about an account being uncollectible as it gets older. We also saw this with Whitehill in our feature story. Whitehill puts accounts over 90 days on its "red flag list" and usually gets senior management involved in helping collect the account at that point.

The $25,000 total for Adorable Junior Garment's estimated uncollectible accounts is the amount of existing receivables that are expected to become uncollectible in the future. This amount is therefore the required balance in Allowance for Doubtful Accounts at the balance sheet date. The amount of the bad debts expense adjusting entry is the difference between the required balance and the existing balance in the allowance account. When using the percentage of receivables approach, the balance in the allowance account cannot be ignored.

Helpful hint Because the balance sheet is emphasized in the percentage of receivables approach, the existing balance in the allowance account must be considered when calculating the bad debts expense in the adjusting entry.

If the trial balance shows Allowance for Doubtful Accounts with a credit balance of $1,000, an adjusting entry for $24,000 ($25,000 – $1,000) is necessary, as follows:

Dec. 31	Bad Debts Expense	24,000	
	Allowance for Doubtful Accounts		24,000
	To adjust allowance account to total estimated uncollectibles.		

A	=	L	+	OE
−24,000				−24,000

Cash flows: no effect

After the adjusting entry is posted, Adorable Junior Garment's accounts will show the following:

Bad Debts Expense		Allowance for Doubtful Accounts	
Dec. 31 Adj. 24,000		Dec. 31 Bal. 1,000	
		31 Adj. 24,000	
		Dec. 31 Bal. 25,000	

Occasionally, the allowance account will have a debit balance before recording the adjusting entry. This happens when write-offs in the year are higher than the previous estimates for bad debts (we will discuss write-offs in the next section). If there is debit balance, prior to recording the adjusting entry, the debit balance is added to the required balance when the adjusting entry is made. If there had been a $500 debit balance in the Adorable Junior Garment allowance account before adjustment, the adjusting entry would have been for $25,500 to arrive at a credit balance in the allowance account of $25,000.

An aging schedule, rather than a percentage of total receivables, is normally used in this approach. An aging schedule can be easily obtained from a computerized accounts receivable system. While preparing this schedule by hand takes a lot of time, the schedule can be done in minutes on a computer. Most companies have aging schedules prepared already, as this helps them closely monitor the age of their receivables. As noted in our feature story, Whitehill Technologies prepares an aging schedule every week to closely monitor how collectible its accounts receivable are and to identify problem accounts.

Whether it is done with an aging schedule or a percentage of total receivables, the percentage of receivables approach normally gives a better estimate of the net realizable value of the accounts receivable than does the percentage of sales approach. But the percentage of receivables approach does not do as good a job as the percentage of sales approach in matching bad debts expense to the period in which the sale takes place. Because a balance sheet account (Accounts Receivable) is used to calculate the required balance in another balance sheet account (Allowance for Doubtful Accounts), the percentage of receivables approach is also often called the **balance sheet approach**.

Both the percentage of sales and the percentage of receivables approaches are generally accepted. The choice is a management decision. It depends on how much emphasis management wishes to give to matching expenses and revenues on the one hand, and to the net realizable value of the accounts receivable on the other. Most companies prefer using the percentage of receivables approach. Illustration 8-5 compares the two approaches.

Illustration 8-5 ►

Comparison of approaches for estimating uncollectibles

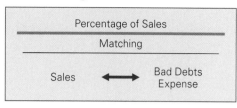

Income Statement Approach

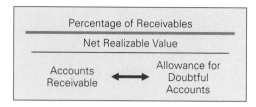

Balance Sheet Approach

Under both approaches, it is necessary to review the company's past experience with credit losses. It also should be noted that, unlike in our example with Adorable Junior Garment, the two approaches normally result in different amounts in the adjusting entry.

2. Recording the Write-Off of an Uncollectible Account

Companies use various methods for collecting past-due accounts, including letters, calls, and legal actions. In the feature story, Whitehill Technologies uses both e-mail and telephone calls to follow up accounts that are overdue. Whitehill's senior management gets involved if an account is 90 days overdue, and the company does not hesitate to cut off technical support in order to encourage payment.

When all the ways of collecting a past-due account have been tried and collection appears impossible, the account should be written off. To prevent premature write-offs, each write-off should be approved in writing by management. To keep good internal control, the authorization to write off accounts should not be given to someone who also has responsibilities related to cash or receivables.

To illustrate a receivables write-off, assume that the vice-president of finance of Adorable Junior Garment authorizes the write-off of a $4,500 balance owed by a delinquent customer, Kids Online, on March 1, 2008. The entry to record the write-off is as follows:

Cash flows: no effect

Mar. 1	Allowance for Doubtful Accounts	4,500	
	Accounts Receivable—Kids Online		4,500
	Write-off of uncollectible account.		

Bad Debts Expense is not increased (debited) when the write-off occurs. Under the allowance method, every account write-off is debited to the allowance account rather than to Bad Debts Expense. A debit to Bad Debts Expense would be incorrect because the expense was already recognized when the adjusting entry was made for estimated bad debts last year.

Instead, the entry to record the write-off of an uncollectible account reduces both Accounts Receivable and Allowance for Doubtful Accounts. After posting, using an assumed balance of $230,000 in Accounts Receivable on February 29, 2008, the general ledger accounts will appear as follows:

Accounts Receivable				Allowance for Doubtful Accounts			
Feb. 29 Bal.	230,000	Mar. 1	4,500	Mar. 1	4,500	Jan. 1 Bal.	25,000
Mar. 1 Bal.	225,500					Mar. 1 Bal.	20,500

A write-off affects only balance sheet accounts. The write-off of the account reduces both Accounts Receivable and Allowance for Doubtful Accounts. Net realizable value in the balance sheet remains the same, as shown below:

	Before Write-Off	After Write-Off
Accounts receivable	$230,000	$225,500
Less: Allowance for doubtful accounts	25,000	20,500
Net realizable value	$205,000	$205,000

As mentioned earlier, the allowance account can sometimes end up in a debit balance position after the write-off of an uncollectible account. This can happen if the write-offs in the period are more than the opening balance. It means the actual credit losses were greater than the estimated credit losses. The balance in Allowance for Doubtful Accounts will be corrected when the adjusting entry for estimated uncollectible accounts is made at the end of the period.

3. Recovery of an Uncollectible Account

Occasionally, a company collects cash from a customer after the account has been written off. Two entries are required to record the recovery of a bad debt: (1) The entry made in writing off the account is reversed to restore the customer's account. (2) The collection is recorded in the usual way.

To illustrate, assume that on July 1, 2008, Kids Online pays the $4,500 amount that had been written off on March 1. The entries are as follows:

	(1)		
July 1	Accounts Receivable—Kids Online	4,500	
	Allowance for Doubtful Accounts		4,500
	To reverse write-off of Kids Online account.		
	(2)		
July 1	Cash	4,500	
	Accounts Receivable—Kids Online		4,500
	To record collection from Kids Online.		

A	=	L	+	OE
+4,500				
−4,500				

Cash flows: no effect

A	=	L	+	OE
+4,500				
−4,500				

↑ Cash flows: +4,500

Note that the recovery of a bad debt, like the write-off of a bad debt, affects only balance sheet accounts. The net effect of the two entries is a debit to Cash and a credit to Allowance for Doubtful Accounts for $4,500. Accounts Receivable is debited and later credited for two reasons. First, the company must reverse the write-off. Second, Kids Online did pay, so the accounts receivable account in the general ledger and Kids Online's account in the subsidiary ledger, if a subsidiary ledger is used, should show this payment as it will need to be considered for deciding what credit to give to Kids Online in the future.

Summary of Allowance Method

In summary, there are three types of transactions that you may need to record when valuing accounts receivable using the allowance method:

1. Estimates of uncollectible accounts receivable are recorded as adjusting entries at the end of the period by debiting Bad Debts Expense and crediting Allowance for Doubtful Accounts. The amount to record can be calculated using either the percentage of sales approach or the percentage of receivables approach.
2. Write-offs of actual uncollectible accounts are recorded in the next accounting period by debiting Allowance for Doubtful Accounts and crediting Accounts Receivable.

3. Later recoveries, if any, are recorded in two separate entries. The first reverses the write-off by debiting Accounts Receivable and crediting Allowance for Doubtful Accounts. The second records the normal collection of the account by debiting Cash and crediting Accounts Receivable.

These entries are summarized in the following T accounts:

Accounts Receivable		Allowance for Doubtful Accounts	
Beginning balance	Cash collections	Write-offs	Beginning balance
Credit sales	Write-offs		Later recoveries
Later recoveries			Bad debt adjusting entry
Ending balance			Ending balance

BEFORE YOU GO ON . . .

▶Review It

1. How does the allowance method respect the matching principle?
2. Explain the differences between the percentage of sales and the percentage of receivables approaches.
3. How do write-offs and subsequent recoveries affect net income and the net realizable value of the accounts receivable when they are recorded?

▶Do It

The unadjusted trial balance at December 31 for Woo Wholesalers Co. shows the following selected information:

	Debit	Credit
Accounts receivable	$120,000	
Allowance for doubtful accounts		$ 2,000
Net credit sales		820,000

(a) Prepare the adjusting journal entry to record bad debts expense for each of the following *independent* situations:
   1. Using the percentage of sales approach, Woo estimates uncollectible accounts to be 1% of net credit sales.
   2. Using the percentage of receivables approach, Woo estimates uncollectible accounts to be as follows: 0–30 days, $85,000, 5% uncollectible; 31–60 days, $25,000, 15% uncollectible; and over 60 days, $10,000, 25% uncollectible.
(b) Calculate the net realizable value of Woo's accounts receivable for each of the above situations.

Action Plan

• Percentage of sales: Apply the percentage to net credit sales to determine estimated bad debts expense—the adjusting entry amount. Ignore the balance in the allowance for doubtful accounts.
• Percentage of receivables: Apply percentages to the receivables in each age category to determine total estimated uncollectible accounts. The total amount determined in the aging schedule is the ending balance required in the allowance account, not the amount of the adjustment. Use the existing balance in the allowance account to determine the required adjusting entry.
• Net realizable value is equal to the balance in Accounts Receivable minus the balance in Allowance for Doubtful Accounts after the journal entry to record bad debts expense has been recorded.

Solution

(a) 1. Bad Debts Expense ($820,000 × 1%)   8,200

         Allowance for Doubtful Accounts   8,200

           To record estimate of uncollectible accounts.

    2. Bad Debts Expense ($10,500[1] − $2,000)   8,500

         Allowance for Doubtful Accounts   8,500

           To record estimate of uncollectible accounts.

        [1] ($85,000 × 5%) + ($25,000 × 15%) + ($10,000 × 25%) = $10,500

(b) 1. Net Realizable Value = Accounts Receivable − Allowance for Doubtful Accounts

                             = [$120,000 − ($2,000 + $8,200)]

                             = $109,800

    2. Net Realizable Value = Accounts Receivable − Allowance for Doubtful Accounts

                             = [$120,000 − ($2,000 + $8,500)]

                             = $109,500

Related exercise material: BE8–5, BE8–6, BE8–7, BE8–8, BE8–9, E8–4, E8–5, and E8–6.

the navigator

Notes Receivable

study objective 3

Account for notes receivable.

Credit may also be granted in exchange for a formal credit instrument known as a promissory note. A **promissory note** is a written promise to pay a specified amount of money on demand or at a definite time. Promissory notes may be used (1) when individuals and companies lend or borrow money, (2) when the amount of the transaction and the credit period are longer than normal limits, or (3) in settlement of accounts receivable.

In a promissory note, the party making the promise to pay is called the maker. For the maker of the promissory note, this is a note payable. The party to whom payment is to be made is called the payee. The payee may be specifically identified by name, or may be designated simply as the bearer of the note. For the payee of the promissory note, this is a note receivable.

The promissory note gives these details: the names of the parties, the amount of the loan, the loan period, the interest rate, and whether interest is repayable monthly or at maturity (the note's due date) along with the principal. Other details might include whether any security is pledged as collateral for the loan and what happens if the maker defaults (does not pay).

Students often find it difficult to understand the difference between a note receivable and an account receivable. An account receivable is an informal promise to pay, while a note receivable is a written promise to pay, which gives the payee a stronger legal claim. In addition, a note is a negotiable instrument (similar to a cheque), which means it can be transferred to another party by endorsement (signature of the payee). An account receivable results from a credit sale, while a note receivable can result from financing a purchase, lending money, or extending an account receivable beyond normal amounts or due dates. An account receivable is usually due in a short period of time (e.g., 30 days), while a note can extend for longer periods of time (e.g., 30 days to many years). An account receivable does not incur interest unless the account is overdue. A note usually bears interest for the entire period.

There are also similarities between notes and accounts receivable. Both are credit instruments. Both are valued at their net realizable values. Both can be sold to another party. The basic issues in accounting for notes receivable are the same as those for accounts receivable, as follows:

1. Recognizing notes receivable
2. Disposing of notes receivable

Recognizing Notes Receivable

To illustrate the basic entry for notes receivable, we will assume that on May 31, Wolder Company (the payee) accepts a $10,000 note receivable from Higly Inc. (the maker), in settlement of an account receivable. The note has an annual interest rate of 6 percent and is due in four months, on September 30, at which time interest is also due.

The entry for the receipt of the note by Wolder Company is as follows:

	A	=	L	+	OE
	+10,000				
	−10,000				

Cash flows: no effect

May 31	Notes Receivable—Higly	10,000	
	Accounts Receivable—Higly		10,000
	To record acceptance of Higly note.		

If a note is exchanged for cash instead of an account receivable, the entry is a debit to Notes Receivable and a credit to Cash for the amount of the loan.

The note receivable is recorded at its principal value (the value shown on the face of the note). No interest revenue is reported when the note is accepted because, according to the revenue recognition principle, revenue is not recognized until it is earned. Interest is earned (accrued) as time passes.

Recording Interest

As we learned in Chapter 3, the basic formula for calculating interest on an interest-bearing note is the following:

Illustration 8-6 ▶

Formula for calculating interest

Principal Value of Note	×	Annual Interest Rate	×	Time in Terms of One Year	=	Interest
$10,000	×	6%	×	$\frac{4}{12}$	=	$200

The interest rate specified in a note is an annual rate of interest. The time factor in the above formula gives the fraction of the year that the note has been outstanding. As we did in past chapters, to keep it simple we will assume that interest is calculated in months rather than days. Illustration 8-6 shows the calculation of interest revenue for Wolder Company and interest expense for Higly Inc. for the term of the note.

If Wolder Company's year end was June 30, the following adjusting journal entry would be required to accrue interest for the month of June:

	A	=	L	+	OE
	+50				+50

Cash flows: no effect

June 30	Interest Receivable	50	
	Interest Revenue ($10,000 × 6% × $\frac{1}{12}$)		50
	To accrue interest on Higly note receivable.		

Notice that interest on a note receivable is not debited to the Notes Receivable account. Instead, a separate account for the interest receivable is used. Since the note is a formal credit instrument, its recorded value stays the same as its face value.

Valuing Notes Receivable

Like accounts receivable, notes receivable are reported at their net realizable value. Each note must be analyzed to determine how likely it is to be collected. If eventual collection is doubtful, bad debts expense and an allowance for doubtful notes must be recorded in the same way as is recorded for accounts receivable. Some companies use only one allowance account for both accounts and notes, and call it Allowance for Doubtful Accounts.

Disposing of Notes Receivable

Notes are normally held to their maturity date, at which time the principal plus any unpaid interest is collected. This is known as honouring (paying) the note. Sometimes, the maker of the note defaults and an adjustment to the accounts must be made. This is known as dishonouring (not paying) the note.

Honouring of Notes Receivable

A note is honoured when it is paid in full at its maturity date. The amount due at maturity is the principal of the note plus interest for the length of time the note is outstanding (assuming interest is due at maturity rather than monthly). If Higly Inc. honours the note when it is due on September 30, the maturity date, the entry by Wolder Company to record the collection is:

Sept. 30	Cash	10,200	
	Notes Receivable—Higly		10,000
	Interest Revenue		150
	Interest Receivable		50
	To record collection of Higly note.		

A	=	L	+	OE
+10,200				+150
−10,000				
−50				

↑ Cash flows: +10,200

Recall that one month of interest revenue, $50 ($10,000 × 6% × $\frac{1}{12}$), was accrued on June 30, Wolder's year end. Consequently, only three months of interest revenue, $150 ($10,000 × 6% × $\frac{3}{12}$), is recorded in this period.

Dishonouring of Notes Receivable

A **dishonoured note** is a note that is not paid in full at maturity. Since a dishonoured note receivable is no longer negotiable, the Notes Receivable account must be reduced by the principal of the note. The payee still has a claim against the maker of the note for both the principal and any unpaid interest and will transfer the amount owing to an Accounts Receivable account if there is hope that the amount will eventually be collected.

To illustrate, assume that on September 30 Higly Inc. says that it cannot pay at the present time but Wolder Company expects eventual collection. Wolder would make the following entry at the time the note is dishonoured:

Sept. 30	Accounts Receivable—Higly	10,200	
	Notes Receivable—Higly		10,000
	Interest Revenue		150
	Interest Receivable		50
	To record dishonouring of Higly note where collection is expected.		

A	=	L	+	OE
+10,200				+150
−10,000				
−50				

Cash flows: no effect

Wolder will continue to follow up with Higly. If the amount owing is eventually collected, Wolder will simply debit Cash and credit Accounts Receivable. If Wolder decides at a later date that it will never collect this amount from Higly, Wolder will write off the account receivable in the same way we learned earlier in the chapter—debit Allowance for Doubtful Accounts, and credit Accounts Receivable.

On the other hand, Wolder could directly write the note off on September 30 if it decided there was no hope of collection. Assuming Wolder uses one allowance account for both accounts and notes, it would record the following:

A	=	L	+	OE
+10,050				
−10,000				
−50				

Cash flows: no effect

Sept. 30	Allowance for Doubtful Accounts	10,050	
	Notes Receivable—Higly		10,000
	Interest Receivable		50
	To record dishonouring of Higly note where collection is not		
	expected.		

No interest revenue is recorded, because collection will not occur. The interest receivable that previously had been accrued is also written off.

ACCOUNTING IN ACTION ▶ Across the Organization Insight

Is China at risk of a massive financial crisis? According to the accounting firm Ernst & Young, uncollectible notes—called non-performing loans—in the Chinese financial system have reached a staggering U.S. $911 billion. What has caused this level of bad loans?

Politics is being blamed. The Communist party is relying on the lending practices of the state-controlled banks to ensure the survival of a one-party state. As ideological indoctrination can no longer be used to keep its members' loyalty, the Communist party is instead using political patronage. To keep them happy, party officials are appointed to executive positions in state-owned enterprises, where they are expected to prove that they are competent managers. This then requires the party to give these state-owned enterprises access to capital, mainly bank loans, even if an enterprise undertakes projects that are unlikely to succeed.

As a result, it is not surprising that the Chinese central bank reported that politically directed lending is the reason for most of its non-performing loans.

Source: Minxin Pei, "Politics Blamed for China's Trillion-Dollar Bad Debts," *The Australian*, May 9, 2006.

 If you were a loans officer at a bank, how would you decide whether or not to make a loan to a company?

BEFORE YOU GO ON . . .

▶Review It

1. Explain the differences between an account receivable and a note receivable.
2. How is interest calculated for a note receivable?
3. At what value are notes receivable reported on the balance sheet?
4. Explain the difference between honouring and dishonouring a note receivable.

▶Do It

On May 1, Gambit Stores accepts from J. Nyznyk a $3,400, 3-month, 5% note in settlement of Nyznyk's overdue account. Interest is due at maturity. Gambit has a June 30 year end. (a) What are the entries made by Gambit on May 1, June 30, and on the maturity date August 1, assuming Nyznyk pays the note at that time? (b) What is the entry on August 1 if Nyznyk does not pay the note and collection is not expected in the future?

Action Plan

- Calculate the accrued interest. The formula is: Face value × annual interest rate × time in terms of one year.
- Record the interest accrued on June 30 to correctly apply the revenue recognition principle. Use Interest Receivable not Notes Receivable for accrued interest.
- If the note is honoured, calculate the interest accrued after June 30 and the total interest on the note. Record the interest accrued and the collection of the note and the total interest.
- If the note is dishonoured, record the transfer of the note and any interest earned to an accounts receivable account if eventual collection is expected or to an allowance account if collection is not expected.

Solution

(a)

May 1	Notes Receivable—J. Nyznyk		3,400	
	Accounts Receivable—J. Nyznyk			3,400
	To replace account receivable with 5% note receivable, due August 1.			
Jun. 30	Interest Receivable		28	
	Interest Revenue ($3,400 × 5% × $\frac{2}{12}$)			28
	To record interest earned to June 30.			
Aug. 1	Cash		3,442	
	Interest Receivable			28
	Notes Receivable—J. Nyznyk			3,400
	Interest Revenue ($3,400 × 5% × $\frac{1}{12}$)			14
	To record collection of Nyznyk note plus interest.			

(b)

Aug. 1	Allowance for Doubtful Accounts		3,414	
	Interest Receivable			14
	Notes Receivable—J. Nyznyk			3,400
	To record dishonouring of Nyznyk note as collection is not expected.			

Related exercise material: BE8–10, BE8–11, BE8–12, E8–7, and E8–8.

Statement Presentation and Management of Receivables

The way receivables are presented in the financial statements is important because receivables are directly affected by how a company recognizes its revenue and bad debts expense. In addition, these reported numbers are critical for analyzing the liquidity of a company and how well a company manages its receivables. In the next sections, we will discuss the presentation, analysis, and management of receivables.

study objective 4

Demonstrate the presentation, analysis, and management of receivables.

Presentation

Each of the major types of receivables should be identified in the balance sheet or in the notes to the financial statements. Short-term receivables are reported in the current assets section of the balance sheet, following cash and short-term investments. Although only the net amount of receivables must be disclosed, it is helpful to report both the gross amount of receivables and the allowance for doubtful accounts either in the statement or in the notes to the financial statements. Notes receivable are often listed before accounts receivable because notes are more easily converted to cash.

On the following page the current assets presentation of receivables for Research in Motion Limited is shown:

RESEARCH IN MOTION LIMITED Balance Sheet (partial) March 4, 2006 (in U.S. thousands)	
Current assets	
Cash and cash equivalents	$ 459,540
Short-term investments	175,553
Trade receivables	315,278
Other receivables	31,861
Inventory	134,523
Other current assets	45,035
Deferred income tax asset	94,789
	$1,256,579

In Note 1 to its financial statements, Research in Motion (RIM) states that its trade receivables include invoiced and accrued revenue and are presented net of an allowance for doubtful accounts of $1,551 thousand. The company also tells us that the allowance for doubtful accounts reflects estimates of probable losses in trade receivables. RIM explains that when it becomes aware of a specific customer's inability to meet its financial obligations, RIM records a specific bad debt provision to reduce the customer's related trade receivable to its estimated net realizable value. If the circumstances of specific customers change, RIM could then adjust its estimates of the recoverability of its trade receivables balances.

If a company has a significant risk of uncollectible accounts or other problems with receivables, it is required to disclose this possibility in the notes to the financial statements. RIM discloses that it depends on several significant customers and on large complex contracts with respect to sales of the majority of its products. RIM states that three customers account for 44 percent of its total trade receivables—one customer for 18 percent or almost $57 million. With trade receivables that large, it clearly makes good sense for RIM to closely monitor each account and calculate its allowance for doubtful accounts accordingly.

In the income statement, bad debts expense is reported in the operating expenses section. Interestingly, we are told in RIM's notes to the financial statements that it had a bad debt recovery (the opposite of an expense) of $552 thousand for the year ended March 4, 2006. This means RIM must have overestimated its bad debts expense in previous years and is now able to recover (reverse) these expenses. This shows just how difficult it can be to accurately estimate uncollectible accounts.

Analysis

Managers need to carefully watch the relationship between sales, accounts receivable, and cash collections. If sales increase, then accounts receivable are also expected to increase. But an unusually high increase in accounts receivable might signal trouble. Perhaps the company increased its sales by loosening its credit policy, and these receivables may be difficult or impossible to collect. The company could also end up with higher costs because of the increase in sales since it may need more cash to pay for inventory and salaries.

Recall that the ability to pay obligations as they come due is measured by a company's liquidity. How can we tell if a company's management of its receivables is helping or hurting the company's liquidity? One way of doing this is to calculate a ratio called the **receivables turnover ratio**. This ratio measures the number of times, on average, that receivables are collected during the period. It is calculated by dividing net credit sales by average gross receivables during the year.

Unfortunately, companies rarely report the amount of net sales made on credit in their financial statements. As a result, net sales (including both cash and credit sales) is used as a substitute. In addition, because some companies do not publicly report their gross accounts receivable, net accounts receivable must be used. As long as the components that are used to calculate a ratio are the same for all companies being compared, however, the comparison is a fair one.

In Illustration 8-7, the substitute figures of total revenue and net accounts receivable were used to calculate the 2006 receivables turnover for Forzani (dollars in thousands).

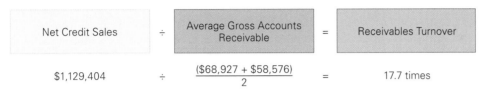

Illustration 8-7 ◀

Receivables turnover

The result indicates an accounts receivable turnover ratio of 17.7 times per year for Forzani. The higher the turnover ratio, the more liquid the company's receivables are.

A popular variation of the receivables turnover ratio is to convert it into the number of days it takes the company to collect its receivables. This ratio, called the **collection period**, is calculated by dividing 365 days by the receivables turnover, as shown for Forzani in Illustration 8-8.

Illustration 8-8 ◀

Collection period

This means that in fiscal 2006 Forzani collected its receivables, on average, in approximately 20.6 days.

The collection period is often used to judge how effective a company's credit and collection policies are. The general rule is that the collection period should not be much longer than the credit term period (i.e., the time allowed for payment).

Both the receivables turnover and the collection period are useful for judging how efficiently a company converts its credit sales to cash. Remember that these measures should also be compared to industry averages, and to previous years.

In addition, these measures should also be analyzed along with other information about a company's liquidity, including the current ratio and inventory turnover. For example, low receivables may result in a low current ratio which might make the company look like it has poor liquidity. But the receivables may be low because they are turning over quickly. In general, the faster the turnover, the more reliable the current ratio is for assessing liquidity.

The collection period can also be used to assess the length of a company's operation cycle. Recall from Chapter 5 that the operating cycle is the average time that it takes to purchase inventory, sell it on account, and then collect cash from customers. In Chapter 6, we learned how to calculate days sales in inventory, which is the average age of the inventory on hand. The combination of the collection period and days sales in inventory is a useful way to measure the length of a company's operating cycle. Using the number of days to sell inventory calculated in Chapter 6, this calculation is shown in Illustration 8-9 for Forzani.

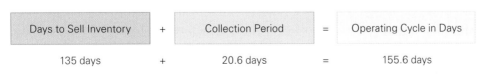

Illustration 8-9 ◀

Operating cycle

This means that in fiscal 2006 it took 155.6 days on average from the time Forzani purchased its inventory until it collected cash.

Accelerating Cash Receipts from Receivables

Normally, accounts receivable are collected in cash and removed from the books. However, as credit sales and receivables increase in size and significance, waiting for receivables to be collected causes increased costs from not being able to immediately use the cash that will be collected. If a company can collect cash more quickly from its receivables, it can shorten the cash-to-cash operating cycle discussed in the previous section.

There are two typical ways to collect cash more quickly from receivables: using the receivables to secure a loan and selling the receivables.

Loans Secured by Receivables

One of the most common ways to speed up cash flow from accounts receivable is to go to a bank and borrow money using accounts receivable as collateral. While this does have a cost (interest has to be paid to the bank on the loan), the cash is available for the company to use earlier. The loan can then be repaid as the receivables are collected. Generally, banks are willing to give financing of up to 75 percent of receivables that are less than 90 days old. Quite often, these arrangements occur through an operating line of credit, which is discussed in a later chapter.

Sale of Receivables

Companies also frequently sell their receivables to another company for cash. There are three reasons for the sale of receivables. The first is their size. To be competitive, sellers often give financing to purchasers of their goods to encourage the sale of the product. But the companies may not want to hold large amounts of receivables. As a result, many major companies in the automobile, truck, equipment, computer, and appliance industries have created wholly owned captive finance companies that accept responsibility for accounts receivable financing. An example is Ford Credit Canada, owned by Ford.

Second, receivables may be sold because they are the only reasonable source of cash. When money is tight, companies may not be able to borrow money in the usual credit markets. Even if credit is available, the cost of borrowing may be too high.

A final reason for selling receivables is that billing and collection are often time-consuming and costly. It is often easier for a retailer to sell its receivables to another party with expertise in billing and collection matters. Credit card companies, such as Visa and MasterCard, specialize in billing and collecting accounts receivable.

Factoring. One specific way to accelerate receivables collection is by sale to a factor. A **factor** is a finance company or bank which buys receivables from businesses and then collects the cash directly from the customer. If the customer does not pay, the business is usually responsible for reimbursing the factor for the uncollected amounts. This is known as selling receivables on a recourse basis.

Securitization of Receivables. An increasingly common way to accelerate receivables collection is to transfer receivables to investors in return for cash through a process called **securitization**. Receivables are sold to an independent trust which holds the receivables as an investment. This transforms the receivables into securities of the trust—which is why the term "securitization of receivables" is used. In some cases, the transfer is treated as a sale of receivables; in other cases, it is treated as a secured loan.

The differences between factoring and securitization are that securitization involves many investors and the cost is lower, the receivables are of higher quality, and the seller usually continues to be involved with collecting the receivables. In factoring, the sale is usually to only one company, the cost is higher, the receivables quality is lower, and the seller does not normally have any involvement with collecting the receivables.

For such companies as Canadian Pacific Railway, Canadian National Railway, and Petro-Canada, securitization of receivables appears to be an increasingly popular way of accelerating cash receipts from their receivables. Each of these companies reports details of the securitization of its receivables in the notes to its financial statements.

ACCOUNTING IN ACTION ▶ Business Insight

On November 15, 2005, Sears Canada Inc. sold the assets and liabilities of its Credit and Financial Services operations, including its Sears Card and Sears MasterCard credit portfolio, to JPMorgan Chase & Co, a global financial services firm. Sears recorded income of $677.2 million on this sale. As part of the sale transaction, Sears and JPMorgan Chase entered into a long-term marketing and servicing alliance with an initial term of ten years. Under the alliance, Sears will receive performance payments from JPMorgan Chase based on a percentage of sales charged to the Sears Card and Sears MasterCard, new account generation, processing of account payments, and a percentage of sales of additional financial products by JPMorgan Chase to Sears Card and Sears MasterCard holders. In 2006, Sears expects that the alliance will generate annual performance payments of approximately $100 million. This amount is expected to partially replace the income previously reported in its Credit and Financial Services operations.

Source: Sears Canada Inc., 2005 Annual Report

 Why would Sears sell its credit card operations to an unrelated company?

BEFORE YOU GO ON . . .

▶Review It

1. Explain where and how accounts and notes receivable are reported on the balance sheet.
2. Where is bad debts expense reported on the income statement?
3. What do the receivables turnover and collection period reveal?
4. Why do companies want to accelerate cash receipts from receivables?

Related exercise material: BE8–13, BE8–14, BE8–15, E8–9, E8–10, E8–11, and E8–12.

Demonstration Problem

Selected transactions for Dylan Co. follow. Dylan's year end is June 30.

Mar. 1 Sold $20,000 of merchandise to Potter Company, terms n/30.

1 Accepted Juno Company's $16,500, 6-month, 6% note for the balance due on account.

11 Potter Company returned $600 worth of goods.

13 Made Dylan Co. credit card sales for $13,200.

15 Made MasterCard credit sales that totalled $6,700. A 3% service fee is charged by MasterCard.

30 Received payment in full from Potter Company.

Apr. 13 Received collections of $8,200 on Dylan Co. credit card sales. Added interest charges of 18% to the remaining balance.

May 10 Wrote off as uncollectible $15,000 of accounts receivable.

June 30 Dylan uses an aging schedule to estimate bad debts. Estimated uncollectible accounts are determined to be $20,000 at June 30. The allowance account has a $3,500 debit balance before the adjustment is recorded.

30 Recorded the interest accrued on the Juno Company note.

July 16 One of the accounts receivable written off in May pays the amount due, $4,000, in full.

Sept. 1 Collected cash from Juno Company in payment of the March 1 note receivable.

Instructions

Prepare the journal entries for the transactions. Dylan Co. uses a periodic inventory system.

Action Plan

- Record accounts receivable at the invoice price.
- Recognize that sales returns and allowances reduce the amount received on accounts receivable.
- Recall that bank credit card sales are cash sales and company credit card sales are credit sales.
- Calculate interest by multiplying the interest rate by the face value by the part of the year that has passed.
- Record write-offs of accounts and recoveries of accounts written off only in balance sheet accounts.
- Consider any existing balance in the allowance account when making the adjustment for uncollectible accounts.
- Recognize any remaining interest on notes receivable when recording the collection of a note.

Solution to Demonstration Problem

Mar. 1	Accounts Receivable—Potter	20,000	
	Sales		20,000
	To record sale on account.		
1	Notes Receivable—Juno	16,500	
	Accounts Receivable—Juno		16,500
	To record acceptance of Juno Company note.		
11	Sales Returns and Allowances	600	
	Accounts Receivable—Potter		600
	To record return of goods.		
13	Accounts Receivable	13,200	
	Sales		13,200
	To record company credit card sales.		
15	Cash	6,499	
	Credit Card Expense (3% × $6,700)	201	
	Sales		6,700
	To record bank credit card sales.		
30	Cash ($20,000 − $600)	19,400	
	Accounts Receivable—Potter		19,400
	To record collection of accounts receivable.		
Apr. 13	Cash	8,200	
	Accounts Receivable		8,200
	To record collection of credit card accounts receivable.		
13	Accounts Receivable [($13,200 − $8,200) × 18% × $\frac{1}{12}$]	75	
	Interest Revenue		75
	To record interest on amount due.		
May 10	Allowance for Doubtful Accounts	15,000	
	Accounts Receivable		15,000
	To record write-off of accounts receivable.		

June 30	Bad Debts Expense ($20,000 + $3,500)	23,500	
	Allowance for Doubtful Accounts		23,500
	To record estimate of uncollectible accounts.		
30	Interest Receivable ($16,500 × 6% × $^4/_{12}$)	330	
	Interest Revenue		330
	To record interest earned.		
July 16	Accounts Receivable	4,000	
	Allowance for Doubtful Accounts		4,000
	To reverse write-off of accounts receivable.		
16	Cash	4,000	
	Accounts Receivable		4,000
	To record collection of accounts receivable.		
Sept. 1	Cash [$16,500 + ($16,500 × 6% × $^6/_{12}$)]	16,995	
	Interest Revenue ($16,500 × 6% × $^2/_{12}$)		165
	Interest Receivable		330
	Note Receivable		16,500
	To record collection of note receivable plus interest.		

Summary of Study Objectives

1. **Record accounts receivable transactions.** Accounts receivable are recorded at the invoice price. They are reduced by sales returns and allowances, and sales discounts. Accounts receivable subsidiary ledgers are used to keep track of individual account balances. When interest is charged on a past-due receivable, this interest is added to the accounts receivable balance and is recognized as interest revenue. Sales using non-bank credit cards result in a receivable, net of the credit card charges, from the credit card company; sales using company credit cards result in a receivable from the customer.

2. **Calculate the net realizable value of accounts receivable and account for bad debts.** The allowance method is used to match expected bad debts expense against sales revenue in the period when the sales occur. There are two approaches that can be used to estimate the bad debts: (1) percentage of sales, or (2) percentage of receivables. The percentage of sales approach emphasizes the matching principle. The percentage of receivables approach emphasizes the net realizable value of the accounts receivable. An aging schedule is usually used with the percentage of receivables approach. Uncollectible accounts are deducted from gross accounts receivable to report accounts receivable at their net realizable value in the balance sheet.

3. **Account for notes receivable.** Notes receivable are recorded at their principal, or face, value. Interest is earned from the date the note is issued until it matures and must be recorded in the correct accounting period. Interest receivable is recorded in a separate account from the note. Like accounts receivable, notes receivable are reported at their net realizable value.

Notes are normally held to maturity. At that time, the principal plus any unpaid interest is due and the note is removed from the accounts. If a note is not paid at maturity, it is said to be dishonoured. If eventual collection is still expected, an account receivable replaces the note receivable and any unpaid interest. Otherwise, the note must be written off.

4. **Demonstrate the presentation, analysis, and management of receivables.** Each major type of receivable should be identified in the balance sheet or in the notes to the financial statements. It is desirable to report the gross amount of receivables and the allowance for doubtful accounts/notes. Bad debts expense is reported in the income statement as an operating expense.

The liquidity of receivables can be evaluated by calculating the receivables turnover and collection period ratios. The receivables turnover is calculated by dividing net credit sales by average gross accounts receivable. This ratio measures how efficiently the company is converting its receivables into sales. The collection period converts the receivables turnover into days, dividing 365 days by the receivables turnover ratio. It shows the number of days, on average, it takes a company to collect its accounts receivable. The combination of the collection period and days sales in inventory is a useful way to measure the length of a company's operating cycle.

There are two typical ways to accelerate the receipt of cash from receivables: using the receivables to secure a loan and selling the receivables either to a factor or by securitizing them.

Glossary

Study Aids: Glossary
Practice Tools: Key Term Matching Activity

Accounts receivable Amounts owed by customers on account. (p. 408)

Aging schedule A list of accounts receivable organized by the length of time they have been unpaid. (p. 416)

Allowance method A method of accounting for bad debts that involves estimating uncollectible accounts at the end of each period. (p. 414)

Bad debts expense An expense account to record uncollectible receivables. (p. 413)

Balance sheet approach Another name for the percentage of receivables approach. (p. 417)

Collection period The average number of days that receivables are outstanding. It is calculated by dividing 365 days by the receivables turnover. (p. 427)

Dishonoured note A note that is not paid in full at maturity. (p. 423)

Factor A finance company or bank that buys receivables from businesses and then collects the payments directly from the customers. (p. 428)

Income statement approach Another name for the percentage of sales approach. (p. 416)

Net realizable value Gross receivables less allowance for doubtful accounts. The net amount of receivables expected to be received in cash. (p. 412)

Notes receivable Claims for which formal instruments of credit are issued as evidence of the debt. (p. 408)

Percentage of receivables approach An approach to estimating uncollectible accounts where the allowance for doubtful accounts is calculated as a percentage of receivables. (p. 416)

Percentage of sales approach An approach to estimating uncollectible accounts where bad debts expense is calculated as a percentage of net credit sales. (p. 415)

Promissory note A written promise to pay a specified amount of money on demand or at a definite time. (p. 421)

Receivables turnover ratio A measure of the liquidity of receivables, calculated by dividing net credit sales by average gross accounts receivable. (p. 426)

Securitization The transfer of assets such as receivables to a company that issues securities as collateral for the receivables. (p. 428)

Trade receivables Accounts and notes receivable that result from sales transactions. (p. 408)

Self-Study Questions

Practice Tools: Self-Assessment Quizzes

Answers are at the end of the chapter.

(SO 1) AP 1. On June 15, Patel Company sells merchandise on account to Bullock Co. for $1,000, terms 2/10, n/30. On June 20, Bullock returns merchandise worth $300 to Patel. On June 24, payment is received from Bullock for the balance due. What is the amount of cash received?
  (a) $680   (c) $700
  (b) $686   (d) $980

(SO 2) AP 2. Sanderson Company has a credit balance of $5,000 in Allowance for Doubtful Accounts before any adjustments are made. Based on a review and aging of its accounts receivable at the end of the period, the company estimates that $60,000 of its receivables are uncollectible. The amount of bad debts expense which should be reported for this accounting period is:
  (a) $5,000.   (c) $60,000.
  (b) $55,000.   (d) $65,000.

3. Assume Sanderson Company has a debit balance of (SO 2) $5,000 in Allowance for Doubtful Accounts before any adjustments are made. Based on a review and aging of its accounts receivable at the end of the period, the company estimates that $60,000 of its receivables are uncollectible. The amount of bad debts expense which should be reported for this accounting period is:
  (a) $5,000.   (c) $60,000
  (b) $55,000.   (d) $65,000.

4. Net sales for the month are $800,000 and bad debts are (SO 2) expected to be 1.5% of net sales. The company uses the percentage of sales approach. If Allowance for Doubtful Accounts has a credit balance of $15,000 before adjustment, what is the balance in the allowance account after adjustment?
  (a) $15,000   (c) $27,000
  (b) $23,000   (d) $12,000

(O 2) AP 5. On January 1, 2008, Allowance for Doubtful Accounts had a credit balance of $18,000. In 2008, $30,000 of uncollectible accounts receivable were written off. On December 31, 2008, the company had accounts receivable of $750,000. Past experience indicates that 3% of total receivables will become uncollectible. What should the adjusted balance of Allowance for Doubtful Accounts be at December 31, 2008?

(a) $4,500   (c) $22,500
(b) $10,500   (d) $40,500

(O 3) AP 6. Sorenson Co. accepts a $1,000, 3-month, 8% promissory note in settlement of an account with Parton Co. The entry to record this transaction is:

(a) Notes Receivable	1,020	
Accounts Receivable		1,020
(b) Notes Receivable	1,000	
Accounts Receivable		1,000
(c) Notes Receivable	1,000	
Sales		1,000
(d) Notes Receivable	1,080	
Accounts Receivable		1,080

(O 3) AP 7. Schlicht Co. holds Osgrove Inc.'s $10,000, 4-month, 9% note. If no interest has been accrued when the note is collected, the entry made by Schlicht Co. is:

(a) Cash	10,300	
Notes Receivable		10,300
(b) Cash	10,900	
Interest Revenue		900
Notes Receivable		10,000

(c) Accounts Receivable	10,300	
Notes Receivable		10,000
Interest Revenue		300
(d) Cash	10,300	
Notes Receivable		10,000
Interest Revenue		300

8. Accounts and notes receivable are reported in the current assets section of the balance sheet at: (SO 4) K
(a) net realizable value.
(b) net book value.
(c) lower of cost and market value.
(d) invoice cost.

9. Moore Company had net credit sales of $800,000 in the year and a cost of goods sold of $500,000. The balance in Accounts Receivable at the beginning of the year was $100,000 and at the end of the year it was $150,000. What were the receivables turnover and collection period ratios, respectively? (SO 4) AP
(a) 4.0 and 91 days   (c) 6.4 and 57 days
(b) 5.3 and 69 days   (d) 8.0 and 46 days

10. Which of the following statements about securitization of accounts receivable is correct? (SO 4) K
(a) Usually the seller continues to be involved with collection of the receivables.
(b) The receivables must be of high quality to qualify for securitization.
(c) Securitization of receivables is a relatively low-cost method of accelerating the receipt of cash.
(d) All of the above are correct.

the navigator

Questions

(SO 1) K 1. Describe the three major types of receivables.

(SO 1) K 2. Why are accounts receivable and notes receivable sometimes called trade receivables?

(SO 1) C 3. (a) What are the advantages of using an accounts receivable subsidiary ledger? (b) Describe the relationship between the general ledger control account and the subsidiary ledger.

(SO 1) C 4. Ashley Dreher is confused about how a retail company should record a credit card sale. She thinks it does not matter if the customer used a bank credit card, a nonbank credit card, or a company credit card—the retail company should always debit Accounts Receivable because the customer is not paying in cash. Is Ashley correct? Explain.

(SO 2) C 5. Rod Ponach is the new credit manager for ACCT Company. He has told management there will be no bad debts in the future because he will do a complete credit check on each customer before the company makes a sale on

credit to the customer. Do you think Rod can completely eliminate bad debts for the company? Discuss.

6. Explain the allowance method of accounting for bad debts. (SO 2) K

7. What is the purpose of the account Allowance for Doubtful Accounts? Although the normal balance of this account is a credit balance, it sometimes has a debit balance. Explain how this can happen. (SO 2) C

8. Soo Eng cannot understand why net realizable value does not decrease when an uncollectible account is written off under the allowance method. Clarify this for Soo Eng. (SO 2) C

9. Explain the difference between the two approaches that may be used in estimating uncollectible accounts under the allowance method. (SO 2) C

10. Explain why the percentage of sales approach is also called the income statement approach and the percentage (SO 2) K

of receivables approach is also called the balance sheet approach.

(SO 2) K 11. Kyoto Company has a credit balance of $3,500 in Allowance for Doubtful Accounts. The estimated uncollectible amount under the percentage of sales approach is $4,100. The total estimated uncollectible amount under the percentage of receivables approach is $5,800. Describe the similarities and the differences in preparing the adjusting journal entry to record the estimated uncollectible accounts under each approach.

(SO 2) C 12. Why is the bad debts expense in the income statement typically not the same amount as the allowance for doubtful accounts amount in the balance sheet?

(SO 2) C 13. When an account receivable that was written off is later collected, two journal entries are usually made. Explain why.

(SO 3) K 14. Explain how notes receivable and accounts receivable are the same and how they are different.

(SO 3) C 15. Why might a company prefer to have a note receivable instead of an account receivable?

(SO 3) C 16. Why are notes receivable recorded at their principal value and not the amount that must be paid at maturity? Why is interest accrued on a note recorded in a separate account from the note receivable?

17. What does it mean if a note is dishonoured? What are the alternatives for the payee in accounting for a dishonoured note? (SO 3)

18. Saucier Company has accounts receivable, notes receivable due in three months, notes receivable due in two years, an allowance for doubtful accounts, sales taxes recoverable, and income tax receivable. How should the receivables be reported on the balance sheet? (SO 4)

19. The president proudly announces that her company's liquidity has improved. Its current ratio increased substantially this year. Does an increase in the current ratio always indicate improved liquidity? What other ratio(s) might you review to determine whether or not the increase in the current ratio is an improvement in the company's financial health? (SO 4)

20. Does an increase in the receivables turnover indicate faster or slower collection of receivables? An increase or decrease in the collection period? (SO 4)

21. Why do companies sometimes sell their receivables? (SO 4)

22. As at December 31, 2005, **Canadian Pacific Railway Limited** had sold $120 million of its accounts receivable to an independent trust in a transaction known as securitization. Why might a company such as Canadian Pacific securitize its receivables? (SO 4)

Brief Exercises

Identify receivables.
(SO 1) K

BE8–1 Six transactions follow. Indicate the transactions that result in a receivable. For each transaction that does result in a receivable, would the receivable be reported as accounts receivable, notes receivable, or other receivables on a balance sheet?

(a) Advanced $10,000 to an employee.
(b) A customer pays $5,000 in advance for goods to be shipped the next month.
(c) Performed services for a customer in exchange for a $15,000 note.
(d) Sold merchandise on account to a customer for $60,000.
(e) Extended a customer's account for three months by accepting a note in exchange for it.
(f) Performed services for a customer who had paid in advance.

Record accounts receivable transactions.
(SO 1) AP

BE8–2 Record the following transactions on the books of Essex Co.:

(a) On July 1, Essex Co. sold merchandise on account to Cambridge Inc. for $14,000, terms 2/10, n/30. The cost of the merchandise sold was $9,000. Essex uses a perpetual inventory system.
(b) On July 3, Cambridge Inc. returned merchandise worth $2,400 to Essex Co. The original cost of the merchandise was $1,550. The merchandise was returned to inventory.
(c) On July 10, Cambridge Inc. paid for the merchandise.

Record accounts receivable transactions.
(SO 1) AP

BE8–3 Record the following transactions on the books of Lough Co.:

(a) On August 1, Lough Co. sold merchandise on account to Veale Inc. for $20,000, terms 2/10, n/30. Lough uses a periodic inventory system.
(b) On August 5, Veale Inc. returned merchandise worth $3,500 to Lough Co.

(c) On September 30, Lough Co. charged Veale Inc. one month's interest for the overdue account. Lough charges 21% on overdue accounts. (Round calculation to the nearest dollar.)

(d) On October 4, Veale Inc. paid the amount owing to Lough Co.

BE8–4 Stewart Department Store accepted a nonbank card in payment of a $200 purchase of merchandise on July 11. The credit card company charges a 3% fee. What entry should Stewart Department Store make? How would this entry change if the payment had been made with a Stewart Department Store credit card instead of a nonbank credit card? A Visa credit card instead of a nonbank credit card? Visa also charges a 3% fee.

Record credit card transactions.
(SO 1) AP

BE8–5 Qinshan Co. uses the percentage of sales approach to record bad debts expense. It estimates that 1.5% of net credit sales will become uncollectible. Credit sales are $900,000 for the year ended April 30, 2008; sales returns and allowances are $50,000; sales discounts are $10,000; and the allowance for doubtful accounts has a credit balance of $7,000. Prepare the adjusting entry to record bad debts expense in 2008.

Record bad debts using percentage of sales approach.
(SO 2) AP

BE8–6 Groleskey Co. uses the percentage of receivables approach to record bad debts expense. It estimates that 4% of total accounts receivable will become uncollectible. Accounts receivable are $500,000 at the end of the year. The allowance for doubtful accounts has a credit balance of $3,000.

Record bad debts using percentage of receivables approach.
(SO 2) AP

(a) Prepare the adjusting entry to record bad debts expense for the year ended December 31.

(b) If the allowance for doubtful accounts had a debit balance of $800 instead of a credit balance of $3,000, what amount would be reported for bad debts expense?

BE8–7 Refer to BE8–6. Groleskey Co. decides to refine its estimate of uncollectible accounts by preparing an aging schedule. Complete the following schedule and prepare the adjusting journal entry using this estimate. Assume Allowance for Doubtful Accounts has a credit balance of $3,000.

Complete aging schedule and record bad debts expense.
(SO 2) AP

Number of Days Outstanding	Accounts Receivable	Estimated % Uncollectible	Estimated Uncollectible Accounts
0–30 days	$315,000	1%	
31–60 days	90,000	4%	
61–90 days	60,000	10%	
Over 90 days	35,000	20%	
Total	$500,000		

BE8–8 At the end of 2007, Searcy Co. has an allowance for doubtful accounts of $54,000. On January 24, 2008, when it has accounts receivable of $680,000, Searcy Co. learns that an $18,000 receivable from Hutley Inc. is not collectible. Management authorizes a write-off.

Record write-off and compare net realizable value.
(SO 2) AP

(a) Record the write-off.

(b) What is the net realizable value of the accounts receivable (1) before the write-off, and (2) after the write-off?

BE8–9 Assume the same information as in BE8–8. Hutley's financial difficulties are over. On March 4, 2008, Searcy Co. receives an $18,000 payment in full from Hutley Inc. Record this transaction.

Record recovery of account written-off.
(SO 2) AP

BE8–10 Rocky Ridge Co. has three outstanding notes receivable at its December 31, 2007, fiscal year end. For each note calculate (a) total interest revenue, (b) interest revenue to be recorded in 2007, and (c) interest revenue to be recorded in 2008.

Calculate interest accrued on notes receivable.
(SO 3) AP

Issue Date	Term	Principal	Interest Rate
1. July 31, 2007	1 year	$16,000	7.50%
2. September 1, 2007	6 months	40,000	8.25%
3. November 1, 2007	15 months	39,000	6.75%

Record notes receivable
transactions.
(SO 3) AP

BE8–11   On March 31, 2008, Raja Co. sold merchandise on account to Opal Co. for $12,000, terms n/30. Raja uses a perpetual inventory system and the merchandise had a cost of $7,500. On May 1, 2008, Opal gave Raja a 7%, 5-month promissory note in settlement of the account. Interest is to be paid at maturity. On October 1, Opal paid the note and accrued interest. Record the above transactions for Raja Co. Raja Co. has a June 30 fiscal year end and adjusts its accounts annually.

Record notes receivable
transactions.
(SO 3) AP

BE8–12   Lee Company accepts a $9,000, 3-month, 7% note receivable in settlement of an account receivable on April 1, 2008. Interest is to be paid at maturity. Lee Company has a December 31 year end and adjusts its accounts annually.

(a) Record (1) the issue of the note on April 1 and (2) the settlement of the note on July 1, assuming the note is honoured.
(b) Repeat part (a) assuming that the note is dishonoured but eventual collection is expected.
(c) Repeat part (a) assuming that the note is dishonoured and eventual collection is not expected.

Record notes receivable
transactions and indicate
statement presentation.
(SO 3, 4) AP

BE8–13   Chant Co. lent Sharp Inc. $100,000 cash in exchange for a 5-year, 5% note on July 1, 2007. Interest is payable quarterly on January 1, April 1, July 1, and October 1 each year. Chant Co. has a December 31 year end. (a) Record Chant's entries related to the note to January 1, 2008. (b) What amounts related to this note will be reported on Chant's December 31, 2007, financial statements?

Prepare current assets
section.
(SO 4) AP

BE8–14   WAF Company's general ledger included the following accounts at November 30, 2008:

Accounts payable	$124,200	Interest receivable	$ 995
Accounts receivable	95,000	Inventory	110,800
Allowance for doubtful		Note receivable—	
accounts	2,850	due April 23, 2009	20,000
Bad debts expense	3,730	Note receivable—	
Cash	34,000	due May 21, 2012	45,000
GST recoverable	1,990	Prepaid expenses	4,950

Prepare the current assets section of the balance sheet.

Calculate and interpret ratios.
(SO 4) AN

BE8–15   The financial statements of **Maple Leaf Foods Inc.** report sales of $6,462,581 thousand for the year ended December 31, 2005. Accounts receivable are $247,014 thousand at the end of the year, and $292,462 thousand at the beginning of the year. Calculate Maple Leaf's receivables turnover and collection period. If the company's receivables turnover and collection period were 23.8 and 15.3 days, respectively, in the previous year, has the company's liquidity improved or weakened?

Exercises

Record accounts receivable
transactions.
(SO 1) AP

E8–1   Links Costumes uses a perpetual inventory system. Selected transactions for April and June follow:

Apr. 6 Sold merchandise costing $3,200 to Pumphill Theatre for $6,500, terms 2/10, n/30.
    8 Pumphill returned $500 of the merchandise. This merchandise had originally cost Links $245 and was returned to inventory.
  16 Pumphill paid Links the amount owing.
  17 Sold merchandise costing $2,700 to EastCo Productions for $5,500, terms 2/10, n/30.
  18 EastCo returned $600 of the merchandise because it was damaged. The merchandise had originally cost Links $290. Links scrapped the merchandise.
June 17 Added interest charges for one month to the amount owning by EastCo. Links charges 21% on outstanding receivables.
  20 EastCo paid the amount owing.

Instructions

Record the above transactions.

E8–2 Transactions follow for the Adventure Sports Co. store and three of its customers in the company's first month of business:

Record accounts receivable transactions. Post to subsidiary and general ledgers.
(SO 1) AP

Mar. 2 Andrew Noren used his Adventure Sports credit card to purchase $570 of merchandise.
   4 Andrew returned $75 of merchandise for credit.
   5 Sold $380 of merchandise to Elaine Davidson, who used her Adventure Sports credit card.
   8 Erik Smistad purchased $421 of merchandise and paid for it in cash.
   17 Andrew Noren used his Adventure Sports credit card to purchase an additional $348 of merchandise.
   28 Erik Smistad used his Adventure Sports credit card to purchase $299 of merchandise.
   29 Elaine Davidson made a $100 payment on her credit card account.

Instructions

(a) Record the above transactions. Adventure Sports uses a periodic inventory system.
(b) Set up general ledger accounts for the Accounts Receivable control account and for the Accounts Receivable subsidiary ledger accounts. Post the journal entries to these accounts.
(c) Prepare a list of customers and the balances of their accounts from the subsidiary ledger. Prove that the total of the subsidiary ledger is equal to the control account balance.

E8–3 Kasko Stores accepts its own credit card, as well as bank and nonbank credit cards. In January and February, the following summary transactions occurred:

Record credit card transactions and indicate statement presentation.
(SO 1, 4) AP

Jan. 5 Made $19,000 of Kasko credit card sales.
   20 Made $4,500 of Visa credit card sales (service charge fee, 3.25%).
   30 Made a $1,000 sale to a customer who used a nonbank credit card (service charge fee, 3.75%).
   31 Made debit card sales (service charge fee, $0.50 per transaction for 50 transactions) totalling $4,000.
Feb. 1 Collected $12,000 on Kasko credit card sales.
   14 Collected the amount owing from the credit card company for the January 30 transaction.
   28 Added interest charges of 24% to outstanding Kasko credit card balances.

Instructions

(a) Record the above transactions for Kasko Stores.
(b) Where are interest revenue and credit card and debit card expenses reported in the income statement?

E8–4 The ledger of Patillo Company at the end of the current year shows Accounts Receivable $90,000; Sales $970,000; Sales Returns and Allowances $40,000; and Sales Discounts $10,000.

Record bad debts using two approaches.
(SO 2) AP

Instructions

(a) If Allowance for Doubtful Accounts has a credit balance of $800 in the trial balance, record the adjusting entry at December 31, assuming bad debts are estimated to be (1) 1% of net sales, and (2) 10% of accounts receivable.
(b) If Allowance for Doubtful Accounts has a debit balance of $600 in the trial balance, record the adjusting entry at December 31, assuming bad debts are estimated to be (1) 0.5% of net sales, and (2) 5% of accounts receivable.

E8–5 Grevina Company has accounts receivable of $92,500 at March 31. An analysis of the accounts shows the following:

Prepare aging schedule and record bad debts.
(SO 2) AP

Month of Sale	Balance
March	$65,000
February	12,600
January	8,500
October, November, and December	6,400
	$92,500

Credit terms are 2/10, n/30. At March 31, Allowance for Doubtful Accounts has a credit balance of $1,200 before adjustment. The company uses the percentage of receivables approach and an aging schedule to estimate uncollectible accounts. The company's percentage estimates of bad debts are as follows:

Age of Accounts	Estimated % Uncollectible
0–30 days outstanding	2%
31–60 days outstanding	10%
61–90 days outstanding	25%
Over 90 days outstanding	50%

Instructions

(a) Prepare an aging schedule to determine the total estimated uncollectible accounts at March 31.
(b) Prepare the adjusting entry at March 31 to record bad debts expense.
(c) What are the advantages and disadvantages to Grevina Company of using an aging schedule to estimate uncollectible accounts, as compared to estimating uncollectible accounts as 10% of total accounts receivable?

Record bad debts, write-off, and recovery; calculate net realizable value.
(SO 2) AP

E8–6 On December 31, 2007, when its Allowance for Doubtful Accounts had a debit balance of $1,000, Ceja Co. estimated that 2% of its $450,000 of accounts receivable would become uncollectible and recorded the bad debts adjusting entry. On May 11, 2008, when Ceja Co. had an Accounts Receivable balance of $471,000, the company determined that Robert Worthy's $1,850 account was uncollectible and wrote it off. On June 12, 2008, Worthy paid the amount previously written off.

Instructions

(a) Prepare the journal entries on December 31, 2007, May 11, 2008, and June 12, 2008.
(b) Post the journal entries to Allowance for Doubtful Accounts and calculate the new balance after each entry.
(c) Calculate the net realizable value of accounts receivable both before and after writing off Robert Worthy's account on May 11.

Record notes receivable transactions.
(SO 3) AP

E8–7 Passera Supply Co. has the following transactions for notes receivable:

Nov. 1 Loaned $24,000 cash to A. Morgan on a 2-year, 8% note.
Dec. 1 Sold goods to Wright, Inc., receiving a $4,500, 3-month, 6% note. Passera uses the periodic method of accounting for inventory.
    15 Received an $8,000, 6-month, 7% note on account from Barnes Company.
    31 Accrued interest revenue on all notes receivable. Interest is due at maturity.
Mar. 1 Collected the amount owing on the Wright note.

Instructions

Record the transactions for Passera Supply Co. (Round calculations to the nearest dollar.)

Record notes receivable transactions.
(SO 3) AP

E8–8 The following are notes receivable transactions for Prejear Co.:

Mar. 1 Received a $10,500, 9-month, 5% note on account from Jones Bros. Interest is due at maturity.
June 30 Accrued interest on the Jones note. June 30 is Prejear's year end and adjustments are recorded annually.
July 1 Lent $3,000 cash to Sarah Lough, receiving a 3-month, 6% note. Interest is due at maturity.
Oct. 1 Sarah Lough defaults on the note. Prejear does not expect to collect the amount owing in the future.
Dec. 1 Jones Bros. defaults on its note. Prejear expects to collect the amount owing in January.

Instructions

Record the transactions for Prejear Co. (Round calculations to the nearest dollar.)

Record notes receivable transactions and indicate statement presentation.
(SO 3, 4) AP

E8–9 Ni Co. has the following notes receivable outstanding at December 31, 2008:

Issue Date	Term	Principal	Interest Rate
1. August 31, 2007	2 years	$15,000	4.50%

Issue Date	Term	Principal	Interest Rate
2. October 1, 2007	18 months	46,000	5.25%
3. May 1, 2008	5 years	22,000	5.75%
4. October 31, 2008	7 months	9,000	4.75%

Interest is payable on the first day of each month for notes with terms of two years or longer. Interest is payable at maturity for notes with terms less than two years.

Instructions

(a) Calculate the interest revenue that Ni Co. will report on its income statement for the year ended December 31, 2008. Indicate where this will be presented on the income statement. (Round calculations to the nearest dollar.)

(b) Calculate the amounts related to these notes that will be reported on Ni Co.'s balance sheet at December 31, 2008. Indicate where they will be presented. Assume all required interest payments have been received on time. (Round calculations to the nearest dollar.)

E8–10 In its first year of operations, AJS Company had sales of $3 million (all on credit) and cost of goods sold of $1,750,000. At year end, February 29, 2008, $600,000 of the sales remained uncollected. The credit manager estimates that $35,000 of these receivables will become uncollectible.

Record bad debts, prepare partial balance sheet, and calculate ratios.
(SO 2, 4) AP

(a) Prepare the journal entry to record the estimated uncollectibles.

(b) Prepare the current assets section of the balance sheet for AJS Company, assuming that in addition to the receivables it has the following: cash of $90,000; merchandise inventory of $365,000; accounts payable of $400,000; GST recoverable of $25,000; notes receivable of $45,000 due on April 22, 2008; and supplies of $10,000.

(c) Calculate the receivables turnover and collection period. (*Hint:* Remember that this is the end of the first year of business.)

E8–11 The following information (in millions) was taken from the December 31 financial statements of **Canadian National Railway Company**:

Calculate ratios.
(SO 4) AN

	2005	2004	2003
Accounts receivable, gross	$ 703	$ 863	$ 584
Allowance for doubtful accounts	80	70	55
Accounts receivable, net	623	793	529
Revenues	7,240	6,548	5,884
Total current assets	1,149	1,710	1,092
Total current liabilities	1,958	2,259	1,977

Instructions

(a) Calculate the 2005 and 2004 current ratios.

(b) Calculate the receivables turnover and average collection period for 2005 and 2004.

(c) Are accounts receivable a material component of the company's current assets?

(d) Comment on any improvement or weakening in CN's liquidity and its management of accounts receivable.

E8–12 Refer to E8–11. In the notes to its financial statements, **Canadian National Railway Company** reports that it has a revolving agreement to sell eligible freight trade and other receivables up to a maximum of $500 million of receivables outstanding at any point in time. At December 31, 2005, the company had sold $489 million of these receivables, compared to $445 million at December 31, 2004. CN has retained the responsibility for servicing, administering, and collecting the freight receivables sold.

Discuss sale of receivables.
(SO 4) C

Instructions

Explain why CN, a financially stable company, securitizes (sells) such a large portion of its receivables.

Problems: Set A

Record accounts receivable
and bad debts transactions.
(SO 1, 2) AP

P8–1A At December 31, 2007, Underwood Imports reported the following information on its balance sheet:

Accounts receivable	$995,000
Less: Allowance for doubtful accounts	59,700

In 2008, the company had the following transactions related to receivables:

1. Sales on account, $2,620,000
2. Sales returns and allowances, $40,000
3. Collections of accounts receivable, $2,700,000
4. Write-offs of accounts deemed uncollectible, $75,000
5. Recovery of bad debts previously written off as uncollectible, $30,000

Instructions

(a) Prepare the summary journal entries to record each of these five transactions.
(b) Enter the January 1, 2008, balances in the Accounts Receivable and Allowance for Doubtful Accounts general ledger accounts. Post the entries to the two accounts and determine the balances at December 31, 2008.
(c) Record bad debts expense for 2008. Uncollectible accounts are estimated at 6% of accounts receivable.
(d) Calculate the net realizable value of accounts receivable at December 31, 2008.

Record accounts receivable
and bad debts transactions.
(SO 1, 2) AP

P8–2A At the beginning of the current period, Hong Co. had a balance of $300,000 in Accounts Receivable and an $18,000 credit balance in Allowance for Doubtful Accounts. In the period, it had sales on account of $1,950,000 and collections of $2,020,000. It wrote off accounts receivable of $29,500 as uncollectible. However, $3,500 of one of the accounts written off as uncollectible was recovered before the end of the current period.

Instructions

(a) Record sales and collections in the period.
(b) Record the write-off of uncollectible accounts and the recovery of accounts written off as uncollectible in the period.
(c) Determine the balance in Accounts Receivable and Allowance for Doubtful Accounts after recording the transactions in (a) and (b).
(d) Record the bad debts expense adjusting entry for the period if Hong Co. estimates that 6% of total accounts receivable will become uncollectible.
(e) What is the net realizable value of receivables at the end of the period?
(f) What is the bad debts expense on the income statement for the period?
(g) Now assume that Hong Co. uses the percentage of sales approach instead of the percentage of receivables approach to estimate uncollectible accounts. Repeat (d) through (f) assuming Hong estimates 1.25% of the credit sales will become uncollectible.

Calculate bad debt amounts
and answer questions.
(SO 2) AP

P8–3A Information for Tisipai Company in 2008 follows:

Total credit sales	$1,650,000
Accounts receivable at December 31	625,000
Accounts receivable written off	24,000
Accounts receivable later recovered	4,000

Instructions

(a) If Tisipai Company does not use the allowance method, what amount will it report for bad debts expense?
(b) Assume instead that Tisipai Company uses the allowance method and estimates its bad debts expense to be 2.25% of credit sales. What amount of bad debts expense will the company record if Allowance for Doubtful Accounts has a credit balance of $3,500 before making the adjustment?

(c) Assume instead that Tisipai Company uses the allowance method and estimates its uncollectible accounts to be $42,000 based on an aging schedule. What amount of bad debts expense will the company record if Allowance for Doubtful Accounts has a credit balance of $3,500 before making the adjustment?

(d) Assume the same facts as in (c), except that there is a $2,250 debit balance in Allowance for Doubtful Accounts. What amount of bad debts expense will the company record?

(e) How does the write-off of an uncollectible account affect the net realizable value of accounts receivable?

(f) Why should companies use the allowance method of accounting for bad debts?

P8–4A   An aging analysis of Hake Company's accounts receivable at December 31, 2007 and 2008, showed the following:

Prepare aging schedule and record bad debts.
(SO 2) AP

Number of Days Outstanding	Estimated % Uncollectible	December 31 2008	December 31 2007
0–30 days	3%	$150,000	$160,000
31–60 days	6%	32,000	57,000
61–90 days	12%	43,000	38,000
Over 90 days	24%	65,000	25,000
Total		$290,000	$280,000

Additional information:

1. At December 31, 2007, the unadjusted balance in Allowance for Doubtful Accounts was a credit of $4,500.
2. In 2008, $21,000 of accounts were written off as uncollectible and $1,500 of accounts previously written off were recovered.

Instructions

(a) Prepare an aging schedule to calculate the estimated uncollectible accounts at December 31, 2007, and at December 31, 2008. Comment on the results.
(b) Record the following transactions:
   1. The adjusting entry on December 31, 2007
   2. The write-off of uncollectible accounts in 2008
   3. The collection of accounts previously written off
   4. The adjusting entry on December 31, 2008
(c) Calculate the net realizable value of Hake's accounts receivable at December 31, 2007, and December 31, 2008.

P8–5A   Imagine Co. uses the allowance method to estimate uncollectible accounts receivable. The computer produced the following aging of the accounts receivable at year end:

Prepare aging schedule and record bad debts.
(SO 2) AP

Customer	Total	Number of Days Outstanding 0–30	31–60	61–90	91–120
Accounts receivable	$385,000	$220,000	$100,000	$40,000	$25,000
Estimated % uncollectible		1%	5%	10%	20%
Estimated uncollectible accounts					

The unadjusted balance in Allowance for Doubtful Accounts is a debit of $10,000.

Instructions

(a) Complete the aging schedule and calculate the total estimated uncollectible accounts from the above information.
(b) Record the bad debts adjusting entry using the above information.
(c) In the following year, $17,800 of the outstanding accounts receivable is determined to be uncollectible. Record the write-off of the uncollectible accounts.

(d) The company collects $6,300 of the $17,800 of accounts receivable that were determined to be uncollectible in (c). No further amounts are expected to be collected. Prepare the journal entry (or entries) to record the recovery of this amount.

(e) Comment on how your answers to parts (a) to (d) would change if Imagine Co. used a percentage of total accounts receivable of 3% instead of aging the accounts receivable.

(f) What are the advantages for the company of aging the accounts receivable rather than applying a percentage to total accounts receivable?

Determine missing amounts.
(SO 2) AN

P8–6A   Armadillo and Company reported the following information in its general ledger at July 31:

Accounts Receivable				Sales	
Beg. bal.	325,000	(b)			(e)
	(a)	(c)			
End. bal.	376,000				

Allowance for Doubtful Accounts				Bad Debts Expense	
		Beg. bal.	22,750	(f)	
	21,550	(d)			
		End. bal.	26,350		

All sales were made on account. Bad debts expense was estimated as 1% of sales. There were no recoveries of accounts previously written off.

Instructions

Determine the missing amounts in Armadillo and Company's accounts. State what each of these amounts represents. You will not be able to determine the missing items in alphabetical order. (*Hint:* To solve this problem, it might help if you reconstruct the journal entries.)

Record accounts receivable and bad debts transactions; discuss statement presentation.
(SO 1, 2, 4) AP

P8–7A   Assiniboia Co. uses the percentage of sales approach to record bad debts expense for its monthly financial statements and the percentage of receivables approach for its year-end financial statements. Assiniboia Co. has a May 31 fiscal year end, closes temporary accounts annually, and uses the periodic inventory system.

On March 31, 2008, after completing its month-end adjustments, it had accounts receivable of $892,500, a credit balance of $47,750 in Allowance for Doubtful Accounts, and a debit balance in Bad Debts Expense of $115,880. In April and May, the following occurred:

April

1. Sold $646,900 of merchandise on credit.
2. Accepted $10,900 of returns on the merchandise sold on credit. These customers were issued credit memos.
3. Collected $696,250 cash on account from customers.
4. Interest charges of $13,860 were charged to outstanding accounts receivable.
5. As part of the month-end adjusting entries, recorded bad debts expense of 3% of net credit sales for the month.

May

1. Credit sales were $763,600.
2. Received $4,450 cash from a customer whose account had been written off in March.
3. Collected $785,240 cash, in addition to the cash collected in (2) above, from customers on account.
4. Wrote off $69,580 of accounts receivable as uncollectible.
5. Interest charges of $12,070 were charged to outstanding accounts receivable.
6. Recorded the year-end adjustment for bad debts. Uncollectible accounts were estimated to be 6% of accounts receivable.

Instructions

(a) Record the above transactions and adjustments.
(b) Show how accounts receivable will appear on the May 31, 2008, balance sheet.

(c) What amount will be reported as bad debts expense on the income statement for the year ended May 31, 2008?

(d) Where are bad debts expense and interest revenue shown on the income statement?

P8–8A On January 1, 2007, Vu Co. had accounts receivable of $146,000, notes receivable of $12,000, interest receivable of $100, and allowance for doubtful accounts of $13,200. The note receivable was a 5-month, 5% note receivable from Annabelle Company dated October 31, 2006; the correct interest has been accrued. Vu Co. prepares financial statements annually for the year ended December 31. Assume interest is due at maturity unless otherwise specified. In the year, the following selected transactions occurred:

Record receivables transactions.
(SO 2, 3) AP

Jan. 2 Sold $16,000 of merchandise to George Company, terms 2/10, n/30.

Feb. 1 Accepted George Company's $16,000, 3-month, 6.5% note for the balance due (see January 2 transaction).

Mar. 31 Received payment in full from Annabelle Company for the amount due.

May 1 Collected George Company note in full (see February 1 transaction).

  25 Accepted Avery Inc.'s $6,000, 3-month, 6% note in settlement of a past-due balance on account. Interest is payable monthly.

June 25 Received one month's interest from Avery Inc. on its note (see May 25 transaction).

July 25 The Avery Inc. note was dishonoured (see May 25 transaction). Avery Inc. is bankrupt and future payment is not expected.

Sept. 1 Sold $10,000 of merchandise to Young Company and accepted a $10,000, 6-month, 5.25% note for the amount due.

Nov. 22 News reports indicate that several key officers of Young Company have been arrested on charges of fraud and embezzlement, and that the company's operations have been shut down indefinitely (see September 1 transaction).

  30 Gave MRC Corp a $5,000 cash loan and accepted MRC's 4-month, 4.5% note.

Dec. 31 Accrued interest is recorded on any outstanding notes at year end.

Instructions

(a) Record the above transactions.

(b) If there have been no further reports on the situation regarding Young Company, do you think the note should be written off? If not, do you think interest should be accrued on the note receivable at year end?

P8–9A Ouellette Co. adjusts its books monthly. On June 30, 2008, the general ledger includes the following account balances:

Record receivable transactions. Show balance sheet presentation.
(SO 1, 3, 4) AP

Notes Receivable	$29,800
Credit Card Receivables	11,500
Interest Receivable	?

Notes receivable include the following:

Issue Date	Maker	Principal	Term	Interest
May 1, 2007	ALD Inc.	$ 6,000	2 years	6.00%
October 31, 2007	KAB Ltd.	10,000	9 months	5.50%
May 31, 2008	DNR Co.	4,800	2 months	6.75%
June 30, 2008	MJH Corp.	9,000	18 months	5.00%

Interest is payable on the first day of each month for notes with terms of one year or longer. Interest is payable at maturity for notes with terms less than one year. In July, the following transactions were completed:

July 1 Received payment of the interest due from ALD Inc.

  5 Made sales of $7,800 on Ouellette credit cards.

  25 Collected $5,400 of Ouellette credit card receivables.

  31 Added $215 to Ouellette credit card customer balances for interest charges on unpaid balances.

July 31 Received notice that the DNR Co. note has been dishonoured. Assume that DNR Co. is expected to pay in the future.

Instructions

(a) Calculate the interest receivable at June 30, 2008.

(b) Record the July transactions and the July 31 adjusting entry for accrued interest receivable.

(c) Enter the balances at July 1 in the receivables accounts. Post the entries to all the receivables accounts.

(d) Show the balance sheet presentation of the receivables accounts at July 31, 2008.

(e) How would the journal entry on July 31 be different if DNR Co. were not expected to pay in the future?

Prepare assets section of balance sheet; calculate and interpret ratios.
(SO 4) AN

P8–10A Norlandia Saga Company's general ledger included the following selected accounts (in thousands) at November 30, 2008:

Accounts payable	$ 682.7	Interest revenue	$ 13.4
Accounts receivable	389.2	Merchandise inventory	420.6
Accumulated amortization—equipment	577.1	Notes receivable—due in 2009	64.0
Allowance for doubtful accounts	18.5	Notes receivable—due in 2012	127.4
Bad debts expense	54.5	Prepaid expenses and deposits	24.1
Cash and cash equivalents	802.2	Sales	3,529.7
Cost of goods sold	441.2	Sales discounts	23.1
Equipment	1,155.2	Supplies	19.9
		Unearned sales revenue	50.3

Additional information:

1. The net realizable value of accounts receivable was $345.1 thousand on November 30, 2007.
2. The receivables turnover was 9.1 the previous year.

Instructions

(a) Prepare the assets section of the balance sheet.

(b) Calculate the receivables turnover and average collection period. Compare these results to the previous year's results and comment on any trends.

Calculate and interpret ratios.
(SO 4) AN

P8–11A Presented here is selected financial information (in U.S. millions) from the 2005 financial statements of **Nike** and **Adidas**:

	Nike	Adidas
Sales	$13,739.7	$6,635.6
Allowance for doubtful accounts, Jan. 1	95.3	91.5
Allowance for doubtful accounts, Dec. 31	80.4	80.7
Accounts receivable balance (gross), Jan. 1	2215.5	1137.8
Accounts receivable balance (gross), Dec. 31	2342.5	1045.5

Instructions

Calculate the receivables turnover and average collection period for both companies and compare the two companies. Comment on the difference in the two companies' collection experiences.

Evaluate liquidity.
(SO 4) AN

P8–12A The following ratios are available for Western Roofing:

	2008	2007	2006
Current ratio	1.6 to 1	1.5 to 1	1.4 to 1
Receivables turnover	6 times	7 times	8 times
Inventory turnover	7 times	6 times	5 times

Instructions

(a) Calculate the collection period, days sales in inventory, and operating cycle for each year.

(b) Has Western Roofing's liquidity improved or weakened over the three-year period? Explain.

Problems: Set B

P8–1B At December 31, 2007, Bordeaux Co. reported the following information on its balance sheet:

Accounts receivable	$960,000
Less: Allowance for doubtful accounts	67,200

Record accounts receivable and bad debts transactions. (SO 1, 2) AP

In the first quarter of 2008, the company had the following transactions related to receivables:

1. Sales on account, $3,200,000
2. Sales returns and allowances, $50,000
3. Collections of accounts receivable, $3,000,000
4. Write-offs of accounts considered uncollectible, $90,000
5. Recovery of accounts previously written off as uncollectible, $18,000

Instructions

(a) Prepare the summary journal entries to record each of these five transactions.
(b) Enter the January 1, 2008, balances in the Accounts Receivable and Allowance for Doubtful Accounts general ledger accounts. Post the entries to the two accounts and determine the balances.
(c) Record bad debts expense for the first quarter of 2008. Uncollectible accounts are estimated at 7% of accounts receivable.
(d) Calculate the net realizable value of accounts receivable at the end of the first quarter.

P8–2B At the beginning of the current period, Huang Co. had a balance of $200,000 in Accounts Receivable and a $16,000 credit balance in Allowance for Doubtful Accounts. In the period, it had net credit sales of $800,000 and collections of $723,000. It wrote off accounts receivable of $21,750 as uncollectible. However, $3,300 of one of the accounts written off as uncollectible was recovered before the end of the current period.

Record accounts receivable and bad debts transactions. (SO 1, 2) AP

Instructions

(a) Record sales and collections in the period.
(b) Record the write-off of uncollectible accounts and the recovery of accounts written off as uncollectible in the period.
(c) Record the bad debts expense adjusting entry for the period if Huang Co. estimates that 2.25% of net credit sales will become uncollectible.
(d) Determine the ending balances in Accounts Receivable and Allowance for Doubtful Accounts.
(e) What is the net realizable value of receivables at the end of the period?
(f) What is the amount of bad debts expense on the income statement for the period?
(g) Now assume that Huang Co. uses the percentage of receivables approach instead of the percentage of sales approach to estimate uncollectible accounts. Repeat (c) through (f) assuming Huang estimates 8% of the ending accounts receivable will become uncollectible.

P8–3B Information on Hohenberger Company for 2008 follows:

Total credit sales	$2,000,000
Accounts receivable at December 31	800,000
Uncollectible accounts written off	35,000
Uncollectible accounts later recovered	6,000

Calculate bad debt amounts and answer questions. (SO 2) AP

Instructions

(a) If Hohenberger Company does not use the allowance method, what amount will it report for bad debts expense?
(b) Assume instead that Hohenberger Company uses the allowance method and estimates its bad debts expense at 2.5% of credit sales. What amount of bad debts expense will Hohenberger Company record if Allowance for Doubtful Accounts has a credit balance of $4,000 before making the adjustment?

(c) Assume instead that Hohenberger Company estimates its bad debts expense based on 6% of total accounts receivable. What amount of bad debts expense will Hohenberger Company record if it has an Allowance for Doubtful Accounts credit balance of $4,000 before making the adjustment?

(d) Assume the same facts as in (c) except that there is a $3,000 debit balance in Allowance for Doubtful Accounts. What amount of bad debts expense will Hohenberger record?

(e) How does the write-off of an uncollectible account affect the bad debts expense for the current period?

(f) How does the collection of an account that had previously been written off affect the net realizable value of accounts receivable?

Prepare aging schedule and record bad debts.
(SO 2) AP

P8–4B An aging analysis of Hagiwara Company's accounts receivable at December 31, 2007 and 2008, showed the following:

Number of Days Outstanding	Estimated % Uncollectible	December 31 2008	December 31 2007
0–30 days	1.5%	$120,000	$137,000
31–60 days	6.0%	32,000	61,000
61–90 days	18.0%	45,000	38,000
Over 90 days	40.0%	78,000	24,000
Total		$275,000	$260,000

Additional information:

1. At December 31, 2007, the unadjusted balance in Allowance for Doubtful Accounts was a credit of $5,700.
2. In 2008, $26,000 of accounts were written off as uncollectible and $1,200 of accounts previously written off were recovered.

Instructions

(a) Prepare an aging schedule to calculate the estimated uncollectible accounts at December 31, 2007, and at December 31, 2008. Comment on the results.

(b) Record the following transactions:
   1. The adjusting entry on December 31, 2007
   2. The write off of uncollectible accounts in 2008
   3. The collection of accounts previously written off
   4. The adjusting entry on December 31, 2008

(c) Calculate the net realizable value of Hagiwara's accounts receivable at December 31, 2007, and December 31, 2008.

Prepare aging schedule and record bad debts.
(SO 2) AP

P8–5B The following is selected information taken from a company's aging schedule to estimate uncollectible accounts receivable at year end:

Customer	Total	Number of Days Outstanding 0–30	31–60	61–90	91–120
Accounts receivable	$560,000	$220,000	$160,000	$100,000	$80,000
Estimated % uncollectible		1%	5%	10%	20%
Estimated uncollectible accounts					

The unadjusted balance in Allowance for Doubtful Accounts is a credit of $7,000.

Instructions

(a) Complete the aging schedule and calculate the total estimated uncollectible accounts.

(b) Record the bad debts adjusting entry using the above information.

(c) In the following year, $32,000 of the outstanding accounts receivable is determined to be uncollectible. Record the write-off of the uncollectible accounts.

(d) The company collects $8,500 of the $32,000 of accounts that were determined to be uncollectible in (c). The company also expects to collect an additional $500. Record the journal entry (or entries) to restore the accounts receivable and the cash collected. Collection of the $500 is expected in the near future.

(e) Explain how establishing an allowance satisfies the matching principle.

P8–6B Kadakus and Company reported the following information in its general ledger at August 31:

Determine missing amounts.
(SO 2) AN

Accounts Receivable						Sales		
Beg. bal.	845,000		(b)				(f)	
	(a)		(c)					
End. bal.	927,500							

Allowance for Doubtful Accounts					Bad Debts Expense	
		Beg. bal.	72,500		45,500	
(d)		(e)				
		End. bal.	79,600			

All sales were made on account. Bad debts expense was estimated as 1% of sales. There were no recoveries of accounts previously written off.

Instructions

Determine the missing amounts in Kadakus and Company's accounts. State what each of these amounts represents. You will not be able to determine the missing items in alphabetical order. (*Hint:* To solve this problem, it might help if you reconstruct the journal entries.)

P8–7B Bassano Company uses the percentage of sales approach to record bad debts expense for its monthly financial statements and the percentage of receivables approach for its year-end financial statements. Bassano Company has an October 31 fiscal year end, closes temporary accounts annually, and uses a periodic inventory system.

Record accounts receivable
and bad debts transactions;
discuss statement
presentation.
(SO 1, 2, 4) AP

On August 31, 2008, after completing its month-end adjustments, it had accounts receivable of $742,500, a credit balance of $27,570 in Allowance for Doubtful Accounts, and bad debts expense of $85,680. In September and October, the following occurred:

September
1. Sold $546,300 of merchandise on account.
2. A total of $9,170 of the merchandise sold on account was returned. These customers were issued credit memos.
3. Collected $592,750 cash on account from customers.
4. Interest charges of $12,020 were charged to outstanding accounts receivable.
5. As part of the month-end adjusting entries, recorded bad debts expense of 2% of net credit sales for the month.

October
1. Credit sales in the month were $639,900.
2. Received $3,450 cash from a customer whose account had been written off in July.
3. Collected $585,420 cash, in addition to the cash collected in (2) above, from customers on account.
4. Wrote off $46,480 of accounts receivable as uncollectible.
5. Interest charges of $12,070 were charged to outstanding accounts receivable.
6. Recorded the year-end adjustment for bad debts. Uncollectible accounts were estimated to be 3% of accounts receivable.

Instructions

(a) Record the above transactions and adjustments.
(b) Show how accounts receivable will appear on the October 31, 2008, balance sheet.
(c) What amount will be reported as bad debts expense on the income statement for the year ended October 31, 2008?
(d) Where are bad debts expense and interest revenue shown on the income statement?

Record receivables
transactions.
(SO 2, 3) AP

P8–8B Bleumortier Company has a March 31 fiscal year end. Selected transactions in the year included the following:

Jan. 2 Sold $9,000 of merchandise to Brooks Company, terms n/30.

Feb. 1 Accepted a $9,000, 3-month, 6% promissory note from Brooks Company for the balance due (see January 2 transaction). Interest must be paid monthly.

    18 Sold $4,000 of merchandise to Mathias Co., terms n/10.

Mar. 1 Collected the monthly interest payment from Brooks Company (see February 1 transaction).

    2 Accepted a $4,000, 3-month, 5.5% note from Mathias Co. for its balance due, with interest payable at maturity.

    31 Accrued interest on any outstanding notes.

Apr. 1 Collected the monthly interest payment from Brooks Company (see February 1 transaction).

May 1 Collected Brooks Company note in full (see February 1 transaction).

June 2 Mathias Co. dishonours its note of March 2. It is expected that Mathias will eventually pay the amount owed.

July 13 Sold $5,000 of merchandise to Tritt Inc. and accepted Tritt's $5,000, 3-month, 7% note for the amount due, with interest payable at maturity.

Oct. 13 The Tritt Inc. note was dishonoured (see July 13 transaction). Tritt Inc. is bankrupt and there is no hope of future settlement.

Instructions

Record the above transactions. (Round calculations to the nearest dollar.)

Record receivable
transactions. Show balance
sheet presentation.
(SO 1, 3, 4) AP

P8–9B Tardif Company adjusts its books monthly. On September 30, 2008, selected ledger account balances are as follows:

Notes Receivable	$32,700
Credit Cards Receivable	16,300
Interest Receivable	?

Notes receivable include the following:

Issue Date	Maker	Principal	Interest	Term
Aug. 1, 2007	FRN Inc.	$ 9,000	5.50%	2 years
May 31, 2008	IMM Ltd.	7,500	5.25%	9 months
Aug. 31, 2008	DRX Co.	6,000	5.00%	2 months
Sept. 30, 2008	MGH Corp.	10,200	6.00%	16 months

Interest is payable on the first day of each month for notes with terms of one year or longer. Interest is payable at maturity for notes with terms less than one year. In October, the following transactions were completed:

Oct. 1 Received payment of the interest due from FRN Inc.

    7 Made sales of $5,800 on Tardif credit cards.

    29 Collected $4,100 of Tardif credit card receivables.

    31 Added $325 to Tardif credit card customer balances for interest charges on unpaid balances.

    31 Received notice that the DRX note had been dishonoured. (Assume that DRX is expected to pay in the future.)

Instructions

(a) Calculate the interest receivable at September 30, 2008.

(b) Record the October transactions and the October 31 adjusting entry for accrued interest receivable.

(c) Enter the balances at October 1 in the receivables accounts, and post the entries to all of the receivables accounts.

(d) Show the balance sheet presentation of the receivables accounts at October 31.

(e) How would the journal entry on October 31 be different if DRX were not expected to pay in the future?

P8–10B Tocksfor Company's general ledger included the following selected accounts (in thousands) at September 30, 2008:

Prepare assets section of balance sheet; calculate and interpret ratios.
(SO 4) AN

Accounts payable	$1,436.4	Interest revenue	$ 26.3
Accounts receivable	787.1	Merchandise inventory	841.2
Accumulated amortization—equipment	1,144.9	Notes receivable—due in 2009	128.0
Allowance for doubtful accounts	47.2	Notes receivable—due in 2012	254.8
Bad debts expense	121.7	Prepaid expenses and deposits	26.8
Cash and cash equivalents	787.3	Sales	6,087.3
Cost of goods sold	880.5	Sales discounts	41.7
Equipment	2,310.4	Supplies	29.0
		Unearned sales revenue	75.1

Additional information:

1. The net realizable value of the accounts receivable was $765.9 thousand on September 30, 2007.
2. The receivables turnover was 8.3 the previous year.

Instructions

(a) Prepare the assets section of the balance sheet.
(b) Calculate the receivables turnover and average collection period. Compare these results to the previous year's results and comment on any trends.

P8–11B Presented here is selected financial information (in millions) from the 2005 financial statements of **Rogers Communications Inc.** and **Shaw Communications Inc.**:

Calculate and interpret ratios.
(SO 4) AN

	Rogers	Shaw
Sales	$7,482.2	$2,209.8
Allowance for doubtful accounts, Jan. 1	94.0	23.0
Allowance for doubtful accounts, Dec. 31	98.5	31.9
Accounts receivable balance (gross), Jan. 1	767.9	142.5
Accounts receivable balance (gross), Dec. 31	989.2	146.6

Instructions

Calculate the receivables turnover and average collection period for both companies. Comment on the difference in their collection experiences.

P8–12B The following ratios are available for Satellite Mechanical:

Evaluate liquidity.
(SO 4) AN

	2008	2007	2006
Current ratio	2.0 to 1	1.8 to 1	1.6 to 1
Receivables turnover	6.5 times	7.3 times	8.7 times
Inventory turnover	6.9 times	7.6 times	8.5 times

Instructions

(a) Calculate the collection period, days sales in inventory, and operating cycle for each year.
(b) Has Satellite Mechanical's liquidity improved or weakened over the three-year period? Explain.

Continuing Cookie Chronicle

(*Note:* This is a continuation of the Cookie Chronicle from Chapters 1 through 7.)

Natalie has been approached by one of her friends, Curtis Lesperance. Curtis runs a coffee shop where he sells specialty coffees, and prepares and sells muffins and cookies. He is very anxious to buy one of Natalie's fine European mixers because he would then be able to prepare larger batches of muffins and cookies. Curtis, however, cannot afford to pay for the mixer for at least 30 days. He has asked Natalie if she would be willing to sell him the mixer on credit.

Natalie comes to you for advice and asks the following questions:

1. Curtis has given me a set of his most recent financial statements. What calculations should I do with the data from these statements and what questions should I ask him after I have analyzed the statements? How will this information help me decide if I should extend credit to Curtis?
2. Is there another alternative other than extending credit to Curtis for 30 days?
3. I am thinking seriously about being able to have my customers use credit cards. What are some of the advantages and disadvantages of letting my customers pay by credit card?

The following transactions occurred in June through August, 2008:

June 1 After much thought, Natalie sells a mixer to Curtis on credit, terms n/30, for $1,250 (cost of mixer $566).

30 Curtis calls Natalie. He is unable to pay the amount outstanding for another month, so he signs a 1-month, 8.25%, note receivable.

July 31 Curtis calls Natalie. He cannot pay today but hopes to have a cheque for her at the end of the week. Natalie prepares the correct journal entry.

Aug. 10 Curtis calls again and promises to pay at the end of August, including interest for two months.

31 Natalie receives a cheque from Curtis in payment of his balance owing plus interest outstanding.

Instructions

(a) Answer Natalie's questions.
(b) Prepare journal entries for the transactions that occurred in June, July, and August.

BROADENING YOUR PERSPECTIVE

Financial Reporting and Analysis

Financial Reporting Problem

BYP8–1 The receivables turnover, collection period, and operating cycle for **The Forzani Group Ltd.** were calculated in this chapter, based on the company's financial statements for the 2006 fiscal year. These consolidated financial statements are presented in Appendix A.

Instructions

(a) Calculate Forzani's receivables turnover, collection period, and operating cycle for the 2005 fiscal year. Note that the company's accounts receivable and inventory at the end of its 2004 fiscal year amounted to $36,319 thousand and $258,816 thousand respectively.
(b) Comment on any significant differences which you observe between the ratios for 2006 (as calculated in the chapter) and 2005 (as calculated above).

Interpreting Financial Statements

BYP8–2 **Suncor Energy Inc.** reported the following information (in millions) in its financial statements for the fiscal years 2003 through 2005:

	2005	2004	2003
Operating revenues (assume all credit)	$9,749	$8,270	$6,329
Accounts receivable (gross)	1,143	630	509
Allowance for doubtful accounts	4	3	4
Total current assets	1,916	1,195	1,279
Total current liabilities	1,935	1,409	1,060

Additional detail about Suncor's receivables includes the following:

The company has a securitization program in place to sell to a third party, on a revolving, fully serviced, and limited recourse basis, up to $340 million of accounts receivable having a maturity of 45 days or less. As at December 31, 2005, $340 million in outstanding accounts receivable had been sold under the program.

Industry averages are as follows: current ratio, 1.45:1; receivables turnover, 7.3 times; and average collection period, 50 days.

Instructions

(a) Calculate the current ratios, receivables turnover ratios, and average collection periods for fiscal 2005 and 2004. Comment on Suncor's liquidity for each of the years and compared to the industry.
(b) In 2005, Suncor's dollar amount of its allowance for doubtful accounts was the same as it was in 2003. Comment on the relevance of this as a percentage of accounts receivable.
(c) Suncor regularly sells a portion of its accounts receivable. Comment on this practice as part of Suncor's management of its accounts receivable.

Critical Thinking

Collaborative Learning Activity

Note to instructors: Additional instructions and material for this group activity can be found on the Instructor Resource Site.

BYP8–3   In this group activity, you will work in pairs to review the following two approaches to estimate bad debts:

1. Percentage of sales
2. Percentage of receivables

Instructions

(a) In your pair, each select one of the above approaches. Temporarily leave your partner and join the "expert" group for that approach.
(b) In the "expert" group, use the handout given to you by your instructor and discuss your approach. Ensure that each group member thoroughly understands it.
(c) Return to your partner and explain your approach.
(d) You may be asked by your instructor to write a short quiz on this topic.

Study Aids:
Working in Groups

Communication Activity

BYP8–4   Toys for Big Boys sells snowmobiles, personal watercraft, ATVs, and the like. Recently, the credit manager of Toys for Big Boys retired. The sales staff threw him a big retirement party— they were glad to see him go because they felt his credit policies restricted their selling ability. The sales staff convinced management that there was no need to replace the credit manager since they could handle this responsibility in addition to their sales positions.

Study Aids:
Writing Handbook

Management was thrilled at year end when sales doubled. However, accounts receivable quadrupled and cash flow halved. The company's average collection period increased from 30 days to 120 days.

Instructions

In a memo to management, explain the financial impact of allowing the sales staff to manage the credit function. Has the business assumed any additional credit risk? What would you recommend the company do to better manage its increasing accounts receivable?

Ethics Case

**Study Aids:
Ethics in Accounting**

BYP8–5 The controller of Proust Company has completed an aging schedule, using the following percentages to estimate the uncollectible accounts: 0–30 days, 5%; 31–60 days, 10%; 61–90 days, 30%; 91–120 days, 50%; and over 120 days, 80%. The president of the company, Suzanne Bros, is nervous because the bank expects the company to sustain its current growth rate of at least 5% over the next two years—the remaining term of its bank loan. President Bros suggests that the controller increase the percentages, which will increase the amount of the required bad debts expense adjustment. The president thinks that the lower net income (because of the increased bad debts expense) will make it easier next year to show a better growth rate.

Instructions

(a) Who are the stakeholders in this case?
(b) Does the president's request create an ethical dilemma for the controller?
(c) Should the controller be concerned with Proust Company's growth rate in estimating the allowance? Explain your answer.

ANSWERS TO CHAPTER QUESTIONS

Answers to Accounting in Action Insight Questions

Business Insight, p. 411

Q: Since the interest rates on company credit cards are so high, why don't all companies have their own credit cards?

A: It might sound like a great idea for a company to have its own credit card if customers are willing to pay interest rates as high as 28.8%. But if a company has its own credit card, it will have to do a credit check on each customer, keep track of all of the customer accounts, absorb any losses if a customer does not pay, and wait for customers to pay so that the cash is available for the company to use.

Across the Organization Insight, p. 424

Q: If you were a loans officer at a bank, how would you decide whether or not to make a loan to a company?

A: The most important thing is to decide whether or not the company will be able to repay the loan. You should find out about the company's business, about how it plans to use the money, and about how it plans to repay the money. You should also evaluate the company's past liquidity and profitability. Loans should not be given because of the political connections of the company's owners or managers.

Business Insight, p. 429

Q: Why would Sears sell its credit card operations to an unrelated company?

A: Companies are always looking for ways to increase profits through either cutting costs or increasing revenues. Sears would have compared the amount it expects to earn in performance payments from JPMorgan Chase to what it earned from the credit card operations, and then concluded that it could earn more on the performance payments. In addition, because JPMorgan Chase already has an extensive credit card operation, it will probably be able to process and manage the credit card receivables at a lower cost than Sears.

Answer to Forzani Review It Question, p. 412

In Note 2(h) on revenue recognition, The Forzani Group Ltd. states that it earns revenue on both sales to customers in stores and from sales to, and service fees from, franchise stores and others. Forzani also states that revenue is recognized on sales to franchise stores at the time of shipment. These sales to franchise stores are probably on credit. Forzani would therefore record a receivable from the franchise store when the merchandise is shipped.

Answers to Self-Study Questions

1. b   2. b   3. d   4. c   5. c   6. b   7. d   8. a   9. c   10. d

Remember to go back to the Navigator Box at the beginning of the chapter to check off your completed work.

concepts for review >>

Before studying this chapter, you should understand or, if necessary, review:

a. The cost principle (Ch. 1, p. 8) and the matching principle (Ch. 3, pp. 105–106).

b. The time period assumption. (Ch. 3, p. 104)

c. What amortization is, and how to make adjustments for it. (Ch. 3, pp. 111–112)

Measuring Value: What's a Historic Building Worth?

Dawson College: www.dawsoncollege.qc.ca

Montreal, Que.—For a college or university, the buildings where classes and other activities take place are some of its most important assets. Look around the campus of your own school. Where did the money for these buildings come from? Who pays to maintain them? How should the cost of the buildings be allocated over their useful lives? And how much are they worth?

For Dawson College in Montreal, the first of these questions is easy. The provincial government financed the 1988 purchase of its current building, the historic former Mother House of the Congrégation de Notre-Dame. With this purchase and the expansions that followed, all the college's facilities were brought together under one roof.

As for the second question, again, the provincial government pays for most of Dawson's expenses. Established in 1969 as the first English-language institution in Quebec's network of CEGEPs (which replaced Grades 12 and 13), Dawson receives an annual allocation of about $1 million, which goes into a capital fund to cover any needed repairs or renovations, explains controller Guy Veilleux, CGA. It has also received lump sums from the government for specific projects, such as the $37-million renovations done after the building was purchased, a $10-million expansion in 1990–91, and another $23-million expansion in 1994–95. In addition, the government allocates specific funds for equipment purchases and renovations that are required when it revises programs.

How the cost of the buildings should be allocated or amortized has been a complicated problem. "For years, there was no amortization of buildings or equipment in our books," says Mr. Veilleux. Until the early 2000s, special accounting principles for government entities did not require accrual accounting. When the public sector accounting principles later changed to require accrual accounting, the government and other public institutions began recognizing the amortization of their physical assets.

In 2000–01, the government instructed its CEGEPs to calculate amortization retroactively from 1995–96 using the declining-balance method. By 2006, Dawson's building had been amortized at about 25 percent of its book value, using a 3 percent amortization rate.

How much the buildings are now worth is the trickiest question. "The value of the building is not the cost. The value of the building that we show on the financial statements includes the original buildings, plus the cost of the acquisitions since then, and less the accumulated amortization over the years," says Mr. Veilleux. However, since the former Mother House is a designated heritage site, some people might consider it priceless.

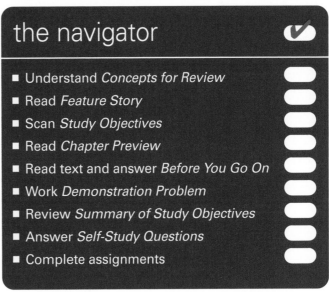

the navigator ✔

- Understand *Concepts for Review*
- Read *Feature Story*
- Scan *Study Objectives*
- Read *Chapter Preview*
- Read text and answer *Before You Go On*
- Work *Demonstration Problem*
- Review *Summary of Study Objectives*
- Answer *Self-Study Questions*
- Complete assignments

chapter 9
Long-Lived Assets

study objectives >>

the navigator

After studying this chapter, you should be able to:

1. Apply the cost principle to property, plant, and equipment.
2. Explain and calculate amortization.
3. Revise periodic amortization.
4. Account for the disposal of property, plant, and equipment.
5. Calculate and record amortization of natural resources.
6. Identify the basic accounting issues for intangible assets.
7. Illustrate the reporting and analysis of long-lived assets.

The accounting for campus buildings at Dawson College has a real impact on the school's reported results. In this chapter, we explain the application of the cost principle of accounting to property, plant, and equipment, as well as to natural resources and intangible assets. We describe the methods that can be used to allocate the cost of an asset over its useful life. In addition, we discuss the accounting for expenditures which occur during the useful life of assets, such as the cost of renovations for Dawson College. We also discuss the disposition of these assets during and at the end of their useful lives.

The chapter is organized as follows:

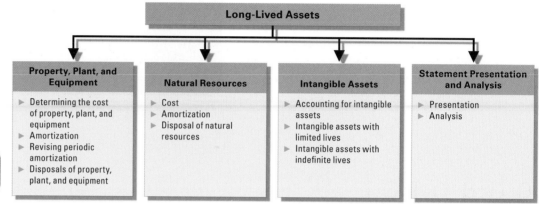

the navigator

Property, Plant, and Equipment

Alternative terminology
Property, plant, and equipment are also commonly known as *fixed assets*; *land, building, and equipment*; or *capital assets*.

Property, plant, and equipment are long-lived assets that the company owns and uses for the production and sale of goods or services to consumers. They have three characteristics: they have a physical substance (a definite size and shape), are used in the operations of the business, and are not intended for sale to customers. Property, plant, and equipment are often subdivided into four classes:

1. Land, such as a building site
2. Land improvements, such as driveways, parking lots, fences, and underground sprinkler systems
3. Buildings, such as stores, offices, factories, and warehouses
4. Equipment, such as store checkout counters, cash registers, coolers, office furniture, factory machinery, and delivery equipment

In the following sections, we will learn about determining the cost of property, plant, and equipment, the amortization of property, plant, and equipment, and the accounting for disposals of property, plant, and equipment.

Determining the Cost of Property, Plant, and Equipment

study objective 1

Apply the cost principle to property, plant, and equipment.

The cost principle requires that property, plant, and equipment be recorded at cost. Cost includes all expenditures that are necessary in order to acquire an asset and make it ready for its intended use. For example, the cost of factory machinery includes the purchase price, freight costs paid by the purchaser, and any testing and installation costs. All of these costs are capitalized (recorded as property, plant, and equipment), rather than expensed, because they will provide benefits over future periods.

Determining which costs to include in a long-lived asset account and which costs not to include is very important. Costs which benefit only the current period are expensed. Such costs are called **operating expenditures**. Costs that benefit future periods are included in a long-lived asset account. These costs are called **capital expenditures**.

Once the asset's cost is established, it becomes the basis of accounting for the asset over its useful life. Current market values are not used after an asset is acquired unless the values permanently decline below net book value (cost less accumulated amortization). We will discuss how to account for permanent declines in market value in a later section of this chapter.

How the cost principle is applied to each of the major classes of property, plant, and equipment is explained next.

 ACCOUNTING IN ACTION ▶ Ethics Insight

Atlas Cold Storage Income Trust needed to tell investors a convincing growth story or its string of acquisitions would have come to a dead stop. From 2001 through the second quarter of 2003, Atlas's actual quarterly results were lower than the unreasonably high target that the company's president and CEO, Patrick Gouveia, had presented to the market. Accounting staff were told to find more earnings. How did they do this? One method was to review all expenses over $1,000 and to instead treat them as capital expenditures. After an investigation in 2003, it was determined that more than $5 million of such expenses had been incorrectly capitalized. Atlas's earnings for 2001 through the second quarter of 2003 have long since been corrected and restated, but the investigation into the actions of several members of senior management during that time continues.

? Why is it wrong to treat expenses as capital expenditures?

Land

The cost of land includes (1) the purchase price, (2) closing costs such as surveying and legal fees, and (3) the costs of preparing the land for its intended use, such as the removal of old buildings, clearing, draining, filling, and grading. All of these costs (less any proceeds from salvaged materials) are debited to the Land account.

To illustrate, assume that the Budovitch Manufacturing Company acquires real estate for $100,000 cash. The property contained an old warehouse that is removed at a net cost of $6,000 ($7,500 to remove it less $1,500 received for materials from the warehouse that were salvaged and later sold). Additional expenditures include the legal fee of $3,000. The cost of the land is $109,000, calculated as follows:

Land	
Cash price of property	$100,000
Net cost of removing warehouse	6,000
Legal fee	3,000
Cost of land	$109,000

When recording the acquisition, Land is debited for $109,000 and Cash is credited for $109,000 (assuming the costs were paid in cash).

Land Improvements

Land is a unique long-lived asset. Its cost is not amortized—allocated over its useful life—because land has an unlimited useful life. However, costs are often incurred for certain items related to the land that have limited useful lives. **Land improvements** are structural additions made to land, such as driveways, parking lots, fences, and landscaping.

As time passes, land improvements become less able to provide the service they are intended for and they therefore require maintenance and replacement to maintain their value. Because of this, these costs are recorded separately from land. They are instead recorded as land improvements and are amortized over their useful lives.

Buildings

All costs that are related to the purchase or construction of a building are debited to the Buildings account. When a building is purchased, these costs include the purchase price and closing costs (e.g., legal fees). The costs of making a building ready to be used as intended can include expenditures for remodelling, and for replacing or repairing the roof, floors, electrical wiring, and plumbing. These costs also are debited to Buildings.

When a new building is built, cost includes the contract price plus payments for architects' fees, building permits, and excavation costs. The interest costs of financing for the construction project are also included in the cost of the asset when a significant amount of time is needed to get the building ready to be used. In these circumstances, interest costs are considered as necessary as materials and labour. Only the interest costs which occur during the construction period are included, however. After construction is finished, future interest payments on funds that were borrowed to finance the cost of the constructed building are debited to Interest Expense.

Equipment

The "equipment" classification is a broad one that can include delivery equipment, office equipment, machinery, vehicles, furniture and fixtures, and other similar assets. The cost of these assets includes the purchase price, freight charges and insurance during transit that are paid by the purchaser, and the costs of assembling, installing, and testing the equipment. These costs are treated as capital expenditures because they benefit future periods.

Such annual costs as motor vehicle licences and insurance on company trucks and cars are treated as operating expenditures because they are recurring expenditures that do not benefit future periods.

To illustrate, assume that 1 Stop Florists purchases a used delivery truck on January 1, 2008, for $24,500 cash. Related expenditures include painting and lettering, $500; a motor vehicle licence, $80; and a one-year insurance policy, $2,600. The cost of the delivery truck is $25,000, calculated as follows:

Delivery Truck	
Cash price	$24,500
Painting and lettering	500
Cost of delivery truck	$25,000

The cost of the motor vehicle licence is recorded as an expense and the cost of the insurance policy is recorded as a prepaid asset. The entry to record the purchase of the truck and related expenditures, assuming they were all paid for in cash, is as follows:

A	=	L	+	OE
+25,000				−80
+2,600				
−27,680				

↓ Cash flows: −27,680

Jan. 1	Delivery Truck	25,000	
	Licence Expense	80	
	Prepaid Insurance	2,600	
	Cash		27,680
	To record purchase of delivery truck and related expenditures.		

Basket Purchase

Property, plant, and equipment are often purchased together for a single price. This is known as a **basket purchase**. We need to know the cost of each individual asset in order to journalize the purchase, and to later calculate the amortization of each asset. When a basket purchase occurs, we determine individual costs by allocating the total price paid for the group of assets to each individual asset based on its relative fair market value.

Alternative terminology
A basket purchase is also known as a *lump-sum purchase*.

To illustrate, assume Sega Company acquired a building and a parcel of land on July 31 for $300,000, paying $50,000 cash and incurring a mortgage payable for the balance. The land was recently appraised at $120,000. The building was appraised at $200,000. The $300,000 cost should be allocated based on fair market values (i.e., appraised values) as shown in Illustration 9-1.

Illustration 9-1 ◀

Allocating cost in a basket purchase

	Fair Market Value	Allocated Percentage		Allocated Cost	
Land	$120,000	37.5%	($120,000 ÷ $320,000)	$112,500	($300,000 × 37.5%)
Building	200,000	62.5%	($200,000 ÷ $320,000)	187,500	($300,000 × 62.5%)
Totals	$320,000	100.0%		$300,000	

The journal entry to record this purchase is as follows:

July 31	Land		112,500	
	Building		187,500	
	Cash			50,000
	Mortgage Payable			250,000
	To record purchase of land and building, with costs allocated based on appraised values of $120,000 and $200,000, respectively.			

A	=	L	+	OE
+112,500		+250,000		
+187,500				
−50,000				

Cash flows: −50,000

BEFORE YOU GO ON . . .

▶Review It

1. What are the major classes of property, plant, and equipment?
2. Explain the difference between operating and capital expenditures.
3. What types of costs are included in each major class of property, plant, and equipment?
4. What is a basket purchase?
5. What is the cost of each type of capital asset that The Forzani Group Ltd. reports in Note 3 to its balance sheet? The answer to this question is at the end of the chapter.

▶Do It

Assume that factory machinery is purchased on November 6 for $10,000 cash and a $40,000 note payable. Related cash expenditures include insurance during shipping, $500; the annual insurance policy, $750; and installation and testing, $1,000. Prepare the journal entry to record these expenditures.

Action Plan

- Capitalize expenditures that are made to get the machinery ready for its intended use.
- Expense operating expenditures that benefit only the current period, or are recurring costs.

Solution

Factory Machinery	
Purchase price	$50,000
Insurance during shipping	500
Installation and testing	1,000
Cost of machinery	$51,500

The entry to record the purchase and related expenditures is:

Nov. 6	Factory Machinery	51,500	
	Prepaid Insurance	750	
	Cash ($10,000 + $500 + $750 + $1,000)		12,250
	Note Payable		40,000
	To record purchase of factory machinery and related expenditures.		

Related exercise material: BE9–1, BE9–2, BE9–3, BE9–4, and E9–1.

Amortization

study objective 2

Explain and calculate amortization.

Alternative terminology
Amortization is also commonly known as *depreciation*.

As we learned in Chapter 3, amortization is the process of allocating the cost of a long-lived asset to expense over the asset's useful life (i.e., its service life) in a rational and systematic way. The cost is allocated in this way so that expenses are properly matched with revenues in accordance with the matching principle.

You will recall that amortization is recorded through an adjusting journal entry which debits Amortization Expense and credits Accumulated Amortization. Amortization expense is an operating expense on the income statement. Accumulated amortization appears on the balance sheet as a contra account to the related asset account. This contra asset account is similar in purpose to the one used in Chapter 8 for the allowance for doubtful accounts. Both contra accounts reduce assets to their carrying values: *net realizable value* for accounts receivable, and *net book value* for property, plant, and equipment.

It is important to understand that amortization is a process of cost allocation, not a process of determining an asset's real value. Illustration 9-2 shows this. There is no attempt to measure the change in an asset's market value while it is owned, because property, plant, and equipment are not for resale. Current market values are not relevant (unless a permanent decline in value has occurred). So, the net book value of property, plant, or equipment (cost less accumulated amortization) may be very different from its market value. We saw this in our feature story where Dawson College's former Mother House building has a book value much lower than its market value.

It is also important to understand that amortization does not result in the accumulation of cash for the replacement of the asset. The balance in Accumulated Amortization only represents the total amount of the asset's cost that has been allocated to expense so far: it is not a cash fund. Cash is neither increased nor decreased by the adjusting entry to record amortization.

Illustration 9-2 ►

Amortization as an allocation concept

Three classes of property, plant, and equipment are amortized: land improvements, buildings, and equipment. Each of these classes is considered an amortizable asset because the usefulness to the company and the revenue-producing ability of each class decreases during the asset's useful life. Because land has an unlimited useful life, land is not amortized. Its life is unlimited because its ability to produce revenue is generally the same over time. In fact, in many cases, the usefulness of land increases because of the scarcity of good land sites. Thus, land is not an amortizable asset.

During an amortizable asset's useful life, its revenue-producing ability declines because of physical factors such as wear and tear. A delivery truck that has been driven 100,000 kilometres is less useful to a company than one driven only 1,000 kilometres.

A decline in revenue-producing ability may also occur because of economic factors, such as obsolescence. For example, many companies replace their computers long before they wear out, because improvements in hardware and software make their old computers obsolete. It is important to understand that amortization only approximates the decline in an asset's ability to produce revenue. It does not exactly measure the true effects of physical or economic factors.

Factors in Calculating Amortization

In Chapter 3, we learned that amortization expense was calculated by dividing the cost of an amortizable asset by its useful life. At that time, we ignored the added complexity of residual value in the calculation of amortization. In this chapter, we will include this factor by deducting residual value from the asset's cost as part of determining the asset's amortizable cost. Consequently, there are now three factors that affect the calculation of amortization:

1. Cost. The factors that affect the cost of an amortizable asset were explained earlier in this chapter. Recall that property, plant, and equipment are recorded at cost, which respects the cost principle. This includes all costs incurred to get the asset ready for use.
2. Useful life. **Useful life** is an estimate of the expected productive life, also called the *service life*, of the asset. Useful life can be expressed in terms of time, units of activity (such as machine hours), or units of output. Useful life is an estimate. In making the estimate, management considers such factors as the intended use of the asset, its expected need for repair and maintenance, and its vulnerability to obsolescence (i.e., the chances of its becoming obsolete). The company's past experience with similar assets often helps in estimating the expected useful life.
3. Residual value. **Residual value** is an estimate of the asset's value at the end of its useful life. This value may be based on the asset's worth as scrap or on its expected trade-in value. Residual value is not amortized, since the amount is expected to be recovered at the end of the asset's useful life. Like useful life, residual value is an estimate. In making the estimate, management considers when and how it plans to dispose of the asset and its experience with similar assets.

Alternative terminology
Residual value is also sometimes called *salvage value*.

Illustration 9-3 summarizes these three factors.

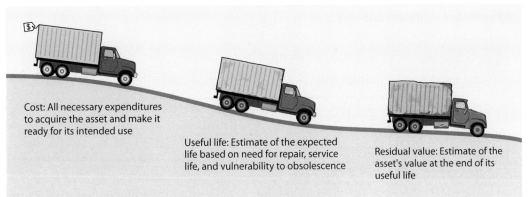

Illustration 9-3 ◄

Three factors in calculating amortization

Cost: All necessary expenditures to acquire the asset and make it ready for its intended use

Useful life: Estimate of the expected life based on need for repair, service life, and vulnerability to obsolescence

Residual value: Estimate of the asset's value at the end of its useful life

Amortization Methods

Amortization is generally calculated using one of the following methods:

1. Straight-line
2. Declining-balance
3. Units-of-activity

Each method is acceptable under generally accepted accounting principles. Management chooses the method that it believes will best measure an asset's contribution to revenue during its useful life. Once a method is chosen, it should be applied consistently over the useful life of the asset. Consistency makes the comparison of financial statements easier. Consistency is also the reason why Dawson College in our feature story retroactively recorded amortization back to 1995–96 when it started recording amortization in 2000–01. If Dawson had not done this, it would have been difficult to compare its financial statements in 2000–01 with the year before and other past years.

Companies may use one method for one type of long-lived asset and another method for a different type of long-lived asset—for example, straight-line amortization for buildings and declining-balance for equipment. Regardless of how many methods are used, nearly every company uses the straight-line method of amortization for some of its long-lived assets, if not all of them. In Canada, 94 percent of public companies use the straight-line method of amortization.

To learn how to calculate the three amortization methods and to compare them, we will use the following data for the small delivery truck bought by 1 Stop Florists on January 1, 2008:

Cost (as shown on page 458)	$25,000
Expected residual value	$2,000
Estimated useful life (in years)	5
Estimated useful life (in kilometres)	200,000

Straight-Line. Under the **straight-line method**, amortization expense is the same for each year of the asset's useful life. As mentioned earlier in the chapter, residual value is deducted from the cost of the asset to determine an asset's **amortizable cost**, the total amount that can be amortized. Amortizable cost is divided by the asset's useful life to calculate the annual amortization expense.

The calculation of amortization expense in the first year for 1 Stop Florists' delivery truck is shown in Illustration 9-4.

Illustration 9-4 ▶

Formula for straight-line method

Alternatively, we can calculate an annual percentage rate at which to amortize the delivery truck by dividing 100% by the useful life in years. In this case, the straight-line amortization rate is 20% (100% ÷ 5 years). When an annual rate is used, the amortizable cost of the asset is multiplied by the straight-line amortization rate to calculate the annual amortization expense, as shown in the amortization schedule in Illustration 9-5.

Illustration 9-5 ◀

Straight-line amortization
schedule

1 STOP FLORISTS Straight-line Amortization Schedule					
				End of Year	
Year	Amortizable Cost	× Amortization Rate	= Amortization Expense	Accumulated Amortization	Net Book Value
					$25,000
2008	$23,000	20%	$ 4,600	$ 4,600	20,400
2009	23,000	20%	4,600	9,200	15,800
2010	23,000	20%	4,600	13,800	11,200
2011	23,000	20%	4,600	18,400	6,600
2012	23,000	20%	4,600	23,000	2,000
			$23,000		

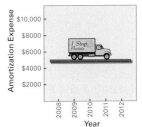

Note that the amortization expense of $4,600 is the same each year. Also note that the column total for amortization expense is equal to the amortizable cost of the asset, and that the book value at the end of the useful life is equal to the estimated $2,000 residual value.

What happens when an asset is purchased during the year, rather than on January 1 as in our example? In that case, it is necessary to prorate the annual amortization for the part of the year that the asset was used. If 1 Stop Florists had purchased the delivery truck on April 1, 2008, the truck would have been used for nine months in 2008. The amortization for 2008 would be $3,450 ($23,000 × 20% × $\frac{9}{12}$). Note that amortization is normally rounded to the nearest month. Since amortization is an estimate only, calculating it to the nearest day gives a false sense of accuracy.

To keep things simple, some companies establish a convention for partial-period amortization, rather than calculating amortization monthly. Companies may choose to record a full year's amortization in the year of acquisition and none in the year of disposal. Others may record a half year's amortization in the year of acquisition and a half year's amortization in the year of disposal. Whatever policy is chosen for partial-year amortization, the impact is not significant in the long run if the policy is used consistently.

As indicated earlier, the straight-line method of amortization is the most popular. It is simple to apply, and it correctly matches expenses with revenues if the asset is used consistently throughout its service life. Assets that give the same benefits all the time during their useful lives generally do not become less productive as they are used. Examples include buildings, and office furniture and fixtures.

Declining-Balance. The **declining-balance method** produces a decreasing annual amortization expense over the asset's useful life. It is called the "declining-balance" method because the periodic amortization is calculated based on the declining book value—or net book value—of the asset (cost less accumulated amortization). Annual amortization expense is calculated by multiplying the book value at the beginning of the year by the amortization rate. The amortization rate remains constant from year to year, but the rate is applied to a book value that declines each year.

Book value for the first year is the cost of the asset, because the balance in accumulated amortization at the beginning of the asset's useful life is zero. In the following years, the book value is the difference between cost and the accumulated amortization at the beginning of the year. Unlike the other amortization methods, the declining-balance method does not use amortizable cost. Residual value is not used in determining the amount that the declining-balance amortization rate is applied to. Residual value does, however, limit the total amortization that can be taken. Amortization stops when the asset's book value equals its expected residual value.

Varying rates of amortization may be used, depending on how fast the company wants to amortize the asset. You will find rates such as one time (single), two times (double), and even three times (triple) the straight-line rate of amortization. An amortization rate that is often used is double the straight-line rate. This method is referred to as the double declining-balance method. If 1 Stop Florists uses the double declining-balance method, the amortization rate is 40% (2 × the straight-line rate of 20%). Illustration 9-6 shows the calculation of amortization on the delivery truck for the first year.

Illustration 9-6 ▶

Formula for double declining-balance method

Net Book Value at Beginning of Year	×	Straight-Line Rate × 2	=	Annual Amortization Expense
$25,000	×	40%	=	$10,000

Illustration 9-7 shows the amortization schedule under this method.

Illustration 9-7 ▶

Double declining-balance amortization schedule

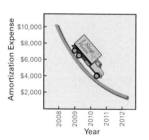

1 STOP FLORISTS
Double Declining-Balance Amortization Schedule

Year	Net Book Value Beginning of Year	× Amortization Rate	= Amortization Expense	Accumulated Amortization (End of Year)	Net Book Value (End of Year)
					$25,000
2008	$25,000	40%	$10,000	$10,000	15,000
2009	15,000	40%	6,000	16,000	9,000
2010	9,000	40%	3,600	19,600	5,400
2011	5,400	40%	2,160	21,760	3,240
2012	3,240	40%	1,240*	23,000	2,000
			$23,000		

*The calculation of $1,296 ($3,240 × 40%) is adjusted to $1,240 so that net book value will equal the residual value.

You can see that the delivery truck is 70% amortized ($16,000 ÷ $23,000) at the end of the second year. Under the straight-line method it would be 40% amortized ($9,200 ÷ $23,000) at that time. Because the declining-balance method produces a higher amortization expense in the early years than the later years, it is considered an accelerated amortization method.

The declining-balance method respects the matching principle. The higher amortization expense in early years is matched with the higher benefits received in these years. A lower amortization expense is recognized in later years when the asset contributes less to revenue. Also, some assets lose their usefulness rapidly because of obsolescence. In these cases, the declining-balance method gives a more appropriate amortization amount than the straight-line method.

When an asset is purchased during the year, the first year's declining-balance amortization must be prorated. For example, if 1 Stop Florists had purchased the delivery truck on April 1, 2008, the amortization for the partial year would be $7,500 ($25,000 × 40% × 9/12). The net book value for calculating amortization in 2009 would then become $17,500 ($25,000 − $7,500). The amortization for 2009 would be $7,000 ($17,500 × 40%). Future calculations would follow from these amounts until the net book value equalled the residual value.

While the declining-balance method is not as popular as the straight-line method, it is still chosen by many companies when it provides the best match of cost and benefit. In other cases, declining-balance is chosen because it must be used for income tax purposes (discussed later in this chapter) and it is simpler to use the same method for both accounting and income tax purposes. Dawson College, in the feature story, uses the declining-balance method of amortization for its buildings. It uses an amortization rate of 3 percent, which means that its buildings are amortized over an average useful life of 33⅓ years.

Units-of-Activity. Under the **units-of-activity method**, useful life is not expressed as a time period; instead, useful life is expressed as the total units of activity or production that is expected from the asset. The units-of-activity method is ideal for equipment whose activity can be measured in units of output, kilometres driven, or hours in use. The units-of-activity method is generally not suitable for buildings or furniture, because amortization of these assets is more a result of time than of use.

Alternative terminology The units-of-activity method is often called the *units-of-production method.*

In this method, the total units of activity for the entire useful life are estimated. This amount is divided into the amortizable cost to determine the amortizable cost per unit. The amortizable cost per unit is then multiplied by the actual units of activity during the year to calculate the annual amortization expense.

To illustrate, assume that the 1 Stop Florists delivery truck is driven 30,000 kilometres in the first year of a total estimated life of 200,000 kilometres. Illustration 9-8 shows the calculation of amortization expense in the first year.

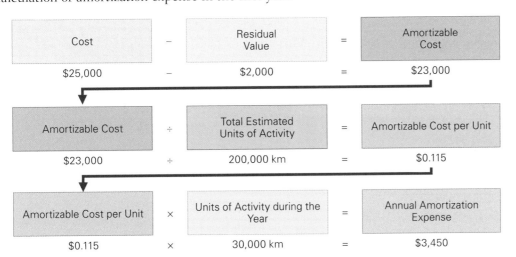

Illustration 9-8 ◀

Formula for units-of-activity method

Cost	–	Residual Value	=	Amortizable Cost
$25,000	–	$2,000	=	$23,000

Amortizable Cost	÷	Total Estimated Units of Activity	=	Amortizable Cost per Unit
$23,000	÷	200,000 km	=	$0.115

Amortizable Cost per Unit	×	Units of Activity during the Year	=	Annual Amortization Expense
$0.115	×	30,000 km	=	$3,450

Illustration 9-9 shows the units-of-activity amortization schedule, using assumed units of activity (kilometres driven) for the later years.

Illustration 9-9 ◀

Units-of-activity amortization schedule

1 STOP FLORISTS
Units-of-Activity Amortization Schedule

Year	Units of Activity	×	Amortizable Cost/Unit	=	Amortizable Expense	End of Year Accumulated Amortization	End of Year Net Book Value
							$25,000
2008	30,000		$0.115		$3,450	$ 3,450	21,550
2009	60,000		$0.115		6,900	10,350	14,650
2010	40,000		$0.115		4,600	14,950	10,050
2011	50,000		$0.115		5,750	20,700	4,300
2012	20,000		$0.115		2,300	23,000	2,000
	200,000				$23,000		

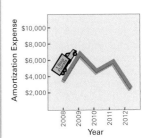

As Illustration 9-9 shows, in this example the total actual units of activity equal the original estimated total units of activity of 200,000 kilometres. But in most real life situations, the total actual units of activity do not exactly equal the total estimated units of activity. This means that the final year's amortization will have to be adjusted—as we saw in the declining-balance method in Illustration 9-7—so that the ending net book value is equal to the estimated residual value.

The units-of-activity method amortization calculations are the same whether the asset is purchased at the beginning of the year or during the year. The actual units of activity already show how much the asset was used during the year. Therefore, the amortization calculations do not need to be adjusted for partial periods as is done in the straight-line and declining-balance methods.

The units-of-activity method is much less popular than the other methods, for two reasons: (1) as already discussed, it can only be used for assets whose activity can be measured in units of output, and (2) even when an asset's activity can be measured in units of output, it is still often difficult to make a reasonable estimate of total activity. Later in this chapter, however, we will see that this method is widely used to amortize natural resources. Although it has limitations, the units-of-activity method results in the best matching of expenses with revenues when the productivity of the asset varies significantly from one period to another.

Comparison of Amortization Methods

Illustration 9-10 presents a comparison of annual and total amortization expense for 1 Stop Florists under each of the three amortization methods. In addition, if we assume for simplicity that net income before deducting amortization expense is $50,000 for each of the five years, we can clearly see the impact that the choice of method has on net income.

Illustration 9-10 ▶

Comparison of amortization methods

Year	Straight-Line Amortization Expense	Straight-Line Net Income	Double Declining-Balance Amortization Expense	Double Declining-Balance Net Income	Units-of-Activity Amortization Expense	Units-of-Activity Net Income
2008	$4,600	$ 45,400	$10,000	$ 40,000	$ 3,450	$ 46,550
2009	4,600	45,400	6,000	44,000	6,900	43,100
2010	4,600	45,400	3,600	46,400	4,600	45,400
2011	4,600	45,400	2,160	47,840	5,750	44,250
2012	4,600	45,400	1,240	48,760	2,300	47,700
	$23,000	$227,000	$23,000	$227,000	$23,000	$227,000

Recall that straight-line amortization results in the same amount of amortization expense and net income each year. Declining-balance results in a higher amortization expense in early years, and therefore lower income, and a lower amortization expense in later years and higher income. Results with the units-of-activity method vary, depending on how much the asset is used each year. While the amortization expense and net income will be different each year for each method, *total* amortization expense and net income after the five-year period are the same for all three methods.

Each method is acceptable because each one recognizes the decline in service potential of the asset in a rational and systematic manner. Which method is best? There is no easy answer to this question.

Helpful hint Practical considerations, rather than theoretical ones, often influence a manager's choice of amortization method—how easy it is to use, how convenient, and tradition.

The matching principle requires that the cost of a long-lived asset should be matched to the revenue produced by that asset. Since the pattern of revenue production is different for each type of asset, the amortization method should be chosen based on the revenue pattern of the specific asset. For an asset that generates revenues fairly consistently over time, the straight-line method is appropriate. The declining-balance method best fits assets that are more productive—that generate larger revenues—in the earlier years of their life. The units-of-activity method applies well to assets whose usage is very different each year.

ACCOUNTING IN ACTION ► Business Insight

Why does Morris Formal Wear use the units-of-activity method for its tuxedos? The reason is that the Ottawa-based family business wants to track wear and tear on each of its 5,200 tuxedos individually. Each tuxedo has a bar code, like a box of cereal at the grocery store. When a tux is rented, a clerk runs its code across an electronic scanner. At year end, the computer adds up the total rentals for each of the tuxedos, then divides this number by expected total use to calculate the rate. For instance, on a two-button black tux, Morris expects a life of 30 rentals. In one year, the tux was rented 13 times. The amortization rate for that period was 43 percent (13 ÷ 30) of the amortizable cost.

? Is the units-of-activity method the best amortization method for Morris Formal Wear to use for its tuxedos or would you recommend another method?

Amortization and Income Tax

For accounting purposes, a company should choose the amortization method that best matches revenues to expenses. The Canada Revenue Agency (CRA), however, does not permit a choice among the three amortization methods. Instead, the CRA allows taxpayers to deduct a specific amount of amortization expense when they calculate their taxable income. Income tax regulations require the taxpayer to use the single declining-balance method on the tax return, regardless of what method is used in the financial statements.

In addition, the CRA does not allow taxpayers to estimate the useful lives of assets or amortization rates. It groups assets into various classes and states maximum amortization rates for each class. Amortization allowed for income tax purposes is calculated on a class (group) basis and is called **capital cost allowance (CCA)**. Capital cost allowance is an optional deduction from taxable income. This means that you may see a company deduct amortization on its income statement (because it must do this to fulfill the matching principle), but not deduct CCA for income tax purposes.

As part of its policy to reduce the number of alternative treatments, the CRA also sets partial-year amortization rules. Only half of the CCA is allowed in the year that an asset is acquired.

BEFORE YOU GO ON . . .

►**Review It**

1. What is the relationship of amortization to (a) cost allocation, (b) asset valuation, and (c) cash accumulation? If there is no relationship, state this.
2. How are annual amortization and net income different each year over the useful life of an asset, and in total after the entire life of an asset, under each of the three amortization methods?
3. When a company chooses an amortization method, what should it base its decision on?

►**Do It**

On October 1, 2008, Iron Mountain Ski Company purchases a new snow grooming machine for $52,000. The machine is estimated to have a five-year useful life and a $4,000 residual value. It is also estimated to have a total useful life of 6,000 hours. It is used 1,000 hours in the year ended December 31, 2008, and 1,300 hours in the year ended December 31, 2009. How much amortization expense should Iron Mountain Ski record in each of 2008 and 2009 under each amortization method: (a) straight-line, (b) double declining-balance, and (c) units-of-activity?

Action Plan

- Under straight-line amortization, annual amortization expense is equal to the amortizable cost (cost less residual value) divided by the estimated useful life.

• Under double declining-balance amortization, annual amortization expense is equal to double the straight-line rate of amortization times the net book value of the asset at the beginning of the year. Residual values are ignored in this method.
• Under the straight-line and declining-balance methods, the annual amortization expense must be prorated if the asset is purchased during the year.
• Under units-of-activity amortization, the amortizable cost per unit is equal to the total amortizable cost divided by the total estimated units of activity. The annual amortization expense is equal to the amortizable cost per unit times the actual usage in each year.

Solution

	2008	2009
Straight-line	$2,400	$ 9,600
Double declining-balance	5,200	18,720
Units-of-activity	8,000	10,400

(1) Straight-line: ($52,000 − $4,000) ÷ 5 years = $9,600 per year
2008: $9,600 × 3/12 = $2,400

(2) Double declining-balance: 100% ÷ 5 years = 20% straight-line rate
20% × 2 = 40% double declining-balance rate
2008: $52,000 × 40% × 3/12 = $5,200
2009: ($52,000 − $5,200) × 40% = $18,720

(3) Units-of-activity: ($52,000 − $4,000) ÷ 6,000 hours = $8.00 per hour
2008: 1,000 × $8.00 = $8,000
2009: 1,300 × $8.00 = $10,400

Related exercise material: BE9–5, BE9–6, BE9–7, BE9–8, BE9–9, E9–2, E9–3, and E9–4.

Revising Periodic Amortization

Recall that the three factors that affect the calculation of amortization are the asset's cost, useful life, and residual value. During the useful life of a long-lived asset, the annual amortization expense needs to be revised if there are changes to any of these factors. Amortization therefore needs to be revised if there are (1) capital expenditures during the useful life of the asset, (2) impairments in the market value of the asset, and/or (3) changes in the asset's estimated useful life or residual value. In the following sections, we discuss each of these items and then show how to revise amortization calculations.

Capital Expenditures during Useful Life

Earlier in the chapter, we learned that companies can have both operating and capital expenditures when a long-lived asset is purchased. Similarly, during the useful life of a long-lived asset, a company may incur costs for ordinary repairs, or for additions or improvements.

Ordinary repairs are costs to *maintain* the operating efficiency and expected productive life of the unit. They are usually fairly small amounts that occur frequently. Motor tune-ups and oil changes, repainting a building, and the replacement of worn-out gears on machinery are examples. Such repairs are debited to Repair (or Maintenance) Expense as they occur. Ordinary repairs are **operating expenditures**.

Additions and improvements are costs that are incurred to *increase* the operating efficiency, productive capacity, or expected useful life of the asset. These costs are usually large and happen less often. Additions and improvements that increase the company's investment in productive facilities are not expensed as they occur—they are capitalized. As capital expenditures, they are generally debited to the appropriate property, plant, or equipment account. The capital expenditure will be amortized over the remaining life of the original structure or the useful life of the addition, if the capital expenditure's useful life does not depend on the useful life of the original asset. Additions and improvements can therefore change an asset's annual amortization, compared to the original amortization estimate.

In our feature story, Dawson College spent $37 million on renovations and $33 million on two expansions. Thus, according to the explanation just given, these would be treated as capital expenditures and would have resulted in revisions to the college's amortization of its buildings.

Impairments

As noted earlier in the chapter, the book value of property, plant, or equipment is rarely the same as its market value. The market value is normally not relevant since property, plant, and equipment assets are not purchased for resale, but rather to be used in operations over long periods of time. Consequently, the asset is carried at cost (less the accumulated amortization after its acquisition) in accordance with the cost principle.

In some circumstances, however, the market value of a long-lived asset falls far below its book value and is not expected to recover. This may happen because a machine has become obsolete, or the market for a product made by a machine has dried up or become very competitive. If the decline in market value is permanent and the net book value of the asset is not recoverable an **impairment loss** has occurred. The amount of the impairment loss is the amount by which the book value of the asset is greater than its market value.

The lower of cost and market rule does not apply automatically to property, plant, and equipment, as it does to inventory. Because inventory is expected to be converted into cash during the year, it is important to value it annually at whichever value is lower, its cost or market (i.e., saleable) value. In contrast, property, plant, and equipment are used in operations over a longer term and are not available for resale. The going concern assumption assumes that a company will recover at least the cost of its long-lived assets. This is why these assets are only written down to their market value when there is a permanent impairment in their value. Write-downs do not happen often, and are subject to certain recoverability tests before any decrease in value can be recorded. Also note that if the fair market value later increases, the book value is *not* adjusted for any recovery in value.

To illustrate the write-down of a long-lived asset, assume that on December 31 Piniwa Company reviews its equipment for possible impairment. It owns equipment with a cost of $800,000 and accumulated amortization of $200,000. The equipment's market value is currently $500,000 and it is considered to be permanently impaired and the net book value is not recoverable. The amount of the impairment loss is determined by comparing the asset's net book value to its market value as follows:

Net book value ($800,000 – $200,000)	$600,000
Market value	500,000
Impairment loss	$100,000

The journal entry to record the impairment is:

Dec. 31	Loss on Impairment	100,000	
	Accumulated Amortization—Equipment		100,000
	To record impairment loss on equipment.		

A	=	L	+	OE
–100,000				–100,000

Cash flows: no effect

Assuming that the asset will continue to be used in operations, the impairment loss is reported on the income statement as part of operating income rather than as "other expense." Often the loss is combined with amortization expense on the income statement.

The Accumulated Amortization account is credited for the impairment loss, not the asset account; recording the loss this way keeps a record of the asset's original cost. In addition, future amortization calculations will need to be revised because of the reduction in the asset's net book value.

Changes in Estimated Useful Life or Residual Value

Management should periodically review its estimates of the useful life and residual value of the company's amortizable assets. If wear and tear or obsolescence indicates that the estimates are too low or too high, the estimates should be changed. As happens with capital expenditures and impairments, a change in estimated useful life or residual value will also cause a revision to the amortization calculations.

Revised Amortization Calculations

A revision of amortization is known as a change in estimate. Changes in estimates are made for current and future years only. They are not made retroactively for past periods. Thus, when a change in amortization is made, (1) there is no correction of previously recorded amortization expense, and (2) amortization expense for current and future years is revised. The rationale for this treatment is that the original calculation made in the past was based on the best information available at that time. The revision is based on new information which should affect only future periods. In addition, if past periods were often restated, users would feel less confident about financial statements.

To calculate the new annual amortization expense, we must first calculate the asset's net book value at the time of the change. This is equal to the asset's original cost minus the accumulated amortization to date, plus any capital expenditures, minus any impairment in value. We must also determine the revised estimated residual value and estimated remaining useful life.

To illustrate how to revise straight-line amortization, assume that 1 Stop Florists decides on December 31, 2011—before recording its amortization for 2011—to extend the estimated useful life of its truck by one more year (to December 31, 2013) because of its good condition. As a result of owning the truck an extra year, the estimated residual value is expected to decline from its original estimate of $2,000 to $700. Recall that the truck was purchased on January 1, 2008, for $25,000 and originally had an estimated useful life of five years.

The net book value at December 31, 2011—before recording amortization for 2011—is $11,200 [$25,000 − (3 × $4,600)]. This is also the amount shown in Illustration 9-5 as the net book value at December 31, 2010. The remaining useful life of three years is calculated by taking the original useful life of five years, subtracting the three years where amortization has already been recorded, and adding the additional estimated years of useful life—in this case one year. The new annual amortization is $3,500, calculated as in Illustration 9-11.

Illustration 9-11 ▶

Formula for revised straight-line amortization

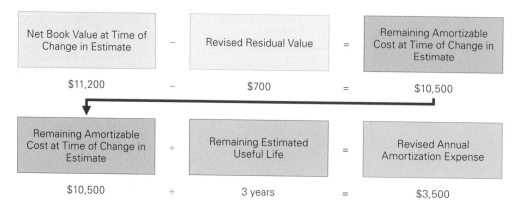

As a result of the revision to the truck's estimated useful life and residual value, 1 Stop Florists will record amortization expense of $3,500 on December 31 of 2011, 2012, and 2013. The company will not go back and change the amortization for 2008, 2009, and 2010. Accumulated amortization will now equal $24,300 [($4,600 × 3) + ($3,500 × 3)] at the end of the six-year useful life instead of the $23,000 that was originally calculated. The $1,300 increase in accumulated amortization is because the estimated residual value was revised and decreased by $1,300 ($2,000 − $700).

If the units-of-activity amortization method is used, the calculation is the same as we just saw except that the remaining useful life is expressed as units rather than years. If the declining-balance method is used, the revised rate would be applied to the net book value at the time of the change in estimate. The rate must be revised because the useful life has changed.

In our feature story, we are told that in 2000–01 Dawson College retroactively calculated amortization from 1995–96. Based on what you have just learned, this retroactive change would appear to be incorrect. However, the retroactive change in 2000–01 was the result of recording amortization for the first time. Before this, Dawson had not recorded amortization. This type of change is known as a change in accounting policy, instead of a change in estimate. Changes in accounting policy usually apply to past periods.

BEFORE YOU GO ON . . .

▶Review It

1. What are the differences between operating and capital expenditures?
2. What is an impairment loss? How is it calculated?
3. Why is an impairment loss credited to the Accumulated Amortization account rather than directly to the asset account?
4. Are revisions of periodic amortization made to prior periods, future periods, or both? Explain.

▶Do It

On August 1, 1993, just after its year end, The Fine Furniture Company purchased a building for $500,000. The company used straight-line amortization to allocate the cost of this building, estimating a residual value of $50,000 and a useful life of 30 years. After 15 years of use, on August 1, 2008, the company was forced to replace the roof at a cost of $25,000 cash. The residual value was expected to remain at $50,000 but the total useful life was now expected to increase to 40 years. Prepare journal entries to record (1) amortization for the year ended July 31, 2008; (2) the cost of the addition on August 1, 2008; and (3) amortization for the year ended July 31, 2009.

Action Plan

- Understand the difference between an operating expenditure (benefits only the current period) and a capital expenditure (benefits future periods).
- Capital expenditures are normally recorded in the same asset account, not in a separate asset account.
- To revise annual amortization, calculate the net book value (cost less accumulated amortization) at the revision date. Note that the cost of any capital expenditure will increase the book value of the asset to be amortized.
- Subtract any revised residual value from the net book value at the time of the change in estimate (plus the capital expenditure in this case) to determine the amortizable cost.
- Allocate the revised amortizable cost over the remaining (not total) useful life.

Solution

(1)

July 31, 2008	Amortization Expense [($500,000 − $50,000) ÷ 30]	15,000	
	Accumulated Amortization—Building		15,000
	To record annual amortization expense.		

(2)

Aug. 1, 2008	Building	25,000	
	Cash		25,000
	To record replacement of roof.		

(3)

Cost:	$500,000
Less: Accumulated amortization $15,000 per year × 15 years	225,000
Net book value before replacement of roof, August 1, 2008	275,000
Add: Capital expenditure (roof)	25,000
Net book value after replacement of roof, August 1, 2008	300,000
Less: Revised residual value	50,000
Revised amortizable cost	250,000
Divide by: Remaining useful life (40 − 15)	÷25 years
Revised annual amortization	$ 10,000

July 31, 2009	Amortization Expense	10,000	
	Accumulated Amortization—Building		10,000
	To record revised annual amortization expense.		

Related exercise material: BE9–10, BE9–11, E9–5, E9–6, and E9–7.

Disposals of Property, Plant, and Equipment

study objective 4

Account for the disposal of property, plant, and equipment.

Companies dispose of property, plant, or equipment that is no longer useful to them. Illustration 9-12 shows three methods of disposal.

Illustration 9-12 ▶

Methods of property, plant, and equipment disposal

Retirement
Equipment is scrapped or discarded.

Sale
Equipment is sold.

Exchange
Existing equipment is traded for new equipment.

Whatever the disposal method, the company must take the following four steps to record the retirement, sale, or exchange of the property, plant, or equipment:

Step 1: Update amortization

If the disposal occurs in the middle of the accounting period, amortization must be updated for the part of the year that has passed between the last time adjusting entries were recorded and the date of the disposal. Recall that amortization is recorded by debiting Amortization Expense and crediting Accumulated Amortization. Note that the update period will never be more than one year, since adjusting entries are made at least annually.

Step 2: Calculate the net book value

Calculate the net book value after updating the accumulated amortization for any partial year amortization calculated in Step 1 above:

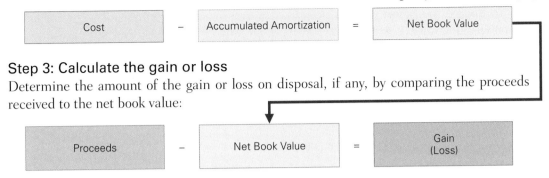

Step 3: Calculate the gain or loss

Determine the amount of the gain or loss on disposal, if any, by comparing the proceeds received to the net book value:

If the proceeds of the sale are more than the net book value of the property, plant, or equipment, there is a gain on disposal. If the proceeds of the sale are less than the net book value of the asset sold, there is a loss on disposal.

Step 4: Record the disposal

Record the disposal, removing the cost of the asset and the accumulated amortization from the accounts. The accumulated amortization account balance is decreased by the total amortization that has been recorded for the asset up to its disposal date. This is the same amount that was used to calculate the net book value in Step 2 above. Record the proceeds (if any) and the gain or loss on disposal (if any). Gains on disposal are recorded as credits because credits increase owner's equity; losses on disposal are recorded as debits because debits decrease owner's equity.

> Dr. Cash (or other account)
> Dr. Accumulated Amortization
> Dr. Loss on Disposal **OR** Cr. Gain on Disposal
>   Cr. Property, plant, or equipment account

In the following sections, we will illustrate the accounting for each of the three disposal methods described in Illustration 9-12, using these four steps.

Retirement of Property, Plant, and Equipment

Instead of being sold or exchanged, some assets are simply retired at the end of their useful lives. For example, some productive assets used in manufacturing may have highly specialized uses and consequently have no general market when the company no longer needs the asset. In this case, the asset is simply retired.

When an asset is retired, there are no proceeds for the company. The accumulated amortization account is decreased (debited) for the full amount of amortization taken over the life of the asset. The asset account is reduced (credited) for the original cost of the asset. Quite often, the net book value will equal zero; however, a journal entry is still required to remove the asset and its related amortization account from the books.

To illustrate the retirement of a piece of property, plant, and equipment, assume that on August 1, 2008, Baseyev Enterprises retires its printing equipment, which cost $31,200. At the time of purchase, on August 1, 2004, the printing equipment was expected to have a four-year useful life and no residual value. Baseyev used straight-line amortization and the annual amortization expense was $7,800 per year ($31,200 ÷ 4) or $650 per month ($7,800 ÷ 12). The balance in the account Accumulated Amortization at Baseyev's year end, December 31, 2007, was $26,650 ($650/month × 41 months). Straight-line amortization for the seven months from December 31, 2007 to August 1, 2008 is $4,550 ($650/month × 7 months).

To update the amortization since the last time adjusting journal entries were made, which would have been at Baseyev's year-end, December 31, 2007, a journal entry to record the seven months of amortization is made, as follows:

Aug. 1	Amortization Expense		4,550	
	Accumulated Amortization—Printing Equipment			4,550
	To record amortization expense for the first 7 months of 2008.			

After this journal entry is posted, the balance in Accumulated Amortization is $31,200 ($26,650 + $4,550). The printing equipment is now fully amortized with a net book value of zero (cost of $31,200 − accumulated amortization of $31,200).

The entry to record the retirement of the printing equipment is:

A	=	L	+	OE
+31,200				
−31,200				

Cash flows: no effect

Aug. 1	Accumulated Amortization—Printing Equipment		31,200	
	Printing Equipment			31,200
	To record retirement of fully amortized printing equipment.			

What happens if a company is still using a fully amortized asset? In this case, the asset and its accumulated amortization continue to be reported on the balance sheet, without further amortization, until the asset is retired. Reporting the asset and related amortization on the balance sheet informs the reader of the financial statements that the asset is still being used by the company. Once an asset is fully amortized, even if it is still being used, no additional amortization should be taken. Accumulated amortization on a piece of property, plant, and equipment can never be more than the asset's cost.

If a piece of property, plant, and equipment is retired before it is fully amortized and no residual value is received, a loss on disposal occurs (a gain is not possible on retirement). Assume that Baseyev Enterprises retires its printing equipment on January 1, 2008. The loss on disposal is calculated by subtracting the net book value of the asset from the proceeds that are received. In this case, there are no proceeds and the net book value is $4,550 (cost of $31,200 − accumulated amortization of $26,650), resulting in a loss of $4,550:

Proceeds	−	Net Book Value	=	Gain (Loss)
$0	−	$4,550	=	$(4,550)
		($31,200 − $26,650)		

The entry to record the retirement of equipment is as follows:

Jan. 1	Accumulated Amortization—Printing Equipment		26,650	
	Loss on Disposal		4,550	
	Printing Equipment			31,200
	To record retirement of printing equipment at a loss.			

This loss is reported in the other expenses section of a multiple-step income statement. You should also note that there will never be a gain when an asset is retired: the proceeds are always zero and therefore can never be greater than the net book value of the retired asset.

Sale of Property, Plant, and Equipment

In a disposal by sale, the four steps listed earlier are followed. Both gains and losses on disposal are common when an asset is sold. Only by coincidence will the net book value and the fair market value (the proceeds) of the asset be the same when the asset is sold. We will illustrate the sale of office furniture at both a gain and a loss in the following sections.

Gain on Disposal. To illustrate a gain, assume that on April 1, 2008, Baseyev Enterprises sells office furniture for $15,000 cash. The office furniture had originally been purchased on January 1, 2004, at a cost of $60,200. At that time, it was estimated that the office furniture would have a residual value of $5,000 and a useful life of five years.

The first step is to update any unrecorded amortization. Annual amortization using the straight-line method is $11,040 [($60,200 − $5,000) ÷ 5]. The entry to record the amortization expense and update accumulated amortization for the first three months of 2008 is as follows:

April 1	Amortization Expense ($11,040 × ³⁄₁₂)	2,760	
	Accumulated Amortization—Office Furniture		2,760
	To record amortization expense for the first 3 months of 2008.		

A	=	L	+	OE
−2,760				−2,760

Cash flows: no effect

The second step is to calculate the net book value on April 1, 2008. As at December 31, 2007, the office furniture had accumulated amortization of $44,160 ($11,040 × 4). After the accumulated amortization balance is updated on April 1, 2008 to $46,920 ($44,160 + $2,760), the net book value of the office furniture is $13,280 (cost of $60,200 − accumulated amortization of $46,920).

The third step is to calculate the gain or loss on disposal. A $1,720 gain on disposal is determined as follows:

Proceeds	−	Net Book Value	=	Gain (Loss)
$15,000	−	$13,280 ($60,200 − $46,920)	=	$1,720

The fourth step is the entry to record the sale of the office furniture as follows:

April 1	Cash	15,000	
	Accumulated Amortization—Office Furniture	46,920	
	Gain on Disposal		1,720
	Office Furniture		60,200
	To record the sale of office furniture at a gain.		

A	=	L	+	OE
+15,000				+1,720
+46,920				
−60,200				

↑ Cash flows: +15,000

The gain on disposal is reported in the other revenues section of a multiple-step income statement.

Loss on Disposal. Assume that instead of selling the office furniture for $15,000, Baseyev sells it for $9,000. In this case, a loss of $4,280 is calculated as follows:

Proceeds	−	Net Book Value	=	Gain (Loss)
$9,000	−	$13,280 ($60,200 − $46,920)	=	$(4,280)

The entry to record the sale of the office furniture is as follows:

A	=	L	+	OE
+9,000				−4,280
+46,920				
−60,200				

↑ Cash flows: +9,000

April 1	Cash	9,000	
	Accumulated Amortization—Office Furniture	46,920	
	Loss on Disposal	4,280	
	Office Furniture		60,200
	To record the sale of office furniture at a loss.		

As noted earlier in the chapter, the loss on disposal is reported in the other expenses section of the income statement.

Exchanges of Property, Plant, and Equipment

Some long-lived assets are sold for cash when they are no longer needed. Others are exchanged for new assets. In an exchange of assets, the new asset is usually purchased by trading in an old asset, and a **trade-in allowance** is given to reduce the purchase price of the new asset. Cash may also be involved. The cash is usually a payment for the difference between the trade-in allowance and the purchase price of the new asset.

Instead of being sold for cash, therefore, the old asset is sold for a trade-in allowance on the purchase of the new asset. The new asset is seen as being purchased for cash plus the value of the old asset.

⁎The trade-in allowance amount, however, is often affected by price concessions for the new asset and therefore rarely reflects the fair market value of the asset that is given up. Consequently, as fair market value is what matters, trade-in allowances are ignored for accounting purposes.

The accounting for exchange transactions depends on whether the exchange is a **monetary exchange of assets** or a **nonmonetary exchange of assets**. A monetary exchange is an exchange of nonmonetary assets with a significant amount of cash involved in the transaction. A nonmonetary exchange is an exchange of nonmonetary assets with little or no cash involved in the transaction.

The accounting differs for each type of exchange transaction, as explained in the following sections.

Monetary Exchanges of Assets. If the cash part of an exchange of long-lived assets is significant, the exchange is considered a monetary exchange. The exchange is viewed as both a sale of the old asset and a purchase of the new asset. The new asset is recorded at the fair market value of the asset given up plus any cash paid (or less any cash received). The old asset is seen as having been sold for proceeds equivalent to its fair market value. Accounting for the exchange of assets in these situations allows gains and losses to be recognized because the company's economic situation has changed as a result of entering into the transaction.

Gains and losses from a monetary exchange are determined just as they are for the sale of a piece of property, plant, and equipment. The gain or loss is the difference between the net book value and the fair market value of the asset given up. When the book value is more than the market value, a loss results. When the book value is less than the market value, a gain results.

In summary, the procedure to account for monetary exchanges is as follows:

Step 1: Update any unrecorded amortization expense to the date of the exchange.
Step 2: Calculate net book value (cost − accumulated amortization).
Step 3: Calculate any gain or loss on disposal [fair market value − net book value = gain (loss)].
Step 4: Record the exchange as follows:
      • Remove the cost and the accumulated amortization of the asset that is given up.
      • Record any gain or loss on disposal.

- Record the new asset at the fair market value of the old asset plus any cash paid (or less any cash received).
- Record the cash paid or received.

To illustrate a monetary exchange of long-lived assets, assume that Chilko Company exchanged old computers for new computers on October 1, 2008. The original cost of the old computers was $61,000 on January 1, 2006. Amortization is calculated using the straight-line method, over a three-year useful life, with an estimated residual value of $1,000. The fair market value of the old computers on October 1 is $5,000.

The list price of the new computers was $51,000. Chilko received an $8,000 trade-in allowance from the computer retailer for the old computers and paid $43,000 cash ($51,000 − $8,000) for the new computers. Chilko's year end is December 31.

The first step is to update the amortization for the nine months ended October 1, 2008. Annual amortization expense is $20,000 [($61,000 − $1,000) ÷ 3], so amortization for nine months is $15,000 ($20,000 × $\frac{9}{12}$).

Oct. 1	Amortization Expense	15,000	
	Accumulated Amortization—Computers		15,000
	To record amortization expense for the first 9 months of 2008.		

A	=	L	+	OE
−15,000				−15,000

Cash flows: no effect

After this entry is posted, the balance in Accumulated Amortization on October 1, 2008, is $55,000 [$20,000 (in 2006) + $20,000 (in 2007) + $15,000 (in 2008)]. The accumulated amortization can also be calculated as follows: $20,000 × 2.75 years = $55,000. Be sure to watch the dates and time periods carefully when calculating partial period amortization: thus, the ".75" is for the nine months of amortization in the current year.

On October 1, 2008, the net book value is $6,000 (cost of $61,000 − accumulated amortization of $55,000). The loss on disposal on the old computers is determined by comparing the net book value to the fair market value, which represents the proceeds in this situation:

Proceeds (Fair Market Value)	−	Net Book Value	=	Gain (Loss)
$5,000	−	$6,000 ($61,000 − $55,000)	=	$(1,000)

The entry to record the exchange of computers is as follows:

Oct. 1	Computers (new)	48,000	
	Accumulated Amortization—Computers	55,000	
	Loss on Disposal	1,000	
	Computers (old)		61,000
	Cash		43,000
	To record exchange of computers, plus cash.		

A	=	L	+	OE
+48,000				−1,000
+55,000				
−61,000				
−43,000				

Cash flows: −43,000

Note that the exchange of computers is not netted; rather, it is shown as a separate increase and decrease to the general ledger account Computers. The cost of the new computers ($48,000) is determined by the fair market value of the old computers ($5,000) plus the cash paid ($43,000). The list price of $51,000 and the trade-in allowance of $8,000 are ignored in determining the real cost of the new computers.

Nonmonetary Exchanges of Assets. Generally, nonmonetary exchanges of long-lived assets are accounted for in the same way as monetary exchanges of long-lived assets. However, if the transaction does not change the operations of the business, or the fair values cannot be determined, the exchange of the long-lived assets cannot be recorded at fair value. In such cases, the new long-lived asset is recorded at the net book value of the old asset that was given up, plus any cash paid (or less any cash received). Net book value is used in these circumstances because the new asset is basically substituted or swapped for the old asset. As the net book value of the old asset is used for the net book value of the new asset, and the exchange has therefore not changed the operations of the business significantly, no gain or loss is recorded.

The accounting for nonmonetary exchanges of assets is complex. This type of exchange is also uncommon. Further discussion of nonmonetary exchanges of long-lived assets is left for an intermediate accounting course.

BEFORE YOU GO ON . . .

▶Review It

1. What is the proper way to account for the retirement, sale, or exchange of a piece of property, plant, and equipment?
2. What is the formula to calculate a gain or loss on disposal?
3. When is an exchange of assets considered a monetary exchange? A nonmonetary exchange?

▶Do It

Overland Trucking has a truck that was purchased on January 1, 2004, for $80,000. The truck had been amortized on a straight-line basis with an estimated residual value of $5,000 and an estimated useful life of five years. Overland has a December 31 year end. Assume each of the following four independent situations:

1. On January 1, 2009, Overland retires the truck.
2. On May 1, 2008, Overland sells the truck for $9,500 cash.
3. On October 1, 2008, Overland sells the truck for $9,500 cash.
4. On November 1, 2008, Overland exchanges the old truck, plus $60,000 cash, for a new truck. The old truck has a fair market value of $7,000. The new truck has a list price of $70,000, but the dealer will give Overland a $10,000 trade-in allowance on the old truck.

Prepare the journal entry to record each of these situations.

Action Plan

- Update any unrecorded amortization for dispositions during the fiscal year.
- Compare the proceeds with the asset's net book value to determine if there has been a gain or loss.
- Record any proceeds received and any gain or loss. Remove both the asset and any related accumulated amortization from the accounts.
- Determine the cash paid in an exchange situation as the difference between the list price and the trade-in allowance.
- Record the cost of the new asset in an exchange situation as the fair market value of the asset given up, plus the cash paid.

Solution

$$\frac{\$80,000 - \$5,000}{5 \text{ years}} = \$15,000 \text{ annual amortization expense}$$

(1) Retirement of truck:

Jan. 1, 2009	Accumulated Amortization ($15,000 × 5 years)	75,000	
	Loss on Disposal [$0 – ($80,000 – $75,000)]	5,000	
	Truck		80,000
	To record retirement of truck.		

(2) Sale of truck for $9,500:

May 1, 2008	Amortization Expense ($15,000 × ⁴⁄₁₂)	5,000	
	Accumulated Amortization		5,000
	To record amortization for 4 months.		
	Cash	9,500	
	Accumulated Amortization—Truck ($15,000 × 4.3333 years)	65,000	
	Loss on Disposal [$9,500 – ($80,000 – $65,000)]	5,500	
	Truck		80,000
	To record sale of truck at a loss.		

(3) Sale of truck for $9,500:

Oct. 1, 2008	Amortization Expense ($15,000 × ⁹⁄₁₂)	11,250	
	Accumulated Amortization		11,250
	To record amortization for 9 months.		
	Cash	9,500	
	Accumulated Amortization—Truck ($15,000 × 4.75 years)	71,250	
	Gain on Disposal [$9,500 – ($80,000 – $71,250)]		750
	Truck		80,000
	To record sale of truck at a gain.		

(4) Exchange of truck:

Nov. 1, 2008	Amortization Expense ($15,000 × ¹⁰⁄₁₂)	12,500	
	Accumulated Amortization		12,500
	To record amortization for 10 months.		
	Truck (new) ($7,000 + $60,000)	67,000	
	Accumulated Amortization—Truck ($15,000 × 4.83333 years)	72,500	
	Loss on Disposal [$7,000 – ($80,000 – $72,500)]	500	
	Truck (old)		80,000
	Cash ($70,000 – $10,000)		60,000
	To record exchange of trucks, plus cash.		

Related exercise material: BE9–12, BE9–13, BE9–14, E9–8, and E9–9.

Natural Resources

Natural resources consist of standing timber and underground deposits of oil, gas, and minerals. Canada is rich in natural resources, ranging from the towering rainforests in coastal British Columbia to the world's largest nickel deposits in Voisey's Bay, Labrador. These long-lived assets have two characteristics that make them different from other long-lived assets: (1) they are physically extracted in operations such as mining, cutting, or pumping; and (2) only an act of nature can replace them. Because of these characteristics, natural resources are frequently called wasting assets.

Natural resources are tangible assets, similar to property, plant, and equipment. A key distinction between natural resources and property, plant, and equipment is that natural resources physically lose substance, or deplete, as they are used. For example, there is less of a tract of timberland (a natural resource) as the timber is cut and sold. When we use equipment, its physical substance remains the same regardless of the product it produces.

study objective 5

Calculate and record amortization of natural resources.

Cost

The acquisition cost of a natural resource is determined in the same way as the cost of property, plant, and equipment. The cost includes all expenditures necessary in acquiring the resource and preparing it for its intended use. The cost of a natural resource can also be increased by future removal and site restoration cleanup costs, which are often large. These costs, known as asset retirement obligations, are usually required in order to return the resource as closely as possible to its natural state at the end of its useful life.

The accounting for asset retirement obligations and the allocation of these obligations over the useful life of the natural resource is complicated. Further discussion of these concepts is left to an intermediate accounting course. We will, however, look at how the acquisition cost of a natural resource is allocated over its useful life in the next section.

Amortization

The units-of-activity method (learned earlier in the chapter) is generally used to calculate the amortization of wasting assets. Under the units-of-activity method, the total cost of the natural resource minus its residual value is divided by the number of units estimated to be in the resource. The result is an amortizable cost per unit of product. The amortizable cost per unit is then multiplied by the number of units extracted, to determine the annual amortization expense.

To illustrate, assume that Rabbit Lake Company invests $5.5 million in a mine that is estimated to have 10 million tonnes of uranium and a $200,000 residual value. In the first year, 800,000 tonnes of uranium are extracted. Illustration 9-13 shows the formulas and calculations.

Illustration 9-13 ▶

Formula for units-of-activity method for natural resources

Alternative terminology
Amortization for natural resources is also known as *depletion* because the assets physically deplete as the resource is extracted.

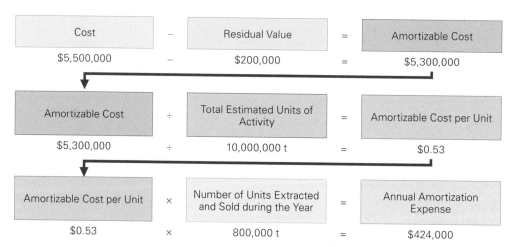

The amortization expense for the amount of the resource that has been extracted is initially charged (debited) to an inventory account. Note that this is not the same as how we record amortization for property, plant, and equipment. In the case of natural resources, the amortization expense is recorded initially as a current asset, not as an expense. Natural resources are accounted for in this way because the resource extracted is available for sale—similar to merchandise that has been purchased or manufactured for sale, as we learned in Chapter 5.

The entry to record amortization of the uranium mine for Rabbit Lake Company's first year of operation, ended December 31, 2008, is as follows:

Dec. 31	Inventory ($0.53 × 800,000 t)	424,000	
	Accumulated Amortization—Uranium Mine		424,000
	To record amortization expense on uranium mine.		

A	=	L	+	OE
+242,000				
−242,000				

Cash flows: no effect

All costs of extracting the natural resource—both current period costs, such as labour, and amortization of the natural resource—are recorded as inventory. When sold, the inventory costs are transferred to cost of goods sold and matched with the period's revenue. In other words, the amortization is charged to the income statement only in the period in which the related goods are sold. Amortization related to goods not yet sold remains in inventory and is reported as a current asset.

For example, assume that Rabbit Lake Company does not sell all of the 800,000 tonnes of uranium extracted in 2008. It sells 700,000 tonnes and stores 100,000 tonnes for later sale. In this situation, Rabbit Lake Company would include $371,000 (700,000 × $0.53) in the cost of the resource sold on its income statement. As mentioned before, the cost of labour and other period costs related to the goods sold would also be included in the cost of the resource sold on the income statement. The remaining amortization of $53,000 ($424,000 − $371,000) is for the 100,000 tonnes kept for later sale and will be included in inventory in the current assets section of the company's balance sheet.

Like amortization for property, plant, and equipment, the amortization of a natural resource needs to be revised if there are capital expenditures during the useful life, changes in the total number of units estimated to be in the resource, or impairments.

Often enough, the amortizable cost per unit of a natural resource needs to be revised because the estimated total units of the resource have changed as a result of new information. Natural resources such as oil and gas deposits and some metals have provided the greatest challenges. Estimates of the total units (also called reserves) of these natural resources are mostly knowledgeable guesses and may be revised whenever more information becomes available.

Natural resources must also be reviewed and tested for impairment whenever circumstances make this appropriate. For example, Rabbit Lake Company would need to test the uranium mine for impairment if there was a significant and permanent decline in the selling price of uranium. If there is impairment, the uranium mine must be written down to its market value, an impairment loss must be recorded, and current and future amortization needs to be revised accordingly.

Disposal of Natural Resources

At disposal, just as with property, plant, and equipment, any unrecorded amortization must be updated for the portion of the year up to the date of the disposal. Then proceeds are recorded, the cost and the accumulated amortization of the natural resource are removed, and a gain or loss, if any, is recorded. As mentioned earlier, there may also be site restoration costs at this time, but we leave the accounting for these costs to a future accounting course.

BEFORE YOU GO ON . . .

▶Review It

1. How is amortization expense calculated for natural resources?
2. Explain how amortization expense can be both an asset (inventory) and an expense (cost of goods sold).
3. Why might a company need to revise the amortization of a natural resource?

▶Do It

High Timber Company invests $14 million in a tract of timber land. It is estimated to have 10 million cunits (1 cunit = 100 cubic feet) of timber and a $500,000 residual value. In the first year, 40,000 cunits of timber are cut, and 30,000 of these cunits are sold. Calculate amortization for High Timber's first year of operations and allocate it between inventory and cost of goods sold.

Action Plan

- Use units-of-activity amortization for natural resources.
- Calculate the amortizable cost per unit by dividing the total cost minus the estimated residual value by the total estimated units.
- Multiply the amortizable cost per unit by the number of units cut to determine the total amortization.
- Allocate the amortization related to the units that have been cut but not yet sold to inventory.
- Allocate the amortization related to the units that have been cut and sold to expense.

Solution

1. Amortizable cost per unit: ($14,000,000 − $500,000) ÷ 10,000,000 cunits = $1.35 per cunit
2. Total amortization for the year: $1.35 per cunit × 40,000 cunits cut = $54,000
3. Amortization allocated to inventory: $1.35 per cunit × 10,000 cunits on hand = $13,500
4. Amortization allocated to expense: $1.35 per cunit × 30,000 cunits sold = $40,500

the navigator

Related exercise material: BE9–15 and E9–10.

Intangible Assets

study objective 6

Identify the basic accounting issues for intangible assets.

Similar to property, plant, and equipment and natural resources, intangible assets benefit future periods and are used to produce products or provide services over these periods. However, unlike property, plant, and equipment and natural resources, which are **tangible assets** because they have a physical substance, **intangible assets** involve rights, privileges, and competitive advantages that have no physical substance. In other words, they are not physical things. Many companies' most valuable assets are intangible. Some widely known intangibles are Alexander Graham Bell's patent on the telephone, the franchises of Tim Hortons, the trade name of President's Choice, and the trademark CBC.

There must be proof that an intangible asset exists. This proof can be a contract, licence, or other document. Intangibles may arise from the following sources:

1. Government grants such as patents, copyrights, trademarks, and trade names
2. An acquisition of another business in which the purchase price includes a payment for goodwill
3. Private monopolistic arrangements arising from contractual agreements such as franchises and leases

In the following sections, we discuss the accounting for intangible assets and also learn more about different types of intangible assets.

Accounting for Intangible Assets

Similar to tangible assets, intangible assets are recorded at cost. Cost includes all the costs of acquisition and other costs that are needed to make the intangible asset ready for its intended use—including legal fees and similar charges. Costs that occur within the company to create intangible assets are generally expensed when they are incurred. As a result, intangible assets that appear on a company's balance sheet are usually purchased assets rather than internally developed ones. However, at the time of writing this textbook, new standards had recently been proposed that would allow an internally developed intangible asset to be recognized as an asset if specific criteria are met. Further discussion of these criteria is left for future accounting courses.

Intangible assets can also be similar to tangible assets in other ways: certain intangible assets are like land as they have an indefinite useful life, while other intangible assets are like equipment and have a limited useful life. Just as with tangible assets, only intangible assets with limited useful lives are amortized. To help in deciding which intangibles are amortized and which intangibles are not amortized, we categorize intangible assets as having either a limited life or an indefinite life.

If an intangible asset has a limited useful life, its amortizable cost (cost less residual value) should be allocated over the shorter of the (1) estimated useful life and (2) legal life. Intangible assets, by their nature, rarely have any residual value, so the amortizable cost is normally equal to the cost. In addition, the useful life of an intangible asset is usually shorter than its legal life, so useful life is most often used as the amortization period. Companies must carefully consider the potential obsolescence and the economic value of owning the intangible asset when they estimate its useful life.

Intangible assets are typically amortized on a straight-line basis, which results in the same amortization expense each year. But, as happens with tangible assets, intangible assets also sometimes need to have their amortization revised. This occurs if there are capital expenditures during its useful life, impairments, or changes in the estimated useful life. Intangible assets must be reviewed and tested for impairment whenever circumstances make this appropriate. Recall from earlier in this chapter that there is impairment if the asset's market value permanently falls below its book value. If any impairment is evident, the asset must be written down to its market value and an impairment loss must be recorded. Also recall that if the fair market value later increases, the book value is *not* adjusted for any recovery in value.

If an intangible has an indefinite life, it is not amortized. Intangible assets with indefinite lives are tested more frequently for impairments than are tangible assets or intangible assets with definite lives. Indefinite-life intangible assets should be tested for impairment at least once a year.

At disposal, just as with tangible assets, the cost and the accumulated amortization of the intangible asset are removed, and a gain or loss, if any, is recorded.

Intangible Assets with Limited Lives

Examples of intangible assets with limited lives include patents and copyrights. We also include research and development costs in this section because these costs often lead to the creation of patents and copyrights.

Patents

A **patent** is an exclusive right issued by the Canadian Intellectual Property Office of Industry Canada that allows the patent holder to manufacture, sell, or otherwise control an invention for a period of 20 years from the date of the application. A patent cannot be renewed. But the legal life of a patent may be extended if the patent holder obtains new patents for improvements or other changes in the basic design.

The initial cost of a patent is the cash or cash equivalent price that was paid to acquire it. After it has been acquired, legal costs are often incurred. The saying "A patent is only as good as the money you're prepared to spend defending it" is very true. For example, Lee Valley Tools Ltd., headquartered in Ottawa, recently won patent cases against a German manufacturer and a U.S. mail order firm that took years and a lot of money to settle. Legal costs to successfully defend the patent in an infringement suit are considered necessary to prove the patent's validity. They are added to the patent account and amortized over the remaining life of the patent.

The cost of a patent should be amortized over its 20-year legal life or its useful life, whichever is shorter. As mentioned earlier, the useful life should be carefully assessed by considering whether the patent is likely to become ineffective at contributing to revenue before the end of its legal life.

Copyrights

Copyrights granted by the Canadian Intellectual Property Office give the owner an exclusive right to reproduce and sell an artistic or published work. Copyrights last for the life of the creator plus 50 years. Generally, the useful life of a copyright is significantly shorter than its legal life.

The cost of a copyright consists of the cost of acquiring and defending it. The cost may only be the fee paid to register the copyright. Or, it may amount to a great deal more if a copyright infringement suit is involved. Consider, for example, the costs incurred by the intellectual property industries. For recording labels, film producers, and others, the struggle to enforce copyright laws in the digital age certainly continues to be an uphill battle despite the legal cases that are meant to educate the public about the threat that file sharing poses.

Research and Development Costs

Research and development (R&D) costs are not intangible assets by themselves. But they may lead to patents and copyrights, new processes, and new products. Many companies spend large sums of money on research and development in an ongoing effort to develop new products or processes. For example, in a recent year Research in Motion spent U.S. $158 million on research and development. Nortel Networks spent nearly $1.9 billion.

Research and development costs present two accounting problems: (1) It is sometimes difficult to determine the costs for specific projects. (2) It is also hard to know when future benefits will occur and how much they will be. As a result, accounting distinguishes between research costs and development costs.

Research is planned investigation that is done to gain new knowledge and understanding. All research costs should be expensed when they are incurred.

Development is the use of research findings and knowledge for a plan or design. Development costs with reasonably certain future benefits can be capitalized. Management must intend to produce and market the product or process, a future market must be defined, and there have to be enough resources available to complete the project. Otherwise, development costs must also be expensed.

To illustrate, assume that Laser Scanner Company spent $3 million on research and $2 million on development. These costs resulted in the development of two highly successful patents. The $3 million of research costs are expensed. The development costs of $2 million are capitalized and included in the cost of the patent, since the development was successful.

Deferred Costs and Other Intangible Assets

Other intangible assets that are sometimes found in corporate balance sheets include items such as customer lists, noncompetition agreements, and sports contracts. Companies sometimes use the term "deferred charges" to classify these items. Others use the term "other assets." Accounting for deferred costs is challenging and many of the standards regarding what can and cannot be recorded as a deferred cost are changing. We will leave further discussion of deferred costs to a future accounting course.

Intangible Assets with Indefinite Lives

Examples of intangible assets with indefinite lives include trademarks and trade names, franchises and licences, and goodwill. Intangible assets do not always fit perfectly in a specific category. Sometimes trademarks, trade names, franchises, or licences do have limited lives. In such cases, they would be amortized over the shorter of their legal or useful lives. It is more usual, however, for these intangible assets, along with goodwill, to have indefinite lives.

Trademarks and Trade Names

A **trademark** or **trade name** is a word, phrase, jingle, or symbol that identifies a particular enterprise or product. Trade names like President's Choice, KFC, Nike, Big Mac, the Blue Jays, and TSN create immediate product identification. They also help the sale of a product or service.

The creator can get an exclusive legal right to the trademark or trade name by registering it with the Canadian Intellectual Property Office. This registration gives continuous protection. It may be renewed every 15 years, as long as the trademark or trade name is still being used. In most cases, companies continuously renew their trademarks or trade names. In such cases, as long as the trademark or trade name continues to be marketable, it will have an indefinite useful life.

If the trademark or trade name is purchased, the cost is the purchase price. If the trademark or trade name is developed internally rather than purchased, the cost includes legal fees, registration fees, design costs, successful legal defence costs, and other expenditures that are directly related to securing it.

 ACCOUNTING IN ACTION ▶ Across the Organization Insight

What is the value of a brand? According to Interbrand, an organization that works with companies to help them develop their brands, the top global brand in 2006 is Coca-Cola at $67 billion. And while it is not surprising to see that the top five global brands are all from the United States, it is interesting to note there is not a single Canadian company in the top 100 global list. Even Switzerland, with a much smaller economy, has five brands in the top 100 global list.

In Canada, financial institutions dominate the top 25 Canadian brand names, with RBC valued at $4 billion in the No. 1 spot and Toronto-Dominion in No. 2; there are five other banks and three mutual fund companies on the Canadian list. So why is it that RBC was not on the global list even though it has a higher brand value than such global brands as Starbucks and Heineken? According to Interbrand, when you compare Canada to the U.S., Japan, and South Korea, the level of brand sophistication does not seem to be there. Canadian brands, according to Interbrand, are becoming irrelevant.

Sources: Interbrand and BusinessWeek, *Best Global Brands 2006: A Ranking by Brand Value* (September 2006); Keith McArthur, "Canada's Top Brands: Only the Bold Will Thrive," *The Globe and Mail*, July 24, 2006, B3.

? **Who is responsible for developing a company's brand value? How is it reported on the financial statements?**

Franchises and Licences

When you drive down the street in your Protegé purchased from a Mazda dealer, fill up your gas tank at the corner Petro-Canada station, buy coffee from Tim Hortons, eat lunch at Wendy's, or get your hair cut at Supercuts, you are dealing with franchises. The Forzani Group also uses franchises to sell its products, including Sports Experts, Intersport, Atmosphere, Econosports, RnR, Tech Shop/Pegasus, Nevada Bob's Golf, and Hockey Experts.

A **franchise** is a contractual arrangement between a franchisor and a franchisee. The franchisor gives the franchisee permission to sell certain products, provide specific services, or use certain trademarks or trade names, usually inside a specific geographic area.

Another type of franchise that is granted by a government body allows a company to use public property in performing its services. Examples are the use of city streets for a bus line or taxi service; the use of public land for telephone, power, and cable lines; and the use of airwaves for radio or TV broadcasting. Such operating rights are called **licences**.

When costs can be identified with the acquisition of the franchise or licence, an intangible asset should be recognized. Franchises and licences may be granted for a limited period of time or an indefinite period of time. The accounting treatment of these costs, as with all intangible assets, depends on the useful life.

In addition to the acquisition costs, sometimes a franchise agreement requires annual payments to the franchisor, and these are often proportionate to sales. These payments are called **royalties** and are recorded as operating expenses in the period in which they are incurred.

Goodwill

Usually, the largest intangible asset that appears on a company's balance sheet is goodwill. **Goodwill** is the value of all the favourable attributes that relate to a company. These include exceptional management, a desirable location, good customer relations, skilled employees, high-quality products, fair pricing policies, and harmonious relations with labour unions. Unlike property, plant, and equipment and natural resources, which can be sold individually in the marketplace, goodwill cannot be sold individually as it is part of the business as a whole.

If goodwill can be identified only with the business as a whole, how can it be determined? An accountant could try to put a dollar value on the attributes (exceptional management, a desirable location, and so on), but the results would be very subjective. Subjective valuations would not contribute to the reliability of financial statements. Goodwill is therefore recorded only when there is a purchase of an entire business, because this makes it possible to do an independent valuation.

In recording the purchase of a business, goodwill is the excess of cost over the fair market value of the net assets (assets less liabilities) that are acquired. Because goodwill has an indefinite life, just as the company has an indefinite life, it is not amortized.

Since goodwill is measured using the market value of a company—a subjective valuation which can easily change—it must be tested regularly for impairment just like other intangible assets with indefinite lives. However, because of its nature, goodwill requires a write-down more often than any other type of intangible asset.

BEFORE YOU GO ON . . .

▶**Review It**

1. What are the main differences between accounting for intangible and tangible assets?
2. Give some examples of intangible assets in your everyday surroundings.
3. What are the differences between the amortization policy for intangible assets with limited lives and the policy for those with indefinite lives?

▶**Do It**

The Dummies 'R' Us Company purchased a copyright to a new book series for $15,000 cash on August 1, 2007. The books are expected to have a saleable life of three years. One year later, the company spends an additional $6,000 cash to successfully defend this copyright in court. The company's year end is July 31. Journalize (1) the purchase of the copyright on August 1, 2007; (2) the year-end amortization at July 31, 2008; (3) the legal costs incurred on August 1, 2008; and (4) the year-end amortization at July 31, 2009.

Action Plan

- Amortize intangible assets with limited lives over the shorter of their useful life and legal life (the legal life of a copyright is the life of the author plus 50 years).
- Treat costs to successfully defend an intangible asset as a capital expenditure because they benefit future periods.
- Revise amortization for additions to the cost of the asset, using the net book value at the time of the addition and the remaining useful life.

Solution

(1)

Aug. 1, 2007	Copyright	15,000	
	Cash		15,000
	To record purchase of copyright.		

(2)

July 31, 2008	Amortization Expense ($15,000 ÷ 3)	5,000	
	Accumulated Amortization—Copyright		5,000
	To record amortization expense.		

(3)

Aug. 1, 2008	Copyright	6,000	
	Cash		6,000
	To record costs incurred to defend copyright.		

(4)

July 31, 2009	Amortization Expense	8,000[1]	
	Accumulated Amortization—Copyright		8,000
	To record revised amortization expense.		

1   $15,000 – $5,000 + $6,000 = $16,000 net book value; $16,000 net book value ÷ 2 years remaining = $8,000

Related exercise material: BE9–16, E9–11 and E9–12.

Statement Presentation and Analysis

Presentation

Property, plant, and equipment and natural resources are often combined and reported in the balance sheet as "property, plant, and equipment" or "capital assets." Intangible assets are normally listed separately, after property, plant, and equipment. Goodwill must be disclosed separately. Other intangibles can be grouped under the caption "intangible assets" for reporting purposes.

For assets that are amortized, the balances and accumulated amortization should be disclosed in the balance sheet or notes. In addition, the amortization methods that are used must be described. The amount of amortization expense for the period should also be disclosed. For assets that are not amortized, the book value of each major type of asset should be disclosed in the balance sheet or notes.

Companies must also disclose their impairment policy in the notes to the financial statements. Impairment losses, if any, should be shown on a separate line on the income statement, with the details disclosed in a note.

The following is an excerpt from Enerflex Systems' balance sheet:

ENERFLEX SYSTEMS LTD. Balance Sheet (partial) December 31, 2005 (in thousands)	
Assets	
Rental equipment (note 4)	$ 90,348
Property, plant, and equipment (note 5)	68,959
Intangible assets	7,355
Goodwill	121,378

Additional details on the long-lived assets are included in the notes to the financial statements. For example, note 4 discloses the cost, accumulated amortization, and net book value of Enerflex Systems' rental equipment. Note 5 discloses the cost, accumulated amortization, and net book value of Enerflex Systems' property, plant and equipment, which include land, buildings, equipment, assets under construction, and assets held for sale.

Another note, Enerflex Systems' summary of significant accounting policies, further discloses the amortization methods that are used and the estimated useful lives of the company's long-lived assets. This note also states that major renewals and improvements in rental equipment and property, plant, and equipment are capitalized. It also includes information on Enerflex Systems' policies on testing its long-lived assets for impairment. Rental equipment and property, plant, and equipment are assessed for impairment whenever changes in events or changes in circumstances indicate that the net book value of the asset may not be recovered. Intangible assets and goodwill are assessed for impairment at least annually. The company did not record any impairment losses in 2005.

Analysis

Typically, long-lived assets are a substantial portion of a company's total assets. We will use two ratios to assess the profitability of total assets: asset turnover and return on assets.

Asset Turnover

The **asset turnover** ratio indicates how efficiently a company uses its assets—that is, how many dollars of sales are generated by each dollar that is invested in assets. It is calculated by dividing net sales by average total assets. If a company is using its assets efficiently, each dollar of assets will create a high amount of sales. When we compare two companies in the same industry, the one with the higher asset turnover is operating more efficiently. The asset turnover ratio for fiscal 2006 for The Forzani Group ($ in thousands) is calculated in Illustration 9-14.

Illustration 9-14 ▶

Asset turnover

Net Sales	÷	Average Total Assets	=	Asset Turnover
$1,129,404	÷	($653,206 + $608,154) ÷ 2	=	1.8 times

The asset turnover ratio shows that each dollar invested in assets produced $1.80 in sales for Forzani. This ratio varies greatly among different industries—from those that have a large investment in assets (e.g., utility companies) to those that much less invested in assets (e.g., service companies). Asset turnover ratios, therefore, should only be compared for companies that are in the same industry.

Return on Assets

The **return on assets** ratio measures overall profitability. This ratio is calculated by dividing net income by average total assets. The return on assets ratio indicates the amount of earnings that is generated by each dollar invested in assets. A high return on assets indicates a profitable company. Illustration 9-15 shows the return on assets for Forzani ($ in thousands).

Net Income	÷	Average Total Assets	=	Return on Assets
$13,757	÷	($653,206 + $608,154) ÷ 2	=	2.2%
		630680		

Illustration 9-15 ◀

Return on assets

Forzani's return on assets was 2.2 percent for 2006. As with other ratios, the return on assets should be compared to previous years, to other companies in the same industry, and to industry averages, to determine how well the company has performed.

BEFORE YOU GO ON . . .

▶Review It

1. How are long-lived assets reported on the financial statements?
2. What information related to long-lived assets is disclosed in the notes to the financial statements?
3. What is the purpose of the asset turnover and return on assets ratios?

Related exercise material: BE9–17, BE9–18, BE9–19, E9–13, and E9–14.

Demonstration Problem 1

DuPage Company purchases a factory machine at a cost of $17,500 on June 1, 2008. The machine is expected to have a residual value of $1,500 at the end of its four-year useful life. DuPage has a December 31 year end.

During its useful life, the machine is expected to be used for 10,000 hours. Actual annual use was as follows: 1,300 hours in 2008; 2,800 hours in 2009; 3,300 hours in 2010; 1,900 hours in 2011; and 700 hours in 2012.

Instructions

Prepare amortization schedules for the following methods: (a) straight-line, (b) units-of-activity, and (c) declining-balance using double the straight-line rate.

Practice Tools:
Demonstration Problems

Action Plan

- Deduct the residual value in the straight-line and units-of-activity methods, but not in the declining-balance method.
- In the declining-balance method, the amortization rate is applied to the net book value (cost – accumulated amortization). The residual value is not used in the calculations except to make sure the net book value is not reduced below the residual value.
- When the asset is purchased during the year, the first year's amortization for the straight-line and declining-balance methods must be adjusted for the part of the year that the asset is owned. No adjustment is required for the units-of-activity method. In the straight-line method, the final year must also be adjusted.
- Amortization should never reduce the net book value of the asset below its expected residual value.

Solution to Demonstration Problem 1

(a) Straight-Line Method

Year	Amortizable Cost	×	Amortization Rate	=	Amortization Expense	Accumulated Amortization	Net Book Value
							$17,500
2008	$16,000ᵃ		25%ᵇ × ⁷⁄₁₂		$2,333	$ 2,333	15,167
2009	16,000		25%		4,000	6,333	11,167
2010	16,000		25%		4,000	10,333	7,167
2011	16,000		25%		4,000	14,333	3,167
2012	16,000		25% × ⁵⁄₁₂		1,667	16,000	1,500

ᵃ $17,500 – $1,500 = $16,000
ᵇ 100% ÷ 4 years = 25%

(b) Units-of-Activity Method

Year	Units of Activity	×	Amortizable Cost/Unit	=	Amortization Expense	Accumulated Amortization	Net Book Value
							$17,500
2008	1,300		$1.60ᵃ		$2,080	$ 2,080	15,420
2009	2,800		1.60		4,480	6,560	10,940
2010	3,300		1.60		5,280	11,840	5,660
2011	1,900		1.60		3,040	14,880	2,620
2012	700		1.60		1,120	16,000	1,500

ᵃ $17,500 – $1,500 = $16,000 amortizable cost ÷ 10,000 total units = $1.60/unit

(c) Declining-Balance Method

Year	Net Book Value Beginning of Year	×	Amortization Rate (25% × 2)	=	Amortization Expense	Accumulated Amortization	Net Book Value End of Year
							$17,500
2008	$17,500		50% × ⁷⁄₁₂		$5,104	$ 5,104	12,396
2009	12,396		50%		6,198	11,302	6,198
2010	6,198		50%		3,099	14,401	3,099
2011	3,099		50%		1,549	15,950	1,550
2012	1,549		50%		50ᵃ	16,000	1,500

ᵃ Adjusted to $50 because ending book value should not be less than the expected residual value.

www.wiley.com/canada/weygandt

Practice Tools:
Demonstration Problems

Demonstration Problem 2

On January 1, 2005, Skyline Limousine Co. purchased a speciality limo for $78,000. The vehicle is being amortized by the straight-line method using a four-year service life and a $4,000 residual value. The company's fiscal year ends on December 31.

Instructions

Prepare the journal entry or entries to record the disposal of the limo, assuming that it is:

(a) retired on January 1, 2009.
(b) sold for $15,000 on July 1, 2008.
(c) traded in on a new limousine on January 1, 2008, for a trade-in allowance of $25,000 and cash of $52,000. The fair market value of the old vehicle was $20,000.

Solution to Demonstration Problem 2

$$\frac{\$78,000 - \$4,000}{4 \text{ years}} = \$18,500 \text{ annual amortization expense}$$

(a)

Jan. 1, 2009	Accumulated Amortization ($18,500 × 4 years)	74,000	
	Loss on Disposal [$0 – ($78,000 – $74,000)]	4,000	
	Limo		78,000
	To record retirement of limo.		

(b)

July 1, 2008	Amortization Expense ($18,500 × $\frac{6}{12}$)	9,250	
	Accumulated Amortization		9,250
	To record amortization for 6 months.		
	Cash	15,000	
	Accumulated Amortization ($18,500 × 3.5 years)	64,750	
	Gain on Disposal [$15,000 – ($78,000 – $64,750)]		1,750
	Limo		78,000
	To record sale of limo.		

(c)

Jan. 1, 2008	Limo (new) ($20,000 + $52,000)	72,000	
	Accumulated Amortization ($18,500 × 3 years)	55,500	
	Loss on Disposal [$20,000 – ($78,000 – $55,500)]	2,500	
	Limo (old)		78,000
	Cash		52,000
	To record exchange of limousines, plus cash.		

Summary of Study Objectives

1. **Apply the cost principle to property, plant, and equipment.** The cost of property, plant, and equipment includes all costs that are necessary to acquire the asset and make it ready for its intended use. All costs that benefit future periods (i.e., capital expenditures) are included in the cost of the asset. In a basket purchase situation, cost is allocated to each individual asset using their relative fair market values.

2. **Explain and calculate amortization.** Amortization is the allocation of the cost of a long-lived asset to expense over its useful life (i.e., service life) in a rational and systematic way. Amortization is not a process of valuation and it does not result in an accumulation of cash. There are three commonly used amortization methods:

Method	Effect on Annual Amortization	Calculation
Straight-line	Constant amount	(Cost – residual value) ÷ estimated useful life (in years)
Declining-balance	Decreasing amount	Net book value at beginning of year × declining-balance rate
Units-of-activity	Varying amount	(Cost – residual value) ÷ total estimated units of activity × actual activity during the year

Each results in the same amount of amortization over the useful life of the asset.

3. **Revise periodic amortization.** A revision to amortization will be required if there are (1) capital expenditures during the useful life of the asset, (2) impairments in the market value of the asset, and/or (3) changes in the asset's estimated useful life or residual value. Revisions of periodic amortization are made in present and future periods, not retroactively. The new annual amortization is determined by dividing the amortizable cost (net book value less the revised residual value) at the time of the revision by the remaining useful life.

4. **Account for the disposal of property, plant, and equipment.** The accounting for the disposal of a piece of property, plant, or equipment through retirement or sale is as follows:

(a) Update any unrecorded amortization.
(b) Calculate the net book value.
(c) Calculate any gain (proceeds > net book value) or loss (proceeds < net book value) on disposal.
(d) Eliminate the asset and accumulated amortization accounts at the date of disposal. Record the proceeds received and the gain or loss, if any.

When an exchange of long-lived assets changes the operations of a company, the steps in accounting for the disposal are similar to the steps for the sale of an asset. Proceeds from the asset that is given up are equal to the asset's fair market value. The new asset that is received in the exchange is recorded at the total of the fair market value of the asset given up, plus any cash paid.

5. ***Calculate and record amortization of natural resources.*** Natural resources generally use the units-of-activity method of amortization. Amortizable cost (cost less residual value) is calculated on a per unit basis by dividing the total amortizable cost by the number of units estimated to be in the resource. The amortizable cost per unit is multiplied by the number of units that have been extracted to determine the annual amortization. The amortization and any other costs to extract the resource are recorded as inventory until the resource is sold. At that time, the costs are transferred to cost of resource sold on the income statement. Revisions to amortization will be required for capital expenditures during the asset's useful life, impairments, and changes in the total estimated units of the resource.

6. ***Identify the basic accounting issues for intangible assets.*** The accounting for intangible assets and the accounting for tangible assets are much the same. The straight-line method is used for amortizing intangible assets with limited useful lives. Intangible assets are normally amortized over the shorter of their useful life or their legal life. When an intangible asset has an indefinite life, it is not amortized but is tested every year for impairment.

7. ***Illustrate the reporting and analysis of long-lived assets.*** It is common for property, plant, and equipment, and natural resources to be combined under the heading Property, Plant, and Equipment. Intangibles are shown separately under the heading Intangible Assets or are listed separately. The balances of the major classes of assets and accumulated amortization (if the asset is amortizable) should be disclosed either in the balance sheet or in the notes. The amortization methods that are used should be described. The amount of amortization expense and any impairment losses for the period should be disclosed.

The asset turnover ratio (net sales ÷ average total assets) is one measure that is used by companies to show how efficiently they are using their assets to generate sales revenue. A second ratio, return on assets (net income ÷ average total assets), calculates how profitable the company is in terms of using its assets to generate net income.

Glossary

Study Aids: Glossary
Practice Tools: Key Term Matching Activity

Additions and improvements Costs that are incurred to increase the operating efficiency, productive capacity, or expected useful life of property, plant, or equipment. (p. 468)

Amortizable cost The total cost to be amortized. It is equal to the cost of a long-lived asset less its residual value. (p. 462)

Asset turnover A measure of how efficiently a company uses its total assets to generate sales. It is calculated by dividing net sales by average total assets. (p. 488)

Basket purchase The acquisition of a group of assets for a single price. Individual asset costs are determined by allocating relative fair market values. (p. 459)

Capital cost allowance (CCA) The amortization of long-lived assets that is allowed by the *Income Tax Act* for income tax purposes. It is calculated on a class (group) basis and mainly uses the declining-balance method with maximum rates specified for each class of assets. (p. 467)

Capital expenditures Expenditures related to long-lived assets that benefit the company over several account periods. (p. 457)

Copyright An exclusive right granted by the federal government allowing the owner to reproduce and sell an artistic or published work. (p. 484)

Declining-balance method An amortization method that applies a constant rate to the declining net book value of the asset. This method produces a decreasing annual amortization expense over the useful life of the asset. (p. 463)

Franchise A contractual arrangement under which the franchisor grants the franchisee the right to sell certain products, offer specific services, or use certain trademarks or trade names, usually inside a specific geographical area. (p. 486)

Goodwill The amount paid to purchase another company that is more than the market value of the company's net identifiable assets. It represents the value of the favourable attributes that relate to a company. (p. 486)

Impairment loss The loss that results when the net book value of an asset is not recoverable and market value permanently declines below the asset's net book value. (p. 469)

Intangible assets Rights, privileges, and competitive advantages that result from owning long-lived assets that have no physical substance. (p. 482)

Land improvements Structural additions to land that have limited useful lives, such as paving, fencing, and lighting. (p. 457)

Licences Operating rights to use public property, granted by a government agency to a company. (p. 486)

Monetary exchange of assets An exchange of similar assets, including a significant amount of money as part of the exchange. (p. 476)

Natural resources Long-lived tangible assets, such as standing timber and underground deposits of oil, gas, and minerals, that are physically extracted and are only replaceable by an act of nature. Also called wasting assets. (p. 479)

Nonmonetary exchange of assets An exchange of similar assets that includes little or no money as part of the exchange. (p. 476)

Operating expenditures Expenditures that benefit only the current period. They are immediately charged against revenues as expenses. (p. 457)

Ordinary repairs Expenditures to maintain the operating efficiency and productive life of the unit. (p. 468)

Patent An exclusive right issued by the federal government that enables the recipient to manufacture, sell, or otherwise control an invention for a period of 20 years from the date of the application. (p. 483)

Property, plant, and equipment Identifiable, long-lived tangible assets, such as land, land improvements, buildings, and equipment, that the company owns and uses for the production and sale of goods or services to consumers. (p. 456)

Research and development (R&D) costs Expenditures that may lead to patents, copyrights, new processes, and new products. (p. 484)

Residual value An estimate of the asset's value at the end of its useful life. (p. 461)

Return on assets An overall measure of profitability that indicates the amount of income that is earned from each dollar invested in assets. It is calculated by dividing net income by average total assets. (p. 489)

Royalties Recurring payments that may be required under a franchise agreement and are paid by the franchisee to the franchisor for services provided (e.g., advertising, purchasing), and are often proportionate to sales. (p. 486)

Straight-line method An amortization method in which the amortizable cost of an asset is divided by the estimated useful life. This method produces the same periodic amortization for each year of the asset's useful life. (p. 462)

Tangible assets Long-lived resources that have physical substance, are used in the operations of the business, and are not intended for sale to customers. Tangible assets include property, plant, and equipment and natural resources. (p. 482)

Trade-in allowance A price reduction offered by the seller when a used asset is exchanged for a new asset as part of the deal. (p. 476)

Trademark (trade name) A word, phrase, jingle, or symbol that distinguishes or identifies a particular enterprise or product. (p. 485)

Units-of-activity method An amortization method in which useful life is expressed in terms of the total estimated units of production or use expected from the asset. Amortization expense is calculated by multiplying the amortizable cost per unit (cost less residual value divided by total estimated activity) by the actual activity that occurs during the year. (p. 465)

Useful life An estimate of the expected productive life of an asset. It is also called the service life. (p. 461)

Self-Study Questions

 Practice Tools: Self-Assessment Quizzes

Answers are at the end of the chapter.

(SO 1) AP 1. Asura Company purchased land, a building, and equipment for a package price of $200,000. The fair market value of the land at the time of acquisition was $75,000. The fair market value of the building was $80,000. The fair market value of the equipment was $50,000. What costs should be debited to the three accounts Land, Building, and Equipment, respectively?
  (a) $66,667; $66,667; and $66,666
  (b) $73,171; $78,049; and $48,780
  (c) $75,000; $80,000; and $50,000
  (d) $200,000; $0; and $0

(SO 2) AP 2. Cuso Company purchased equipment on January 1, 2007, at a total cost of $40,000. The equipment has an estimated residual value of $10,000 and an estimated useful life of five years. If the straight-line method of amortization is used, what is the amount of accumulated amortization at December 31, 2008, the end of the second year of the asset's life?
  (a) $6,000   (c) $18,000
  (b) $12,000   (d) $24,000

3. Kant Enterprises purchases a truck for $33,000 on July (SO 2) AP 1, 2008. The truck has an estimated residual value of $3,000, and an estimated useful life of five years, or a total mileage of 300,000 kilometres. If 50,000 kilometres are driven in 2008, what amount of amortization expense would Kant record at December 31, 2008, assuming it uses the units-of-activity method?
  (a) $2,500   (c) $5,000
  (b) $3,000   (d) $5,333

(SO 2) AP **4.** Refer to the data for Kant Enterprises in question 3. If Kant uses the double declining-balance method of amortization, what amount of amortization expense would it record at December 31, 2008?
(a) $6,000
(b) $6,600
(c) $12,000
(d) $13,200

(SO 3) K **5.** When there is a change in estimated useful life and/or residual value:
(a) the amortization of past years should be corrected.
(b) the amortization of current and future years should be revised.
(c) only the amortization of future years should be revised.
(d) None of the above

(SO 4) AP **6.** Oviatt Company sold equipment for $10,000. At that time, the equipment had a cost of $45,000 and accumulated amortization of $30,000. Oviatt should record:
(a) a $5,000 loss on disposal.
(b) a $5,000 gain on disposal.
(c) a $15,000 loss on disposal.
(d) a $15,000 gain on disposal.

(SO 4) AP **7.** St. Laurent Company exchanged an old machine with a book value of $39,000 and a fair market value of $35,000 for a new machine. The new machine had a list price of $47,500. St. Laurent was offered a trade-in allowance of $37,500, and paid $10,000 cash in the exchange. At what amount should the new machine be recorded on St. Laurent's books?
(a) $35,000
(b) $45,000
(c) $47,500
(d) $49,000

the navigator

(SO 5) **8.** On April 1, 2007, Shady Tree Farm Company purchased a Christmas tree farm that has an estimated 100,000 harvestable Christmas trees. The purchase price was $500,000 and the tree farm is expected to have an estimated residual value of $50,000. During the first year of operations, ended January 31, 2008, Shady Tree Farm cut and sold 10,000 trees. What amount of amortization should be included in cost of goods sold for the year ended January 31?
(a) $37,500
(b) $40,500
(c) $45,000
(d) $50,000

(SO 6) **9.** Pierce Company had $150,000 of development costs in its laboratory that were related to a patent granted on January 2, 2008. On July 31, 2008, Pierce paid $35,000 for legal fees in a successful defence of the patent. The total amount debited to Patents through July 31, 2008, should be:
(a) $35,000.
(b) $150,000.
(c) $185,000.
(d) None of the above

(SO 7) **10. WestJet Airlines Ltd.** reported net sales of $1,395 million, net income of $24 million, and average total assets of $2,045 million in 2005. What are WestJet's return on assets and asset turnover?
(a) 0.68% and 1.2 times
(b) 1.7% and 1.2 times
(c) 1.2% and 1.5 times
(d) 1.2% and 0.68 times

Questions

(SO 1) C **1.** Susan Leung is uncertain about how the cost principle applies to long-lived assets. Explain this to Susan.

(SO 1) C **2.** ACW Company purchases land and a building for $430,000. The company spends $45,000 to remove the building and $30,000 to grade the land so that it is ready for the construction of a new building. Explain how to account for each of these costs.

(SO 1) C **3.** Some people believe that the market values of property, plant, and equipment are more relevant than historical cost for decisions made by such users as creditors, investors, and managers. Why has the cost principle survived even if it does not seem very useful?

(SO 1) C **4.** Jacques asks why the total cost in a basket purchase has to be allocated to the individual assets. For example, if we purchase land and a building for $250,000, why can we not just debit an account called Land and Building for $250,000?

(SO 2) **5.** What is the purpose of amortization? What are some common misunderstandings about amortization?

(SO 2) **6.** Cecile is studying for her next accounting exam. She asks for your help on two questions: (a) What is residual value? (b) How is residual value used in calculating amortization in each of the amortization methods? Answer her questions.

(SO 2) **7.** Contrast the effects of the three amortization methods on net book value, amortization expense, and net income (1) in the early years of an asset's life, and (2) over the total life of the asset.

(SO 2) **8.** Ralph has a plan to reduce the amount of income taxes that will have to be paid on his company's income. He has decided to calculate amortization expense using very low estimated useful lives on his property, plant, and equipment. Will Ralph's plan work?

(SO 3) C 9. Explain the difference between operating expenditures and capital expenditures during an asset's useful life and describe the accounting treatment of each.

(SO 3) C 10. What is an impairment loss? Under what circumstances does it occur?

(SO 3) C 11. In the third year of an asset's four-year useful life, the company decides that the asset will have a six-year service life. Should prior periods be restated because of the revised amortization? Explain why or why not.

(SO 4) K 12. How is a gain or loss on the sale of a piece of property, plant, or equipment calculated? Is the calculation the same for an exchange of a piece of property, plant, or equipment?

(SO 4) C 13. Ewing Company owns a machine that is fully amortized but is still being used. How should Ewing account for this asset and report it in the financial statements?

(SO 5) C 14. Explain how annual amortization is (a) calculated and (b) recorded for natural resources.

(SO 5) C 15. Under what circumstances is the amortization of natural resources recorded as a current asset under inventory rather than as an expense?

(SO 6) C 16. What are the characteristics of an intangible asset?

17. Flin Company recently purchased a patent. Should Flin (SO 6) C amortize the patent over its legal life or some other period? Explain.

18. Bob Leno, a business student, is working on a case prob- (SO 6) C lem for one of his classes. In this problem, the company needs to raise cash to market a new product it has developed. Saul Cain, an engineering student, takes one look at the company's balance sheet and says, "This company has an awful lot of goodwill. Why don't you recommend that they sell some of it to raise cash?" How should Bob respond to Saul's suggestion?

19. Research and development costs often provide compa- (SO 6) C nies with benefits that last many years. For example, these costs can lead to the development of a product that will increase the company's income for years to come. However, generally accepted accounting principles require that most of these costs be recorded as expenses when they are incurred. Why?

20. How should long-lived assets be reported on the balance (SO 7) K sheet and income statement? What information should be disclosed in the notes to the financial statements?

21. What information do the asset turnover and return on (SO 7) C assets ratios show about a company?

Brief Exercises

BE9–1 The following costs were incurred by Shumway Company in purchasing land: cash price, $50,000; removal of old building, $5,000; legal fees, $2,500; clearing and grading, $3,500; installation of fence, $3,000. What is the cost of the land?

Determine cost of land. (SO 1) AP

BE9–2 Mabasa Company incurs the following costs in purchasing a delivery truck: cash price, $41,750; painting and lettering, $750; motor vehicle licence, $100; installation of trailer hitch $500; one-year accident insurance policy, $2,000. What is the cost of the truck?

Determine cost of truck. (SO 1) AP

BE9–3 In the space provided, indicate whether each of the following items is an operating expenditure (O) or a capital expenditure (C):

Identify operating and capital expenditures. (SO 1) K

(a) ___ Repaired building roof, $500
(b) ___ Replaced building roof, $17,500
(c) ___ Purchased building, $180,000
(d) ___ Purchased supplies, $350
(e) ___ Purchased truck, $35,000

(f) ___ Purchased oil and gas for truck, $75
(g) ___ Replaced tires on truck, $500
(h) ___ Rebuilt engine on truck, $5,000
(i) ___ Added new wing to building, $250,000
(j) ___ Painted interior of building, $1,500

BE9–4 Rainbow Company purchased land, a building, and equipment on January 1, 2008, for $400,000. The company paid $100,000 cash and signed a mortgage note payable for the remainder. Management's best estimate of the value of the land was $127,500, of the building, $255,000, and of the equipment, $42,500. Record the purchase.

Record basket purchase. (SO 1) AP

BE9–5 On January 2, 2008, Mabasa Company acquires a delivery truck at a cost of $43,000. The truck is expected to have a residual value of $3,000 at the end of its four-year useful life. Calculate the amortization using the straight-line method (a) for each year of the truck's life, and (b) in total over the truck's life. Mabasa has a December 31 fiscal year end.

Calculate straight-line amortization. (SO 2) AP

BE9–6   Amortization information for Mabasa Company is given in BE9–5. Use the declining-balance method and assume the declining-balance amortization rate is double the straight-line rate. Calculate the amortization expense (a) for each year of the truck's life, and (b) in total over the truck's life.

BE9–7   Speedy Taxi Service uses the units-of-activity method in calculating amortization on its taxicabs. Each cab is expected to be driven 325,000 kilometres. Taxi 10 cost $33,000 and is expected to have a residual value of $500. Taxi 10 is driven 125,000 kilometres in 2007, and 105,000 kilometres in 2008. Calculate the amortization expense for each year.

BE9–8   Amortization information for Mabasa Company is given in BE9–5. Assuming the delivery truck was purchased on April 9, 2008, calculate the amortization using the straight-line method (a) for each year of the truck's life, and (b) in total over the truck's life. The company prorates amortization to the nearest month.

BE9–9   Amortization information for Mabasa Company is given in BE9–5. Assuming the delivery truck was purchased on April 9, 2008, calculate the amortization using the double declining-balance method (a) for each year of the truck's life, and (b) in total over the truck's life. The company prorates amortization to the nearest month.

BE9–10   AMMA Phone Company owns machinery that cost $90,000 and has accumulated amortization of $54,000. The machinery's market value is $20,000. Record the impairment loss, assuming the net book value is not recoverable and the decline in value is permanent.

BE9–11   On January 2, 2005, Lapointe Company purchased equipment for $60,000. At that time, the equipment was estimated to have a useful life of seven years and a residual value of $4,000. On January 3, 2008, Lapointe upgrades the equipment at a cost of $9,000. Lapointe estimates that the equipment will now have a total useful life of nine years and a residual value of $3,000. The company uses straight-line amortization and has a December 31 fiscal year end. Calculate the 2008 amortization expense.

BE9–12   Ruiz Company retires its delivery equipment, which cost $41,000. No residual value is received. Prepare journal entries to record the transaction if (a) accumulated amortization is also $41,000 on this delivery equipment, and (b) the accumulated amortization is $38,000 instead of $41,000.

BE9–13   Wiley Company sells office equipment on September 30, 2008, for $8,250 cash. The office equipment was purchased on January 5, 2004, at a cost of $72,500, and had an estimated useful life of five years and an estimated residual value of $2,500. Adjusting journal entries are made annually at the company's year end, December 31. Prepare the journal entries to (a) update amortization to September 30, 2008, (b) record the sale of the equipment, and (c) record the sale of the equipment if Wiley Company received $4,500 cash for it.

BE9–14   Subramanian Company has machinery with an original cost of $95,000 and, as at December 31, 2007, accumulated amortization of $78,000. On January 7, 2008, Subramanian exchanges the machinery, plus $62,000 cash, for new machinery. The old machinery has a fair market value of $14,000. The new machinery has a list price of $80,000, but the dealer gave Subramanian an $18,000 trade-in allowance on the old machinery. Record the January 7, 2008, journal entry for the machinery exchange.

BE9–15   Cuono Mining Co. purchased a mine for $7 million that is estimated to have 28 million tonnes of ore and a residual value of $500,000. In the first year, 6 million tonnes of ore are extracted and 5 million tonnes are sold.

(a) Record the amortization and the cost of the ore extracted for the first year, ended August 31, 2008.

(b) Show how the mine and the ore on hand are reported on the balance sheet on August 31, 2008.

BE9–16 Surkis Company purchases a patent for $180,000 cash on January 2, 2008. Its legal life is 20 years and its estimated useful life is 10 years. On January 5, 2009, Surkis paid $9,000 cash to successfully defend the patent in court.

(a) Record the purchase of the patent on January 2, 2008.
(b) Record amortization expense for the year ended December 31, 2008.
(c) Record the legal costs on January 5, 2009.
(d) Calculate amortization expense for 2009.

Record acquisition and amortization, and show balance sheet presentation for patent.
(SO 6) AP

BE9–17 Indicate whether each of the following items is property, plant, and equipment (PPE), a natural resource (NR), or an intangible asset (I). If the item does not fit any of these categories, write NA (not applicable) in the space provided.

Classify long-lived assets.
(SO 7) K

(a) ___ Patent
(b) ___ Land
(c) ___ Oil well
(d) ___ Note receivable, due in 3 months
(e) ___ Licence right
(f) ___ Machinery
(g) ___ Inventory

(h) ___ Cost of goods sold
(i) ___ Trademark
(j) ___ Franchise
(k) ___ Unearned service revenue
(l) ___ Building
(m) ___ Parking lot
(n) ___ Natural gas deposit

BE9–18 Canadian Tire Corporation, Limited reports the following selected information about long-lived assets at December 31, 2005 (in millions):

Prepare partial balance sheet.
(SO 7) AP

Accumulated amortization—buildings	$ 704.4
Accumulated amortization—fixtures and equipment	347.5
Accumulated amortization—leasehold improvements	91.3
Buildings	2,094.4
Fixtures and equipment	528.4
Goodwill	46.2
Land	700.5
Leasehold improvements	265.6
Mark's Work Wearhouse store brands and banners	50.4
Mark's Work Wearhouse franchise agreements	2.0
Other property, plant, and equipment	298.2

Mark's Work Wearhouse store brands, banners, and franchises are considered to have indefinite lives. Prepare a partial balance sheet for Canadian Tire.

BE9–19 Agrium Inc., a global agricultural nutrients producer that is headquartered in Calgary, Alberta, reports the following in its 2005 financial statements (in U.S. millions):

Calculate ratios.
(SO 7) AP

Net sales	$3,294	Total assets, December 31, 2005	$2,785
Net income	$283	Total assets, December 31, 2004	$2,661

Calculate Agrium's return on assets and asset turnover for 2005.

Exercises

E9–1 The following expenditures related to assets were made by Pascal Company:

Classify expenditures.
(SO 1) AP

1. Paid $250 to have the company name and advertising slogan painted on a new delivery truck.
2. Paid $900 for a one-year accident insurance policy on the new delivery truck.
3. Paid $4,000 in legal fees on a purchase of a plant site.
4. Paid $6,600 to demolish an old building on the plant site; residual materials were sold for $1,700.
5. Paid $7,800 in architect fees for work on the new plant.

6. Paid $225,000 for a new plant to be built.
7. Paid $5,600 interest during the construction of the new plant.
8. Paid $17,500 for paving the parking lots and driveways on the plant site.
9. Paid $8,000 for the installation of new factory machinery.
10. Paid $200 for insurance to cover potential damage to the new factory machinery while it was in transit.

Instructions

(a) Explain how the cost principle applies in determining the acquisition cost of property, plant, and equipment.
(b) Write the number of each transaction, and beside each number write the account title that the expenditure should be debited to.

Record basket purchase and calculate amortization.
(SO 1, 2) AP

E9–2   Hohenberger Farms purchased real estate for $575,000. It paid $75,000 cash and incurred a mortgage payable for $500,000. Legal fees of $5,000 were paid in cash. The real estate included land that was appraised at $366,000, buildings appraised at $192,000, and fences and other land improvements appraised at $42,000. The buildings have an estimated useful life of 40 years and a $20,000 residual value. Land improvements have an estimated 10-year useful life and no residual value.

Instructions

(a) Calculate the cost that should be allocated to each asset purchased.
(b) Record the purchase of the real estate.
(c) Calculate the annual amortization expense for the buildings and land improvements assuming Hohenberger Farms uses straight-line amortization.

Calculate amortization using three methods; recommend method.
(SO 2) AP

E9–3   Intercity Bus Lines purchases a bus on January 2, 2007, at a cost of $164,500. Over its five-year useful life, the bus is expected to be driven 375,000 kilometres and to have a residual value of $22,000. The company has a December 31 fiscal year end.

Instructions

(a) Calculate amortization for each year of the bus's life and in total under each of the following methods: (1) straight-line, (2) declining-balance using double the straight-line rate, and (3) units-of-activity. Assume the actual distance driven was 78,000 kilometres in 2007; 76,000 kilometres in 2008; 72,000 kilometres in 2009; 74,000 kilometres in 2010; and 75,000 kilometres in 2011.
(b) Which amortization method should the company use? Why?

Prepare amortization schedules and answer questions.
(SO 2) AP

E9–4   Sitrus Company purchased a new machine on October 4, 2007, at a cost of $86,000. The company estimated that the machine will have a residual value of $8,000. The machine is expected to be used for 10,000 working hours during its four-year life. Sitrus Company has a December 31 year end and prorates amortization to the nearest month.

Instructions

(a) Prepare an amortization schedule for the life of the asset under each of the following methods: (1) straight-line, (2) declining-balance using double the straight-line rate, and (3) units-of-activity. Assume that the actual machine usage was 500 hours in 2007; 2,800 hours in 2008; 2,900 hours in 2009; 2,600 hours in 2010; and 1,300 hours in 2011.
(b) Which method results in the highest amortization expense over the life of the asset?
(c) Which method results in the highest cash flow over the life of the asset?

Record expenditures and impairment losses.
(SO 3) AP

E9–5   The following selected transactions related to property, plant, and equipment are for Bisor Company in 2008. Bisor has a December 31 year end and uses straight-line amortization.

Jan. 10 Paid $70,000 to replace the roof on a building that the company has owned for 20 years. This increased the expected useful life of the building by 10 years.
Apr. 8 Paid $25,000 to repaint the interior of the same building.
Sept. 2 Paid $22,500 for an upgrade to a piece of equipment that produces inventory. Bisor expects the equipment's capacity will be doubled after the upgrade.

Nov. 1 Paid $1,000 to replace the exhaust system on one of Bisor's vehicles.

Dec. 31 After recording annual amortization, Bisor reviewed its property, plant, and equipment for possible impairment. Bisor determined that equipment with a cost of $500,000 and accumulated amortization of $150,000 has a current market value of $230,000. The decline in value is considered permanent and the net book value is not recoverable.

Instructions

Prepare journal entries to record the above transactions.

E9–6 Lindy Weink, the new controller of Lafrenière Company, has reviewed the expected useful lives and residual values of selected amortizable assets at the beginning of 2008. Her findings are as follows:

Calculate and record revised amortization.
(SO 3) AP

Type of Asset	Date Acquired	Cost	Total Useful Life in Years Current	Total Useful Life in Years Proposed	Residual Value Current	Residual Value Proposed
Building	Jan. 1, 1998	$800,000	20	25	$40,000	$62,000
Equipment	Jan. 1, 2006	120,000	5	4	5,000	3,600

After discussion, management agrees to accept Lindy's proposed changes. All assets are amortized by the straight-line method. Lafrenière Company has a December 31 year end.

Instructions

(a) Calculate the annual amortization on each asset using the current useful lives and residual values.
(b) Calculate the accumulated amortization and net book value of each asset on January 1, 2008.
(c) Calculate the revised annual amortization on each asset.

E9–7 Mactaquac Company purchased a piece of high-tech equipment on July 1, 2006, for $30,000 cash. The equipment was expected to last four years and has a residual value of $4,000. Mactaquac uses straight-line amortization and its fiscal year end is June 30.

Record asset addition and amortization.
(SO 3) AP

On July 1, 2007, Mactaquac purchased and installed a new part on the equipment which is expected to increase the equipment's productivity a lot. Mactaquac paid $5,000 cash for the part. It paid an additional $500 for the installation and testing of this part. The equipment is expected to last six years in total now and has a revised residual value of $3,000.

Instructions

(a) Record the annual amortization of the equipment on June 30, 2007.
(b) Record the purchase of the part, and its installation and testing, on July 1, 2007.
(c) Record the annual amortization of the equipment on June 30, 2008.
(d) Calculate the net book value of the equipment on June 30, 2008, after recording the annual amortization.

E9–8 Here are some transactions of Surendal Company for 2008. Surendal Company uses straight-line amortization and has a December 31 year end.

Record disposal of property, plant, and equipment.
(SO 4) AP

Jan. 2 Traded in an old delivery truck for a new delivery truck, receiving an $8,000 trade-in allowance and paying $33,000 cash. The old delivery truck cost $30,000 and had accumulated amortization of $22,500. The fair market value of the old delivery truck was $6,500 on January 2, 2008.

Mar. 31 Retired a piece of machinery that was purchased on January 1, 1999, for $62,000. The machinery had an expected useful life of 10 years with no residual value.

Sept. 1 Received $800 cash from the sale of office equipment that was purchased on January 1, 2006. The equipment cost $5,490 and was amortized over an expected useful life of three years with no residual value.

Instructions

Record the above disposals of property, plant, and equipment. When necessary, include entries to update amortization for partial periods.

Calculate gain or loss on
disposal under different
amortization methods.
(SO 4) AP

E9–9 On January 3, 2006, Hamir Company purchased computer equipment for $16,000. Hamir planned to keep the equipment for four years, and expected the equipment would then be sold for $1,000. On January 5, 2008, Hamir sold the computer equipment for $5,000.

Instructions

(a) Calculate the amortization expense for 2006 and 2007 under (1) the straight-line method and (2) the double declining-balance method.

(b) Calculate the gain or loss on disposal if Hamir had used (1) the straight-line method and (2) the double declining-balance method.

(c) Explain why the gain or loss on disposal is not the same under the two amortization methods.

Record amortization
for natural resources;
show financial statement
presentation.
(SO 5) AP

E9–10 On July 1, 2008, Phillips Inc. invests $520,000 in a mine that is estimated to have 800,000 tonnes of ore. The company estimates that the property will be sold for $90,000 when production at the mine has ended. During the last six months of 2008, 100,000 tonnes of ore are mined but only 75,000 tonnes are sold. Phillips has a December 31 fiscal year end.

Instructions

(a) Explain why the units-of-activity method is recommended for amortizing natural resources.

(b) Record the 2008 amortization.

(c) Show how the mine and any related accounts are reported on the December 31, 2008, income statement and balance sheet.

Apply accounting concepts.
(SO 1, 2, 6) AP

E9–11 An accounting co-op student encountered the following situations at Darko Company:

1. The student learned that Darko is amortizing its buildings and equipment, but not its land. The student could not understand why land was not included, so she prepared journal entries to amortize all of the company's property, plant, and equipment for the current year end.

2. The student decided that Darko's amortization policy on its intangible assets is wrong. The company is currently amortizing its patents but not its goodwill. The student fixed that for the current year end by adding goodwill to her adjusting entry for amortization. She told a fellow student that she felt she had improved the consistency of the company's accounting policies by making these changes.

3. One of the buildings that Darko uses has zero book value but a substantial market value. The co-op student felt that leaving the book value at zero did not benefit the financial information's users—especially the bank—and wrote the building up to its market value. After all, she reasoned, you write down assets if market values are lower. She feels that writing them up if their market value is higher is yet another example of the improved consistency that her employment has brought to the company's accounting practices.

Instructions

Explain whether or not the co-op student's accounting treatment in each of the above situations follows generally accepted accounting principles. Explain what accounting principle or assumption, if any, has been violated and what the appropriate accounting treatment should be.

Record acquisition,
amortization, and impairment
of intangible assets.
(SO 6) AP

E9–12 On December 31, 2007, Whiteway Company owned the following intangible assets:

1. Goodwill purchased on August 21, 2000, for $385,000

2. A patent purchased on January 1, 2006, for $450,000. When the patent was purchased, it had an estimated useful life of five years and a legal life of 20 years.

In 2008, Whiteway had the following transactions related to intangible assets:

Jan. 2 Incurred legal fees of $45,000 to successfully defend the patent.
Apr. 1 Purchased a trademark with an indefinite expected life for $325,000.
July 1 Purchased a 10-year franchise which expires on July 1, 2018, for $250,000.
Sept. 1 Incurred research costs of $185,000.
Dec. 31 Reviewed each intangible asset for impairments. Determined that the value of the goodwill had permanently declined to $300,000.

Instructions

(a) Record these transactions. All incurred costs were for cash.

(b) Record any necessary amortization and impairment losses on December 31, 2008. Whiteway has not previously recorded any impairment losses on its intangible assets.

E9–13 BCE Inc. reported the following selected information as at December 31, 2005 (in millions):

Classify long-lived assets; prepare partial balance sheet. (SO 7) AP

Accumulated amortization—buildings	$ 1,340
Accumulated amortization—finite-life intangible assets	1,574
Accumulated amortization—machinery and equipment	3,685
Accumulated amortization—other property, plant, and equipment	66
Accumulated amortization—satellites	404
Accumulated amortization—telecommunications assets	24,144
Amortization expense	3,114
Buildings	3,157
Cash and cash equivalents	363
Common shares	16,806
Finite-life intangible assets	3,813
Goodwill	7,887
Indefinite-life intangible assets	3,031
Land	94
Machinery and equipment	6,273
Other long-term assets	2,914
Other property, plant, and equipment	200
Plant under construction	1,852
Satellites	1,552
Telecommunications assets	36,334

Instructions

(a) Identify in which financial statement (balance sheet or income statement) and which section (e.g., current assets) each of the above items should be reported.

(b) Prepare the tangible and intangible assets sections of the balance sheet as at December 31, 2005.

E9–14 Sleeman Breweries Ltd. reported the following information for the fiscal years ended December 31, 2005, and January 1, 2005 (in thousands):

Calculate asset turnover and return on assets. (SO 7) AN

	Dec. 31, 2005	Jan. 1, 2005
Net revenues	$206,674	$211,476
Net income	8,097	14,426
Total assets, end of year	308,336	300,152
Total assets, beginning of year	300,152	242,755

Instructions

(a) Calculate Sleeman's asset turnover and return on assets for the two years.

(b) Comment on what the ratios reveal about Sleeman Breweries Ltd.'s effectiveness in using its assets to generate revenues and produce net income.

Problems: Set A

Record property transactions.
(SO 1) AP

P9–1A In 2008, Weisman Company had the following transactions related to the purchase of a property. All transactions are for cash unless otherwise stated.

Feb. 7 Purchased real estate for $275,000, paying $75,000 cash and signing a note payable for the balance. The site had an old building on it and the fair market value of the land and building were $270,000 and $30,000 respectively. Weisman intends to demolish the old building and construct a new building on the site.

9 Paid legal fees of $5,500 on the real estate purchase on February 7.

15 Paid $15,000 to demolish the old building and make the land ready for the construction of the apartment building.

17 Received $4,000 from the sale of material from the demolished building.

Mar. 2 Architect's fees on the apartment building were $18,000.

July 5 The full cost for construction of the apartment building was $650,000. Paid $170,000 cash and signed a note payable for the balance.

31 Interest costs while the building was under construction amounted to $6,500.

Aug. 22 Paid $12,000 for sidewalks and a parking lot for the building.

Sept. 1 Purchased a one-year insurance policy on the finished building for $2,500.

Dec. 31 Interest costs after the building was completed and rented to tenants amounted to $17,500.

Instructions

(a) Record the above transactions.

(b) Determine the cost of the land, land improvements, and building that will appear on Weisman's December 31, 2008, balance sheet.

Calculate partial period
amortization.
(SO 2) AP

P9–2A In recent years, Tarcher Company purchased two machines and uses a different method of amortization for each. Information on the machines is as follows:

Machine	Acquired	Cost	Residual Value	Useful Life in Years	Amortization Method
1	Feb. 21, 2006	$48,940	$4,000	7	Straight-line
2	Sept. 10, 2007	84,000	4,500	10	Declining-balance

The company uses double the straight-line rate for the declining-balance method.

Instructions

(a) If Tarcher has a policy of recording amortization to the nearest month, calculate the amount of accumulated amortization on each machine at December 31, 2008. Round your answers to the nearest dollar.

(b) If Tarcher has a policy of recording a half year of amortization in the year of acquisition and disposal, calculate the amount of accumulated amortization on each machine at December 31, 2008. Round your answers to the nearest dollar.

(c) Which policy should Tarcher follow—recording amortization to the nearest month in the year of acquisition or recording a half year of amortization in the year of acquisition?

(d) How would Tarcher's choice of how to record amortization in the year of acquisition affect amortization calculations if Tarcher used the units-of-activity method to amortize the machines?

Determine cost; calculate and
compare amortization under
different methods.
(SO 1, 2) AP

P9–3A Mazlish Company purchased a machine on account on April 6, 2006, at an invoice price of $180,000. On April 7, 2006, it paid $1,000 for delivery of the machine. A one-year, $2,275 insurance policy on the machine was purchased on April 9, 2006. On April 22, 2006, Mazlish paid $3,200 for installation and testing of the machine. The machine was ready for use on April 30, 2006.

Mazlish estimates that the useful life of the machine will be five years, with a residual value of $11,500. Mazlish estimates that the useful life of the machine, in terms of activity, will be 55,000 units. Mazlish has a December 31 fiscal year end and records amortization to the nearest month.

Instructions

(a) Determine the cost of the machine.

(b) Prepare an amortization schedule for the life of the asset under each of the following assumptions:

1. Mazlish uses the straight-line method of amortization.
2. Mazlish uses the declining-balance method at double the straight-line rate.
3. Mazlish uses the units-of-activity method. Assume actual usage is as follows: 8,500 units in 2006; 12,000 units in 2007; 11,500 units in 2008; 10,500 units in 2009; 9,500 units in 2010; and 3,000 units in 2011.

(c) Which method would result in the lowest net income in 2006? Over the life of the asset?

(d) Which method would result in the lowest cash flow in 2006? Over the life of the asset?

(e) What factors should influence management's choice of amortization method?

P9–4A Sugden Company had the following selected transactions related to property, plant, and equipment in 2008:

Account for operating and capital expenditures and asset impairments.
(SO 1, 3) AP

Feb. 12 Added an elevator and ramps to a building owned by the company to make it wheelchair accessible for $120,000.

Mar. 6 Replaced carpets in the main reception area and hallways for $7,500.

Apr. 10 Converted all toilets and faucets to low-flow fixtures to reduce water consumption for $25,000. The company expects to realize substantial savings in its utility bills in the future.

May 17 Overhauled machinery that originally cost $100,000 for $35,000. This increased the expected useful life of the machinery by three years.

June 28 Replaced the tires on several company vehicles for $5,000.

July 20 Repaired a machine for $10,000. An employee had used incorrect material in the machine which resulted in a complete breakdown.

Aug. 5 Spent $1,600 training a new employee to operate the company's machinery.

Sept. 18 Replaced a conveyor belt with a new high-speed model for $80,000. Sugden expects this will increase operating efficiency.

Nov. 6 Paid $4,600 for a one-year insurance policy.

Dec. 31 After recording annual amortization, Sugden reviewed its property, plant, and equipment for possible impairment, Sugden determined the following:

1. Equipment that originally cost $400,000 and has accumulated amortization of $150,000 has a current market value of $180,000. The decline in value is considered permanent and the net book value is not recoverable.
2. Land that originally cost $275,000 had previously been written down to $225,000 as a result of a permanent decline in value. But because of an unexpected change in circumstances, the current market value of the land is $260,000.

Instructions

Prepare journal entries to record the above transactions. All transactions are paid in cash.

P9–5A On January 4, 2004, Harrington Company acquired equipment costing $650,000. It was estimated at that time that this equipment would have a useful life of eight years and a residual value of $30,000. Harrington uses the straight-line method of amortization and has a December 31 year end.

Record impairment and calculate revised amortization.
(SO 3) AP

On December 31, 2007, after recording the annual amortization expense, Harrington determined that the market value of the equipment had permanently declined to $120,000. In 2008, Harrington also determined that the equipment's useful life would be six years in total, instead of the previously estimated eight. The residual value is still expected to be $30,000 at the end of the equipment's useful life.

Instructions

(a) Calculate the amortization expense for the years 2004 to 2007 and accumulated amortization at December 31, 2007.

(b) Record the impairment loss on December 31, 2007.

(c) Calculate amortization expense for each of 2008 and 2009.

(d) What should accumulated amortization and the net book value of the equipment be at the end of its useful life?

P9–6A Copps Co. owns woodworking equipment that originally cost $220,000 on June 30, 2004. When it was new, it had an estimated useful life of five years and an estimated residual value of $20,000. Copps records straight-line amortization annually on December 31.

In 2008, the following expenditures were made for this equipment:

Jan. 9 Completed an overhaul of the equipment at a cost of $33,000. The work included the installation of new optimizer controls to replace the original controls, which were obsolete. As a result of this work, the total estimated useful life of the equipment was changed to nine years and the estimated residual value was increased to $25,000.

Nov. 18 Painted the equipment to make it look new, $1,500.

Dec. 15 Replaced several bearings and guides which were showing signs of wear, $2,400.

Instructions

(a) Calculate amortization expense for the years 2004 to 2007 and accumulated amortization at December 31, 2007.
(b) Record each of the above transactions for 2008. All transactions are for cash.
(c) Calculate the amortization expense for 2008 and for the remaining years of the equipment's estimated useful life.
(d) What will accumulated amortization and the net book value be at the end of the asset's estimated useful life?

P9–7A Rapid Transportation Ltd. purchased a new bus on January 5, 2007, at a cost of $170,000. The bus has an estimated useful life of three years with a residual value of $26,000. Management is contemplating the merits of using the units-of-activity method of amortization instead of the straight-line method, which it currently uses.

Under the units-of-activity method, management estimates a total estimated useful life of 400,000 kilometres: 155,000 kilometres driven in 2007; 135,000 kilometres in 2008; and 110,000 kilometres in 2009.

Instructions

(a) Prepare amortization schedules for the life of the bus using (1) the straight-line method and (2) the units-of-activity method. Rapid Transportation has a December 31 fiscal year end.
(b) Assume that the bus is sold on December 30, 2008, for $60,000.
  1. Calculate the gain or loss on the sale of the bus under (a) the straight-line method and (b) the units-of-activity method.
  2. Prepare a schedule to show the overall impact of the total amortization expense combined with the gain or loss on sale for the two-year period under each method of amortization (consider the total effect on net income over the two-year period). Comment on your results.

P9–8A Hemmingsen Co. purchased office equipment on March 11, 2006, for $85,000 on account. At that time, it was expected to have a useful life of four years and a $1,000 residual value. The office equipment was disposed of on November 22, 2008, when the company moved to new premises. Hemmingsen Co. uses the straight-line method of amortization and calculates amortization for partial periods to the nearest month. The company has a December 31 year end.

Instructions

(a) Record the acquisition of the office equipment on March 11, 2006.
(b) Record amortization for each of 2006, 2007, and 2008.
(c) Record the disposal on November 22, 2008, under the following assumptions:
  1. It was scrapped as having no value.
  2. It was sold for $35,000.
  3. It was sold for $20,000.
  4. It was traded for new office equipment with a catalogue price of $113,000. Hemmingsen was given a trade-in allowance of $35,000 on the old office furniture and paid the balance in cash. Hemmingsen determined that the fair market value of the old office equipment was $25,000 at the date of the exchange.

P9–9A Menda Investments has a September 30 fiscal year end. It uses straight-line amortization and has a policy of recording amortization for partial periods to the nearest month. The following transactions involved property, plant, and equipment:

Record property, plant, and equipment transactions; prepare partial financial statements.

(SO 2, 3, 4, 7) AP

Oct. 6, 2004 Purchased assets from a recently bankrupt business for $550,000. Paid $100,000 of the purchase price in cash and issued a mortgage payable for the balance. The purchase included land for $280,000; a building for $225,000; and machinery for $45,000.

Sept. 30, 2005 Recorded amortization on the amortizable assets. The building has an estimated useful life of 40 years and no residual value. The machinery has an estimated useful life of 10 years and no residual value.

Sept. 30, 2006 Recorded amortization on the amortizable assets.

Sept. 30, 2007 Reviewed the estimated useful lives and residual values before making the year-end adjusting entries for amortization. As a result of the high usage of the machinery, it was decided that the total estimated useful life should be reduced to five years from the original 10 years. There were no changes in estimates for the building. The annual amortization was then recorded.

June 28, 2008 Purchased new machinery with a list price of $65,000. To make the purchase, the machinery purchased in 2004 was traded in for a $23,000 trade-in allowance and the balance was paid in cash. An independent appraisal stated the fair market value of the old machinery was $18,000. The new machinery has an estimated useful life of five years and no residual value.

Sept. 30, 2008 Recorded the amortization on the amortizable assets.

Instructions

(a) Prepare journal entries to record the above.
(b) Show how property, plant, and equipment would appear on the September 30, 2008, balance sheet.
(c) What accounts and amounts for property, plant, and equipment will be included on the income statement for the year ended September 30, 2008?

P9–10A Due to rapid turnover in the accounting department, some transactions that involved intangible assets were improperly recorded by Hahn Company in the year ended August 31, 2008:

Correct errors in recording intangible asset transactions.

(SO 6) AP

1. Hahn developed an electronic monitoring device for running shoes. It had research costs of $60,000 and development costs of $35,000. It recorded all of these costs in the Patent account.
2. The company registered the patent for the monitoring device. Legal fees and registration costs totalled $21,000. These costs were recorded in the Legal Fees Expense account.
3. The company successfully fought a competitor in court, defending its patent. It incurred $38,000 of legal fees. These costs were recorded in the Legal Fees Expense account.
4. The company sold the rights to manufacture and distribute this monitoring device to Fleet Foot Inc. for an annual fee of $50,000. Hahn recorded the receipt of this fee as a credit to the Patent account.
5. The company recorded $2,250 of annual amortization on the patent over its legal life of 20 years [($60,000 + $35,000 − $50,000) ÷ 20 years]. The expected economic life of the patent is five years. Assume that for amortization purposes all costs occurred at the beginning of the year.
6. At the end of the year, Hahn tested the patent for impairment and found that its market value of $70,000 far exceeded its book value of $42,750 ($60,000 + $35,000 − $50,000 − $2,250). Hahn did not record an entry.

Instructions

Prepare all the journal entries that are needed to correct the errors made during 2008.

Record intangible asset
transactions; prepare partial
balance sheet.
(SO 6, 7) AP

P9–11A The intangible assets section of Ghani Corporation's balance sheet at December 31, 2007, is as follows:

Copyright #1	$36,000	
Less: Accumulated amortization	25,200	$ 10,800
Trademark		54,000
Goodwill		125,000
Total		$189,800

The copyright was acquired in January 2001 and has an estimated useful life of 10 years. The trademark was acquired in January 2007 and is expected to have an indefinite useful life. The following cash transactions may have affected intangible assets during 2008:

Jan. 2 Paid $27,000 in legal costs to successfully defend the trademark against infringement by another company.

July 1 Developed a new product, incurring $210,000 in research costs and $50,000 in development costs. A patent was granted for the product on July 1, and its useful life is equal to its legal life.

Sept. 1 Paid $60,000 to a popular hockey player to appear in commercials advertising the company's products. The commercials will air in September and October.

Oct. 1 Acquired a second copyright for $180,000. The new copyright has an estimated useful life of five years.

Dec. 31 The company determined the fair market value of goodwill to be $85,000. This decline in value is believed to be a permanent impairment.

Instructions

(a) Record the above transactions for 2008.
(b) Record the 2008 amortization expense for intangible assets.
(c) Prepare the intangible assets section of the balance sheet at December 31, 2008.

Record equipment and
natural resource transactions;
prepare partial financial
statements.
(SO 2, 5, 7) AP

P9–12A Cypress Timber Company has a December 31 fiscal year end. The following information related to its Westerlund tract of timber land is available:

1. Cypress purchased a 50,000-hectare tract of timber land at Westerlund on June 7, 2007, for $50 million, paying $10 million cash and signing a 7% mortgage payable for the balance. Principal payments of $8 million and the annual interest on the mortgage are due each December 31. It is estimated that this tract will yield 1 million tonnes of timber. The estimated residual value of the timber tract is $2 million. Cypress expects it will cut all the trees and then sell the Westerlund site in five years.

2. On June 26, 2007, Cypress purchased and installed weighing equipment at the Westerlund timber site for $199,900 cash. The weighing equipment will be amortized on a straight-line basis over an estimated useful life of seven years with a residual value of $20,000. Cypress has a policy of recording amortization for partial periods to the nearest month. The weighing equipment will be moved to a new site after the Westerlund site is harvested.

3. In 2007, Cypress cut 110,000 tonnes of timber and sold 100,000 tonnes.

4. In 2008, Cypress cut and sold 230,000 tonnes of timber.

Instructions

(a) Prepare the 2007 and 2008 journal entries for the above, including year-end adjustments.
(b) Show how property, plant, and equipment, natural resources, and related accounts will be reported on Cypress' December 31, 2008, income statement and balance sheet.

Calculate ratios and
comment.
(SO 7) AN

P9–13A St. Amand Company and St. Helene Company, two companies of roughly the same size, both manufacture sea kayaks. An examination of their financial statements reveals the following information:

	St. Amand Company	St. Helene Company
Net sales	$4,375,000	$2,775,000
Net income	350,000	300,000
Total assets, January 1, 2008	3,780,000	2,540,000
Total assets, December 31, 2008	4,290,000	2,175,000

Instructions

(a) For each company, calculate the asset turnover and return on assets ratios.

(b) Based on your results in part (a), compare the two companies by commenting on how effective they are at using their assets to generate sales and produce net income.

Problems: Set B

P9–1B In 2008, Kadlec Company had the following transactions related to the purchase of a property. All transactions were for cash unless otherwise stated.

Record property transactions. (SO 1) AP

Jan. 22 Purchased real estate for a future plant site for $220,000, paying $55,000 cash and signing a note payable for the balance. On the site, there was an old building and the fair market value of the land and building were $210,000 and $30,000 respectively. Kadlec intends to demolish the old building and construct a new building.

24 Paid $4,500 for legal fees on the real estate purchase.

31 Paid $25,000 to demolish the old building to make room for the new plant.

Feb. 13 Graded and filled the land in preparation for the construction for $8,000.

28 Received $7,500 for residual materials from the demolished building.

Mar. 14 Paid $34,000 in architect fees for the building plans.

31 Paid the local municipality $15,000 for building permits.

Apr. 22 Excavation costs for the new building were $17,000.

June 15 Received a bill from the building contractor for half of the cost of the new building, $300,000. Paid $75,000 in cash and signed a note payable for the balance.

Sept. 14 Received a bill for the remaining $300,000 owed to the building contractor for the construction of the new building. Paid $100,000 cash and signed a note payable for the balance.

30 Interest costs while the building was under construction amounted to $6,700.

Oct. 12 Paved the parking lots, driveways, and sidewalks for $42,000.

20 Installed a fence for $8,000.

Dec. 31 Interest costs after the building was in use amounted to $7,800.

Instructions

(a) Record the above transactions.

(b) Determine the cost of the land, land improvements, and building that will appear on Kadlec's December 31, 2008, balance sheet.

P9–2B In recent years, Flakeboard Company purchased two machines. Various amortization methods were selected. Information on the machines is summarized here:

Calculate partial period amortization. (SO 2) AP

Machine	Acquired	Cost	Residual Value	Useful Life in Years	Amortization Method
1	Mar. 25, 2005	$96,000	$4,000	10	Straight-line
2	Oct. 5, 2007	60,000	8,000	8	Single declining-balance

Instructions

(a) If Flakeboard has a policy of recording amortization to the nearest month, calculate the amount of accumulated amortization on each machine at December 31, 2008. Round your answers to the nearest dollar.

(b) If Flakeboard has a policy of recording a half year's amortization in the year of acquisition and disposal, calculate the amount of accumulated amortization on each machine at December 31, 2008. Round your answers to the nearest dollar.

(c) Should Flakeboard consider recording amortization to the nearest day? Why or why not?

(d) Which policy should Flakeboard follow in the year of acquisition—recording amortization to the nearest whole month or recording a half year of amortization?

Determine cost; calculate and compare amortization under different methods.
(SO 1, 2) AP

P9–3B White-line Company purchased a machine on account on September 3, 2006, at an invoice price of $102,000. On September 4, 2006, it paid $5,200 for delivery of the machine. A one-year, $975 insurance policy on the machine was purchased on September 6, 2006. On September 20, 2006, White-line paid $4,300 for installation and testing of the machine. The machine was ready for use on October 1, 2006.

White-line estimates that the useful life of the machine will be four years, with a residual value of $6,500. It also estimates that, in terms of activity, the useful life of the machine will be 30,000 units. White-line has a December 31 fiscal year end and records amortization to the nearest month.

Instructions

(a) Determine the cost of the machine.

(b) Prepare an amortization schedule for the life of the asset under the following assumptions:
   1. White-line uses the straight-line method of amortization.
   2. White-line uses the declining-balance method at double the straight-line rate.
   3. White-line uses the units-of-activity method. Assume that actual usage is as follows: 2,000 units in 2006; 9,150 units in 2007; 7,650 units in 2008; 6,700 units in 2009; and 4,500 units in 2010.

(c) Which method would result in the highest net income in 2006? Over the life of the asset?

(d) Which method would result in the highest cash flow in 2006? Over the life of the asset?

(e) What factors should influence management's choice of amortization method?

Account for operating and capital expenditures and asset impairments.
(SO 1, 3) AP

P9–4B Arnison Company had the following selected transactions related to property, plant, and equipment in 2008:

Feb. 2 All of the company's light bulbs were converted to energy-efficient bulbs for $2,000. Arnison expects that this will save money on its utility bills in the future.

Mar. 16 A fee of $4,500 was paid to paint machinery after the company changed its logo.

Apr. 14 A new air-conditioning system in the factory offices was installed for $57,000.

May 7 A total of $4,600 was spent for decorative landscaping (planting flowers and shrubs, etc.).

June 16 Windows broken in a labour dispute (not covered by insurance) were replaced for $5,900.

July 18 Paid $15,000 to convert the company's trucks from gasoline to propane. Arnison expects this will substantially reduce the trucks' future operating costs.

Aug. 8 Hired a consultant to train several employees on handling hazardous waste materials and emergency procedures for $5,500.

Sept. 20 A machine was completely overhauled for $20,000. Arnison expects this will increase the useful life of the machine by four years.

Oct. 26 The transmission in a delivery vehicle was repaired for $1,600.

Dec. 31 After recording annual amortization, Arnison reviewed its property, plant, and equipment for possible impairment. Arnison determined the following:
   1. Land that originally cost $200,000 had previously been written down to $75,000 as a result of a permanent decline in value. But because of an unexpected change in circumstances, the current market value of the land is $195,000.
   2. Equipment that originally cost $300,000 and has accumulated amortization of $125,000 has a current market value of $135,000. The decline in value is considered permanent and the net book value is not recoverable.

Instructions

Prepare journal entries to record the above transactions. All transactions are paid in cash.

P9–5B   At the beginning of 2004, Bérubé Company acquired equipment costing $600,000. It was estimated at that time that this equipment would have a useful life of 10 years and a residual value of $50,000. Bérubé uses the straight-line method of amortization and has a December 31 year end.

> Record impairment and calculate revised amortization.
> (SO 3) AP

On December 31, 2007, after recording the annual amortization expense, Bérubé determined that the market value of the equipment had permanently declined to $200,000 and that the asset's net book value is not recoverable. In 2008, Bérubé also determined that the equipment's useful life would be six years in total, instead of the previously estimated 10. The residual value is still expected to be $50,000 at the end of the equipment's useful life.

Instructions

(a) Calculate the amortization expense for the years 2004 to 2007 and accumulated amortization at December 31, 2007.
(b) Record the impairment loss on December 31, 2007.
(c) Calculate amortization expense for the years 2008 and 2009.
(d) What should accumulated amortization and the net book value of the equipment be at the end of its useful life?

P9–6B   Koberstein Company owned processing equipment that had a cost of $125,000 on June 30, 2003. It had an estimated useful life of five years and an estimated residual value of $10,000. Koberstein records straight-line amortization annually on December 31.

> Record operating and capital expenditures and calculate revised amortization.
> (SO 1, 3) AP

In 2008, the following cash expenditures were made on this equipment:

Jan. 7 Completed an overhaul of the equipment at a cost of $15,000. The work included the installation of new computer controls to replace the original controls, which were technologically obsolete. As a result of this work, the estimated useful life of the equipment was changed to seven years and the estimated residual value was changed to $12,000.
July 27 Lubricated and adjusted the equipment to maintain optimum performance, $1,000.
Sept. 19 Replaced several belts, hoses, and other parts which were showing signs of wear, $2,500.

Instructions

(a) Calculate amortization expense for the years 2003 to 2007 and accumulated amortization at December 31, 2007.
(b) Record each of the above transactions.
(c) Calculate the amortization expense for 2008 and the remaining years of the equipment's estimated useful life.
(d) What will accumulated amortization be at the end of the asset's estimated useful life?

P9–7B   Forristal Farmers purchased a piece of equipment on December 28, 2005, for $61,000. The equipment had an estimated useful life of four years and a residual value of $5,000. Management is considering the merits of using the double declining-balance method of amortization instead of the straight-line method of amortization. The president feels that the straight-line method will have a more favourable impact on the income statement.

> Calculate and compare amortization and gain or loss on disposal under straight-line and declining-balance methods.
> (SO 2, 4) AP

Instructions

(a) Prepare an amortization schedule for the life of the equipment under (1) the straight-line method, and (2) the declining-balance method, using double the straight-line rate.
(b) Assume that the equipment is sold on January 3, 2009, for $10,000.
  1. Calculate the gain or loss on the sale of the equipment, under (a) the straight-line method, and (b) the declining-balance method.
  2. Prepare a schedule to show the overall impact of the total amortization expense combined with the gain or loss on sale over the life of the asset under each method of amortization (consider the total effect on net income over the asset's life). Comment on your results.

Record acquisition, amortization, and disposal of equipment.
(SO 2, 4) AP

P9–8B Express Co. purchased delivery equipment on February 4, 2006, for $65,000 on account. The equipment had an estimated useful life of five years, with a residual value of $5,000. The equipment is disposed of on October 25, 2008. Express Co. uses the straight-line method of amortization and calculates amortization for partial periods to the nearest month. The company has a December 31 year end.

Instructions

(a) Record the acquisition of the delivery equipment on February 4, 2006.
(b) Record amortization for each of 2006, 2007, and 2008.
(c) Record the disposal on October 25, 2008, under the following assumptions:
    1. It was scrapped as having no value.
    2. It was sold for $30,000.
    3. It was sold for $40,000.
    4. It was traded for new delivery equipment with a list price of $87,000. Express was given a trade-in allowance of $32,000 on the old delivery equipment and paid the balance in cash. Express determined the fair market value of the old equipment to be $28,000 at the date of the exchange.

Record property, plant, and equipment transactions; prepare partial financial statements.
(SO 2, 3, 4, 7) AP

P9–9B Ledesma Investments has a June 30 fiscal year end. It uses straight-line amortization and has a policy of recording amortization for partial periods to the nearest month. The following transactions involved property, plant, and equipment:

July 3, 2004 Purchased assets from a recently bankrupt business for $750,000. Paid $100,000 of the purchase price in cash and issued a mortgage payable for the balance. The purchase included land for $410,000; a building for $300,000; and machinery for $40,000.

June 30, 2005 Recorded amortization on the amortizable assets. The building has an estimated useful life of 40 years and no residual value. The machinery has an estimated useful life of eight years and no residual value.

June 30, 2006 Recorded amortization on the amortizable assets.

June 30, 2007 Reviewed the estimated useful lives and residual values before making the year-end adjusting entries for amortization. As a result of the high usage of the machinery, it was decided that the total estimated useful life should be reduced to five years from the original eight years. There were no changes in estimates for the building. The annual amortization was then recorded.

Dec. 28, 2007 Purchased new machinery with a list price of $65,000. To make the purchase, the machinery purchased in 2004 was traded in for a $25,000 trade-in allowance and the balance was paid in cash. An independent appraisal stated that the fair market value of the old machinery was $22,000. The new machinery has a useful life of five years and no residual value.

June 30, 2008 Recorded amortization on the amortizable assets.

Instructions

(a) Record the above transactions.
(b) Show how property, plant, and equipment would appear on the June 30, 2008, balance sheet.
(c) What accounts and amounts for property, plant, and equipment will be included on the income statement for the year ended June 30, 2008?

Correct errors in recording intangible asset transactions.
(SO 6) AP

P9–10B Due to rapid turnover in the accounting department, several transactions involving intangible assets were improperly recorded by Riley Co. in the year ended December 31, 2008:

1. Riley developed a new patented manufacturing process early in the year, incurring research and development costs of $120,000. Of this amount, 45% was considered to be development costs that could be capitalized. Riley recorded the entire $120,000 in the Patents account and amortized it using a 15-year estimated useful life.

2. The company purchased a trademark, which was expected to have an indefinite life, for $125,000. At the end of the year, Riley recorded an impairment loss of $25,000 because it believed the trademark was only worth $100,000 since another company had infringed on it. Riley is currently

involved in a legal case to defend its right to use the trademark and the lawyers expect Riley to win the case. If Riley wins, the value of the trademark is expected to recover.

3. On July 1, 2008, Riley purchased a small company and as a result of the purchase recorded goodwill of $250,000. Riley recorded a half-year's amortization on the goodwill in 2008 based on a 40-year useful life. At December 31, 2006, Riley determined that the market value of the goodwill was still $250,000.

4. The company made a $6,000 charitable donation on December 31, 2008, which it debited to goodwill.

5. Several years ago, Riley paid $70,000 for a licence to be the exclusive Canadian distributor of a Danish beer. In 2005, Riley determined there was a permanent impairment of $30,000 in the value of the licence and recorded the loss. In 2008, because of a change in consumer tastes, the value of the licence increased to $80,000. Riley recorded a $30,000 increase in the licence's value by crediting Gain on Licence Market Value and debiting the licence account. Management felt it was better to be conservative and not write up the value higher than the original cost.

Instructions

Prepare the journal entries that are needed to correct the errors made during 2008.

P9–11B The intangible assets reported by Ip Company at December 31, 2007, follow:

Record intangible asset transactions; prepare partial balance sheet.
(SO 6, 7) AP

Patent #1	$70,000	
Less: Accumulated amortization	14,000	$ 56,000
Copyright #1	48,000	
Less: Accumulated amortization	28,800	19,200
Goodwill		210,000
Total		$285,200

Patent #1 was acquired in January 2006 and has an estimated useful life of 10 years. Copyright #1 was acquired in January 2002 and also has an estimated useful life of 10 years. The following cash transactions may have affected intangible assets during the year 2008:

Jan. 2 Paid $22,400 of legal costs to successfully defend Patent #1 against infringement by another company.

June 30 Developed a new product, incurring $220,000 in research costs and $60,000 in development costs, which were paid in cash. Patent # 2 was granted for the product on July 1. Its estimated useful life is equal to its legal life.

Sept. 1 Paid $35,000 to an Olympic athlete to appear in commercials advertising the company's products. The commercials will air in September and October.

Oct. 1 Acquired a second copyright for $80,500 cash. Copyright #2 has an estimated useful life of seven years.

Dec. 31 Determined the fair market value of the goodwill to be $150,000. Ip Company believes that this drop in value is a permanent impairment.

Instructions

(a) Record the above transactions for 2008.
(b) Record the 2008 amortization expense for intangible assets.
(c) Prepare the intangible assets section of the balance sheet at December 31, 2008.

P9–12B Yount Mining Company has a December 31 fiscal year end. The following information related to its Gough Alexander mine is available:

Record equipment and natural resource transactions; prepare partial financial statements.
(SO 2, 5, 7) AP

1. Yount purchased the Gough Alexander mine on March 31, 2007, for $2.6 million cash. On the same day, modernization of the mine was completed at a cash cost of $260,000. It is estimated that this mine will yield 560,000 tonnes of ore. The estimated residual value of the mine is $200,000. Yount expects it will extract all the ore, and then close and sell the mine site in four years.

2. On April 6, 2007, Yount moved equipment to the Gough Alexander mine from another mine site. The equipment was originally purchased on September 29, 2002, at a cost of $500,000.

The equipment was being amortized on a straight-line basis over an estimated useful life of eight years with a residual value of $20,000. Yount has a policy of recording amortization for partial periods to the nearest month. The estimated useful life and residual value of the equipment did not change after the relocation. The equipment will be moved to a new site when the Gough Alexander mine is closed.

3. During 2007, Yount extracted 120,000 tonnes of ore from the mine. It sold 100,000 tonnes.
4. During 2008, Yount extracted and sold 110,000 tonnes of ore from the mine.

Instructions

(a) Prepare the 2007 and 2008 journal entries for the above, including year-end adjustments.
(b) Show how the Gough Alexander mine and related accounts will be reported on Yount's December 31, 2008, income statement and balance sheet.

Calculate ratios and comment.
(SO 7) AN

P9–13B Andruski Company and Brar Company, two companies of roughly the same size, both manufacture in-line skates. An examination of their financial statements reveals the following:

	Andruski Company	Brar Company
Net sales	$1,950,000	$2,300,000
Net income	295,000	310,000
Total assets, start of year	2,250,000	2,465,000
Total assets, end of year	2,800,000	3,295,000

Instructions

(a) For each company, calculate the asset turnover and return on assets ratios.
(b) Based on your results in part (a), compare the two companies by commenting on how effective they are at using their assets to generate sales and produce net income.

Continuing Cookie Chronicle

(*Note:* This is a continuation of the Cookie Chronicle from Chapters 1 through 8.)

Natalie is thinking of buying a van that will only be used for business. The cost of the van is estimated at $34,500. Natalie would spend an additional $2,500 to have the van painted. In addition, she wants the back seat of the van removed so that she will have lots of room to transport her mixer inventory and baking supplies. The cost of taking out the back seat and installing shelving units is estimated at $1,500. She expects the van to last about five years and to drive it for 200,000 kilometres. The annual cost of vehicle insurance will be $2,400. Natalie estimates that at the end of the five-year useful life the van will sell for $6,500. Assume that she will buy the van on August 15, 2008, and it will be ready for use on September 1, 2008.

Natalie is concerned about the impact of the van's cost on her income statement and balance sheet. She has come to you for advice on calculating the van's amortization.

Instructions

(a) Determine the cost of the van.
(b) Prepare an amortization table for 2008, 2009, and 2010 under each of the following amortization methods: (1) straight-line amortization, (2) single declining-balance, and (3) units-of-activity. For units-of-activity, Natalie estimates she will drive the van as follows: 15,000 kilometres in 2008; 45,000 kilometres in 2009; and 50,000 kilometres in 2010. Recall that Cookie Creations has a December 31 year end.
(c) What impact will the three methods of amortization have on Natalie's balance sheet at December 31, 2008? What impact will the three methods have on Natalie's income statement in 2008?
(d) What impact will the three methods of amortization have on Natalie's income statement over the van's total five-year useful life?
(e) Which method of amortization would you recommend Natalie use?

Financial Reporting and Analysis

Financial Reporting Problem

BYP9–1 Refer to the financial statements and the Notes to Consolidated Statements for **The Forzani Group Ltd.**, which are reproduced in Appendix A.

Instructions

(a) Identify the following amounts for the company's capital assets at January 29, 2006: (1) cost, (2) accumulated amortization, and (3) net book value.

(b) What was the amount of net additions of capital assets during the 2006 fiscal year? (*Hint:* Look at the statement of cash flows to determine this amount.)

(c) What amortization methods are used by Forzani for financial reporting purposes? What was the amount of amortization expense reported in the statement of operations for fiscal 2006?

(d) What expected useful life was used for calculating the amortization on the "furniture, fixtures, equipment, and automotive" grouping of capital assets?

(e) What types of intangible assets does Forzani have? Did the company report any impairment losses in 2006?

Interpreting Financial Statements

BYP9–2 **Maple Leaf Foods** is Canada's largest food processor, serving customers across North America and internationally. In 2005, the company announced that it was going to invest $110 million to construct a new pork processing plant in Saskatoon that will replace a 65-year-old plant. The new plant will increase production capacity from the current 17,500 to 20,000 hogs per week on a single shift, with the capacity to process up to 40,000 on a double shift.

Instructions

(a) How should Maple Leaf account for the $110 million spent to replace the older plant in Saskatoon?

(b) Identify and discuss the advantages and disadvantages of each amortization method for Maple Leaf Foods' pork facilities. Which method would you recommend that Maple Leaf use to amortize the Saskatoon plant and equipment? Explain your reason for choosing this method.

(c) Would you still choose the same amortization method in (b) if the plant moves to a double-shift operation? If you do choose the same amortization method, how will amortization expense be affected by the double shift?

Critical Thinking

Collaborative Learning Activity

Note to instructors: Additional instructions and material for this group activity can be found on the Instructor Resource Site.

BYP9–3 In this group activity, you will review the following three amortization methods:

1. Straight-Line
2. Double Declining -Balance
3. Units-of-Activity.

Study Aids:
Working in Groups

Instructions

(a) Your instructor will divide the class into "home" group. Each member of your group will choose one of the above methods and then move to the "expert" group for that method.

(b) In the "expert" group, you will be given a handout explaining your method of amortization. As a group, discuss the handout and ensure that each group member thoroughly understands that method.

(c) Return to your "home" group and explain your method to the other students in the group.

(d) You may be asked by your instructor to write a short quiz on this topic

Communication Activity

**Study Aids:
Writing Handbook**

BYP9–4 Long Trucking Corporation is a medium-sized family-owned trucking company with trucks that are driven across North America. The company owns large garages and equipment to repair and maintain the trucks. Ken Bond, the controller, knows that long-lived assets are reviewed annually for impairment. Ken records an impairment loss of $100,000 and the loss appears on the income statement for the current fiscal year. Jason Long, the owner, reviews the financial statements and wants more information from Ken about the impairment loss.

Instructions

Write a memo to Jason Long that explains (1) why a company may have an impairment loss, (2) the journal entry required for the impairment loss, and (3) how this write-down will affect Long Trucking's balance sheet and income statement in future years.

Ethics Case

**Study Aids:
Ethics in Accounting**

BYP9–5 Finney Container Company has been seeing sales go down for its main product, non-biodegradable plastic cartons. The president, Philip Shapiro, instructs his controller to lengthen the estimated asset lives in order to reduce the amortization expense and increase net income.

A processing line of automated plastic extruding equipment that was purchased for $3 million in January 2006 was originally estimated to have a useful life of five years and a residual value of $200,000. Amortization has been recorded for two years on that basis. The president now wants the equipment's estimated useful life to be changed to nine years (total), and for the company to continue using the straight-line method. The controller is hesitant to make the change, believing it is unethical to increase net income in this way. The president says, "Hey, the useful life is only an estimate. Besides, I've heard that our competition uses a nine-year estimated life on its production equipment."

Instructions

(a) Who are the stakeholders in this situation?

(b) Is the suggested change in asset life unethical, or simply a shrewd business practice by a sharp president?

(c) What would be the impact of the president's proposed change on net income in the year of the change?

ANSWERS TO CHAPTER QUESTIONS

Answers to Accounting in Action Insight Questions

Ethics Insight, p. 457

Q: Why is it wrong to treat expenses as capital expenditures?

A: When expenses are recorded as capital expenditures, this increases net income, owner's equity, and total assets. This makes the company look like it is performing better than it really is and gives investors and creditors false information about its financial health.

Business Insight, p. 467

Q: Is the units-of-activity method the best amortization method for Morris Formal Wear to use for its tuxedos or would you recommend another method?

A: Since Morris Formal Wear wants to track wear and tear on each of its tuxedos, the units-of-activity amortization method is the best choice. Rental tuxedos are the type of long-lived asset that will physically wear out with use much faster than they would become obsolete due to changing tuxedo styles. By keeping track of how many times each tuxedo has been used, instead of just how old they are, the company can make better decisions about when to replace the tuxedos.

Across the Organization Insight, p. 485

Q: Who is responsible for developing a company's brand value? How is it reported on the financial statements?

A: A company's marketing department would be responsible for developing and implementing a brand strategy. Some people argue, however, that if a company wants to be very effective in developing its brand, then the most senior person in the company, usually the chief executive officer (CEO), should be actively involved. The value of a company's brand is usually not reported on the financial statements, because the costs that are incurred to create brand value cannot be separately identified.

Answer to Forzani Review It Question 5, p. 459

Forzani reports (in thousands) land, $3,173; buildings, $20,007; building on leased land, $4,564; furniture, fixtures, equipment, and automotive, $176,670; leasehold improvements, $205,519; and construction in progress, $37.

Answers to Self-Study Questions

1. b   2. b   3. c   4. b   5. b   6. a   7. b   8. c   9. c   10. d

Remember to go back to the Navigator Box at the beginning of the chapter to check off your completed work.

chapter 10

concepts for review >>

Before studying this chapter, you should understand or, if necessary, review:

a. How to make adjusting entries for unearned revenue (Ch. 3, pp. 113–114) and accrued expenses. (Ch. 3, pp. 117–119)

b. The importance of liquidity in evaluating the financial position of a company. (Ch. 4, pp. 182–183)

c. How to account for sales discounts. (Ch. 5, p. 234)

d. Accounting for notes receivable. (Ch. 8, pp. 423–426)

Does Size Matter?

EDMONTON, Alta.—Sometimes the word "big" just isn't enough. Consider the West Edmonton Mall, listed in the Guinness Book of World Records as the world's largest shopping centre at 5.3 million square feet. Located in the west end of the City of Edmonton, it also boasts six other records, including the world's largest parking lot (more than 20,000 cars) and the world's largest indoor theme park (with its triple-loop "Mindbender" roller coaster).

In addition to the theme park, an indoor lake, a five-acre water park, the Fantasyland Hotel, and an NHL-sized arena (second home of the Edmonton Oilers), the mall has more than 800 stores and services. Each of these businesses is a tenant renting space from West Edmonton Mall Property Inc., a privately held and family-owned company.

Needless to say, for a place of this size, the bills are also, well, big. Paul Balchen, West Edmonton Mall controller, estimates that current liabilities usually total between $14 million and $16 million.

Still, it's "much like any other business," Mr. Balchen says, glancing at the mall's balance sheet for July 31, 2005. "We have accounts payable of at least $4 million, and sales taxes—GST only, of course, since this is Alberta—of about $600,000." The next line, accrued liabilities, is another $4 million. That includes a "million-dollar plus power bill," explains Mr. Balchen, "which would be accrued for July but not due until August." Clearly, a mall that covers 48 city blocks uses a lot of electricity!

Then, of course, there is the accrued interest on the long-term obligation for the property itself, which amounts to more than $1 million a month. There's also more than $1 million in property and corporate income taxes.

West Edmonton Mall: www.westedmontonmall.com

The final line on this section of the balance sheet, says Mr. Balchen, is unearned revenue. "That's another million dollars or so," he explains. "Mostly payments from the tenant businesses for the following month or things like advance payments from hockey leagues for use of the ice rink."

"Even though some of the figures appear large, we have the same accounts on our balance sheet as a very small business," Mr. Balchen explains. Large or small, every business needs to keep careful track of its liabilities, pay them in a timely fashion, and plan for the future.

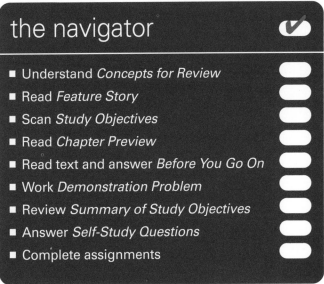

the navigator ✔

- Understand *Concepts for Review*
- Read *Feature Story*
- Scan *Study Objectives*
- Read *Chapter Preview*
- Read text and answer *Before You Go On*
- Work *Demonstration Problem*
- Review *Summary of Study Objectives*
- Answer *Self-Study Questions*
- Complete assignments

chapter | 10

chapter 10
Current Liabilities

study objectives >>

✔ the navigator

After studying this chapter, you should be able to:

1. Account for definitely determinable liabilities.
2. Account for estimated liabilities.
3. Account for contingencies.
4. Prepare the current liabilities section of the balance sheet.
5. Calculate the payroll for a pay period (Appendix 10A).

Whether it is a huge company such as the West Edmonton Mall, or a small company such as your local convenience store, every company has current liabilities. As explained in Chapter 4, a current liability is a debt with two key features: (1) It is likely to be paid within one year. (2) It will be paid from existing current assets (e.g., cash) or by creating other current liabilities. Most companies pay current liabilities out of current assets (e.g., cash), rather than by creating other liabilities (e.g., paying an account payable by issuing a note payable). Debts that do not meet both criteria are classified as long-term liabilities. We will explain current liabilities in this chapter. We will explain long-term liabilities in Chapter 15.

This chapter is organized as follows:

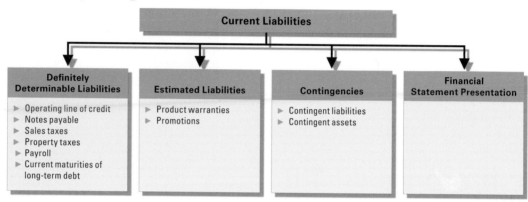

Definitely Determinable Liabilities

study objective 1

Account for definitely determinable liabilities.

Liabilities may be described as definitely determinable, estimated, or contingent. We will discuss definitely determinable liabilities in this section, and the other types of current liabilities in the following sections.

For most liabilities, we know who we owe, when we owe, and how much we owe. We call this type of liability definitely determinable because there is no uncertainty about its existence, amount, or timing. In other words, a **definitely determinable liability** has a known amount, payee, and due date.

Examples of definitely determinable current liabilities include bank indebtedness from operating lines of credit, and notes payable, accounts payable, sales taxes payable, unearned revenue, and current maturities of long-term debt. This category also includes accrued liabilities such as property taxes, payroll, and interest. In our feature story, the West Edmonton Mall reported $4 million of accrued liabilities, including the July power bill and interest owed.

The entries for many of these liabilities have been explained in previous chapters, including the entries for accounts payable and unearned revenues. We will discuss the accounting for other types of current liabilities in this section, including bank indebtedness from an operating line of credit, notes payable, sales taxes payable, property taxes payable, payroll and employee benefits payable, and current maturities of long-term debt.

Operating Line of Credit

Current assets (such as accounts receivable) do not always turn into cash at the exact time that current liabilities (such as accounts payable) must be paid. Consequently, most companies have an **operating line of credit** at their bank to help them manage temporary cash shortfalls. This means that the company has been pre-authorized by the bank to borrow money when it is needed, up to a pre-set limit.

Security, called **collateral**, is usually required by the bank as protection in case the company is unable to repay the loan. Collateral normally includes some, or all, of the company's current assets (e.g., accounts receivable or inventories), investments, or property, plant, and equipment. Forzani has a $175-million operating line of credit that is "collateralized by general security agreements against all existing and future acquired assets of the Company."

Money borrowed through a line of credit is normally borrowed on a short-term basis, and is repayable immediately upon request—that is, on demand—by the bank. In reality, repayment is rarely demanded without notice. A line of credit makes it very easy for a company to borrow money. It does not have to make a call or visit its bank to actually arrange the transaction. The bank simply covers any cheques written in excess of the bank account balance, up to the approved credit limit.

Some companies show a negative, or overdrawn, cash balance at year end as a result of using their line of credit. This amount is usually called bank indebtedness, bank overdraft, or bank advances. No special entry is required to record the overdrawn amount. The normal credits to cash will simply accumulate and be reported as a current liability with an appropriate note disclosure. Interest is usually charged on the overdrawn amount at a floating rate, such as prime plus a specified percentage. The prime rate is the interest rate that banks charge their best customers. This rate is usually increased by a specified percentage according to the risk profile of the company.

Notes Payable

The line of credit described above is similar to a **note payable**. Notes payable are obligations in the form of written promissory notes. Notes payable are often used instead of accounts payable. This gives the lender proof of the obligation in case legal action is needed to collect the debt. Accounts and notes payable that result from purchase transactions (i.e., amounts owed to suppliers) are often called **trade payables**. Notes payable are also frequently issued to meet short-term financing needs.

Helpful hint Notes payable are the opposite of notes receivable, and the accounting is similar.

Notes are issued for varying periods. If they are due for payment within one year of the balance sheet date, they are classified as current liabilities. Most notes are interest-bearing, with interest due monthly or at maturity.

To illustrate the accounting for notes payable, assume that Kok Co. borrows $100,000 from the Caisse Populaire on March 1 for four months, at an interest rate of 6 percent. The note matures on July 1 and interest, along with the principal amount of the note, is payable at maturity.

Kok makes the following journal entry when it signs the note and receives the $100,000:

Mar. 1	Cash	100,000	
	Note Payable		100,000
	To record issue of 4-month, 6% note to Caisse Populaire.		

A	=	L	+	OE
+100,000		+100,000		

↑ Cash flows: +100,000

Interest accrues over the life of the note and, to follow the matching principle, the interest must be recorded in the period when the borrowed money is used. If Kok Co. has a March 31 year end, an adjusting entry is made to recognize interest expense and interest payable of $500 ($100,000 × 6% × $\frac{1}{12}$) at March 31. Recall from Chapter 3 that interest is calculated by multiplying the principal amount by the annual interest rate by the fraction of the year in the accrual.

The adjusting entry is:

A	=	L	+	OE
		+500		−500

Cash flows: no effect

Mar. 31	Interest Expense	500	
	Interest Payable		500
	To accrue interest for March.		

In the March 31 financial statements, the current liabilities section of the balance sheet will show notes payable of $100,000 and interest payable of $500. In addition, interest expense of $500 will be reported as other expenses in the income statement.

At maturity (July 1), Kok Co. must pay the face value of the note ($100,000) plus $2,000 interest ($100,000 × 6% × $\frac{4}{12}$). One month ($500) of this interest has already been accrued. Interest must also be updated for $1,500 ($100,000 × 6% × $\frac{3}{12}$) for the three additional months—April through June—since interest was last recorded. This can be done in a separate journal entry as follows, or in one compound entry:

A	=	L	+	OE
		+1,500		−1,500

Cash flows: no effect

A	=	L	+	OE
−102,000		−100,000		
		−2,000		

⬇ Cash flows: −102,000

July 1	Interest Expense	1,500	
	Interest Payable		1,500
	To accrue interest for April, May, and June.		
1	Note Payable	100,000	
	Interest Payable ($500 + $1,500)	2,000	
	Cash ($100,000 + $2,000)		102,000
	To record payment of Caisse Populaire note and accrued interest.		

Sales Taxes

As a consumer, you are well aware that you pay sales taxes on many of the products you buy at retail stores. The taxes are expressed as a percentage of the sales price. As discussed in earlier chapters and in Appendix B, sales taxes usually take the form of the Goods and Services Tax (GST) and Provincial Sales Tax (PST). Federal GST is assessed at 6 percent across Canada at the time of writing this textbook but the current government has promised to cut the GST by another percentage point within the next five years. Provincial sales tax rates vary from 0 percent to 10 percent across Canada.

In Newfoundland and Labrador, Nova Scotia, and New Brunswick, the PST and GST have been combined into one 14-percent Harmonized Sales Tax (HST). Whether GST, PST, or HST, the retailer collects the tax from the customer when the sale occurs. The retailer then pays (remits) the sales taxes collected to the designated federal and provincial collecting authorities. In the case of GST (or HST), collections may be offset against payments. In such cases, only the net amount owing or recoverable must be paid or refunded.

Depending on the size of the retailer, the sale taxes must be sent to the government monthly, quarterly or, for very small companies, annually. As Paul Balchen notes in our feature story about the West Edmonton Mall, the mall owes no provincial sales tax (Alberta has a 0-percent provincial sales tax rate) but does owe about $600,000 of GST. The mall is large enough to be required to make monthly payments.

The amount of the sale and the amount of the sales tax collected are usually rung up separately on the cash register. The cash register readings are then used to credit sales or services and the correct sales taxes payable accounts. For example, if the March 25 cash register reading for Comeau Company shows sales of $10,000, goods and services tax of $600 ($10,000 × 6% GST rate), and provincial sales tax of $800 ($10,000 × 8% PST rate), the entry is as follows:

Mar. 25	Cash	11,400	
	Sales		10,000
	GST Payable		600
	PST Payable		800
	To record sales and sales taxes.		

A	=	L	+	OE
+11,400		+600		+10,000
		+800		

↑ Cash flows: +11,400

When the sales taxes are remitted, the accounts GST Payable and PST Payable (or HST Payable) are debited and Cash is credited. The company does not report sales taxes as an expense. Sales taxes collected from customers are a liability because the company must forward the amount collected to the federal and provincial collecting authorities. Comeau Company serves only as a collection agent for each of the governments.

Some businesses include sales taxes in the selling price. They do not separate sales taxes from the price of the goods sold. In these businesses, however, sales taxes must still be recorded separately from sales revenues. To find the sales amount, the total receipts are divided by 100 percent plus the sales tax percentage.

To illustrate, assume that Comeau Company's total receipts of $11,400 include GST and PST. The total receipts from the sale are equal to 100 percent of the sales amount plus 14 percent (6% + 8%) of sales, or 1.14 times the sales amount, which gives $11,400. We can use algebra to calculate the sales amount as follows: $11,400 ÷ 1.14 = $10,000. The GST and PST of $600 and $800 can be found by multiplying the sales amount by each of the sales tax rates ($10,000 × 6% = $600, and $10,000 × 8% = $800).

In two provinces, PST is charged on the total selling price plus GST. For example, in Quebec a $100 sale is subject to $6 GST ($100 × 6%) and $7.95 QST [($100 + $6) × 7.5%]. The escalated sales tax rate is 13.95 percent [($6 + $7.95) ÷ $100] rather than 13.5 percent (6% GST + 7.5% QST). Prince Edward Island also charges 10-percent PST on the selling price plus GST. It is important to be careful when getting sales tax amounts from total receipts because of the different rate combinations across Canada.

Helpful hint In Quebec the PST is called QST.

Property Taxes

Businesses that own property pay property taxes. These taxes are charged by the municipal and provincial governments, and are calculated at a specified rate for every $100 of assessed value of property (i.e., land and building). Property taxes generally cover a full calendar year, although bills are not issued until the spring of each year.

To illustrate, assume that Tantramar Management owns land and a building in the city of Regina. Tantramar's year end is December 31 and it makes adjusting entries annually. It receives its property tax bill for $6,000 on March 1, which is due to be paid on May 31.

In March, when Tantramar receives the property tax bill for the calendar year, two months have passed. The company records the property tax expense for the months of January and February and the liability owed at that point as follows:

Mar. 1	Property Tax Expense ($6,000 × 2/12)	1,000	
	Property Tax Payable		1,000
	To record property tax expense for January and February and		
	amount owing.		

A	=	L	+	OE
		+1,000		−1,000

Cash flows: no effect

In May, when Tantramar pays the property tax bill, the company records the payment of the liability recorded on March 1. It also records the expense incurred to date for the months of March, April, and May. As at May 31, five months have passed and should be recorded as property tax expense. The remaining seven months of the year are recorded as a prepayment as shown in the following entry:

A	=	L	+	OE
+3,500		−1,000		−1,500
−6,000				

↓ Cash flows: −6,000

May 31	Property Tax Payable	1,000	
	Property Tax Expense ($6,000 × ³⁄₁₂)	1,500	
	Prepaid Property Tax ($6,000 × ⁷⁄₁₂)	3,500	
	Cash		6,000
	To record payment of property tax, expense for March through May, and amount prepaid for June through December.		

After the payment of the property tax, Tantramar has a zero balance in its liability account but still has a prepayment. Since Tantramar only makes adjusting entries annually, it would not adjust the prepaid property tax account until year end, December 31. At that time, it would make the following entry:

A	=	L	+	OE
−3,500				−3,500

Cash flows: no effect

Dec. 31	Property Tax Expense	3,500	
	Prepaid Property Tax		3,500
	To record property tax expense for June through December.		

There are other acceptable ways to record and adjust property taxes. Some companies would debit Property Tax Expense when the bill is recorded on March 1 and avoid a later adjusting entry. In addition, companies may prepare monthly or quarterly adjusting entries. Whatever way is used, at year end the companies would have the same ending balances. In this case, the accounts Prepaid Property Tax and Property Tax Payable should each have a zero balance and Property Tax Expense should have a balance of $6,000.

Payroll

Every employer has three types of payroll liabilities related to employees' salaries or wages: (1) the net pay owed to employees, (2) employee payroll deductions, and (3) employer payroll deductions.

The first type of liability is the amount of salary or wages owed to employees. Managerial, administrative, and sales personnel are generally paid salaries. Salaries are often expressed as a specific amount per week, per month, or per year. Part-time employees, store clerks, factory employees, and manual labourers are normally paid wages. Wages are based on a rate per hour or on piecework (an amount per unit of product). The terms *salaries* and *wages* are often used interchangeably and the total amount of salaries or wages earned by the employee is called **gross pay**, or gross earnings.

Note that salaries and wages do not include payments made for the services of professionals outside the company such as accountants, lawyers, and architects. Such professionals are independent contractors rather than salaried employees. Payments to them are called fees, rather than salaries or wages. This distinction is important, because government regulations for the payment and reporting of payroll apply only to employees.

The second type of liability is the amount of **payroll deductions** required by law to be withheld from employees' gross pay. Assume that Linfang Wang works 40 hours this week for Pepitone Company, earning $10 per hour. Will Linfang receive a $400 cheque at the end of the week? No, she won't. The reason: Pepitone is required to withhold amounts from Linfang's wages to pay various other parties. Mandatory payroll deductions include amounts withheld for federal and provincial income taxes, Canada Pension Plan (CPP) contributions, and employment insurance (EI) premiums. Companies might also withhold voluntary deductions for health insurance, pensions, union dues, charitable donations, and other purposes.

The difference between an employee's gross pay, or total earnings, less any employee payroll deductions withheld from the earnings is known as **net pay**. This is the amount that the company (the employer) must pay to the employee. Illustration 10-1 on the following page summarizes the types of payroll deductions that most companies usually make and that are the reason for the difference between gross and net pay.

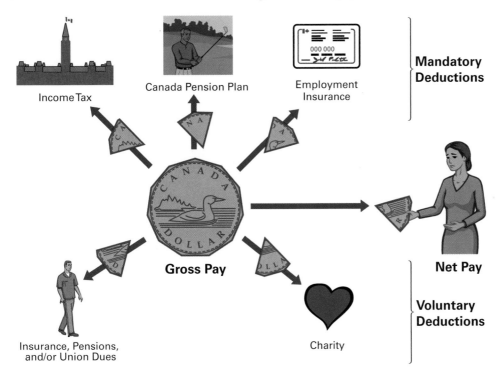

Illustration 10-1 ◀

Employee payroll deductions

In addition to the liabilities from employee payroll deductions, employers also have another type of liability related to payroll deductions. With every payroll, the employer is expected to pay various payroll costs that are charged on certain payroll deductions, such as CPP and EI. For example, employers have to pay the same amount as each employee's CPP contribution and 1.4 times each employee's EI contribution. In addition, the provincial governments require employers to fund a Workplace Health, Safety, and Compensation Plan. These contributions, plus items such as paid vacations and employer-sponsored pensions, are referred to together as **employee benefits**.

In summary, companies like Pepitone must collect payroll deductions from their employees and themselves on behalf of the governments and other third parties. Until these payroll deductions are remitted to the third parties that they are collected for, they are reported as a current liability in the balance sheet.

To illustrate the recording of a weekly payroll, we will assume the information shown in the following journal entry for Pepitone:

Mar. 7	Salaries and Wages Expense	100,000	
	Income Tax Payable		20,427
	CPP Payable		4,950
	EI Payable		1,870
	United Way Payable		2,445
	Union Dues Payable		667
	Salaries and Wages Payable		69,641
	To record payroll and employee deductions for the week ending March 7.		

A	=	L	+	OE
		+20,427		−100,000
		+4,950		
		+1,870		
		+2,445		
		+667		
		+69,641		

Cash flows: no effect

The above journal entry records the gross pay of $100,000 in Pepitone's Salaries and Wages Expense account. The net pay of $69,641 that is owed to employees is recorded in the Salaries and Wages Payable account. In addition, Pepitone records as separate liabilities amounts that it owes for its employee payroll deductions to the governments for income tax, CPP, and EI, and amounts owed to third parties like United Way and for union dues.

Note that while the employee payroll deductions are part of Salaries and Wages Expense, employer payroll contributions are not. Employer payroll contributions are debited instead to a separate expense account, normally called Employee Benefits Expense.

Based on the $100,000 payroll in our Pepitone example, the following entry would be made to record the employer's expense and liability for these employee benefits:

A = L + OE
      +4,950   −8,143
      +2,618
      +575

Cash flows: no effect

Mar. 7	Employee Benefits Expense	8,143	
	CPP Payable		4,950
	EI Payable		2,618
	Workers' Compensation Payable		575
	To record employer's payroll costs on March 7 payroll.		

For now, do not worry about how these amounts were calculated as they are just examples. The detailed calculation of salaries and wages and payroll deductions will be discussed in Appendix 10A to this chapter.

On the same day, or on a later day, Pepitone must also pay its employees. The following entry records the payment of the weekly payroll:

A = L + OE
−69,641 −69,641

⬇ Cash flows: −69,641

Mar. 7	Salaries and Wages Payable	69,641	
	Cash		69,641
	To record payment of March 7 payroll.		

Note that Pepitone is only paying its employees in this entry and not its payroll deductions. Employee and employer deductions will be remitted to government authorities or other third parties when they are due later in the month.

ACCOUNTING IN ACTION ▶ Across the Organization Insight

The battle over employee benefits has grown as benefits have increased faster than wages and salaries. Benefit costs now add up to between 7 and 8 percent of payroll and are increasing by an average of 8 to 12 percent per year. In a recent survey of nearly 1,400 Canadian human resource professionals, limiting benefit costs was cited as their top priority. Many companies have started to look at the impact of sharing benefit costs with employees, but they are moving slowly in order to carefully measure how this affects employee relations.

Source: David Brown, "Employers Approach Benefits Cost Containment with Caution," *Canadian HR Reporter*, January 31, 2005, p. 2.

? Why is it important for a company to offer its employees a meaningful benefit plan? What can a company do to avoid paying unreasonable costs?

Current Maturities of Long-Term Debt

Companies often have a portion of long-term debt that will be due in the current year. That amount is considered a current liability. Assume that on January 1, 2008, Cudini Construction issues a $25,000, 5-year note payable. Each January 1, starting January 1, 2009, $5,000 of the note will be repaid. When financial statements are prepared on December 31, 2008, $5,000 should be reported on the balance sheet as a current liability and the remaining $20,000 of the note should be reported as a long-term liability.

It is not necessary to prepare an adjusting entry to recognize the current maturity of long-term debt. The proper statement classification of each liability account is recognized when the balance sheet is prepared. Forzani reports $5,135 thousand as the "current portion of long-term debt" in the current liabilities section of its balance sheet.

BEFORE YOU GO ON . . .

▶Review It

1. What are the two criteria for classifying a debt as a current liability?
2. What are some examples of current liabilities?
3. Why is sales tax not recorded as revenue to the company that collects it?
4. What is the difference between (1) gross pay and net pay and (2) employee payroll deductions and employer payroll costs?

▶Do It

Prepare the journal entries to record the following transactions. Round any calculations to the nearest dollar.

1. Accrue interest on January 31 (the company's year end) for a $10,000, 3-month, 8% note payable issued on December 1. Interest is payable the first of each month, beginning January 1.
2. The cash register total for sales on April 2 is $256,000. This total includes sales taxes. The GST tax rate is 6% and the PST is 7%. Assume PST is not charged on the GST. Record the sales and sales taxes.
3. A property tax bill of $12,000 for the calendar year is received on May 1 and is due on June 21. Record the entry on May 1, assuming the company has a January 31 year end.
4. A company's gross wages amount to $10,000 per week. The following amounts are deducted from the employees' wages: income tax of $3,965; CPP of $495; EI of $187; and health insurance of $950. The employer's portion of CPP is $495 and of EI, $262. Record the weekly payroll and employee benefits on July 11, assuming cash is paid to the employees but the amounts withheld are still due.

Action Plan

- The formula for interest is as follows: principal (face) value × annual interest rate × time.
- Record sales separately from sales taxes. Divide the total proceeds by 100 percent plus the sales tax rates.
- Record the property tax expense and the property tax payable for amounts incurred (owed) to date.
- Record both the employees' portion of the payroll and the benefits owed by the employer. Employee deductions are not an expense to the employer.

Solution

Date	Account	Debit	Credit
Jan. 31	Interest Expense ($10,000 × 8% × $\frac{1}{12}$)	67	
	Interest Payable		67
	To accrue interest on note payable.		
Apr. 2	Cash	256,000	
	Sales ($256,000 ÷ 113%)		226,549
	GST Payable ($226,549 × 6%)		13,593
	PST Payable ($226,549 × 7%)		15,858
	To record sales and sales taxes.		
May 1	Property Tax Expense ($12,000 × $\frac{3}{12}$)	3,000	
	Property Tax Payable		3,000
	To record property tax for February, March, and April.		

July 11	Wages Expense	10,000	
	Income Tax Payable		3,965
	CPP Payable		495
	EI Payable		187
	Health Insurance Payable		950
	Cash		4,403
	To record payment of wages for week ending July 11.		
July 11	Employee Benefits Expense	757	
	CPP Payable		495
	EI Payable		262
	To record employer's payroll costs on July 11 payroll.		

Related exercise material: BE10–1, BE10–2, BE10–3, BE10–4, BE10–5, E10–1, E10–2, E10–3, and E10–5.

Estimated Liabilities

We learned about definitely determinable liabilities in the last section. With this type of liability, we know who we owe, when we owe, and how much we owe. There is no uncertainty about the liability's existence, amount, or timing.

An **estimated liability** is an obligation that exists but whose amount and timing are uncertain. We know we owe someone, but are not necessarily sure how much and when. We may not even know who we owe. Nonetheless, with this type of liability, the uncertainty is not so great that the company cannot reasonably estimate the liability and match expenses with associated revenues in the correct period. Commonly estimated liabilities include product warranties and promotions. We discuss these two examples in the following sections.

Product Warranties

Product warranties are promises made by the seller to a buyer to repair or replace the product if it is defective or does not perform as intended. Warranties (also known as guarantees) are usually used by manufacturers. For a specified period of time after the date of sale of the item, a manufacturer may promise to repair the item, replace it, or refund the buyer's money under certain conditions.

For example, Apple Computer, Inc. offers a one-year warranty against "defects in materials and workmanship" on the sale of its iPod and iSight products. The company goes on to state that "If a defect arises and a valid claim is received by Apple within the warranty period, at its option, Apple will (1) repair the product at no charge, using new or refurbished replacement parts, (2) exchange the product with a product that is new or which has been manufactured from new or serviceable used parts and is at least functionally equivalent to the original product, or (3) refund the purchase price of the product." As a buyer, it is important to read all warranty contracts carefully because the promises they make can be quite different.

Warranties will lead to future costs for the repair or replacement of defective units. Although the amount and the timing of the future warranty cost are not known, the cost can be reasonably estimated. Based on their previous experience with a particular product, it is usually not that hard for companies such as Apple to estimate the future cost of servicing (honouring) the product's warranty. In addition, recording the estimated cost of product warranties as an expense and a liability in the period where the sale occurs respects the matching principle.

To illustrate the accounting for warranties, assume that Hermann Company sells 10,000 washers and dryers at an average price of $600 in the year ended December 31, 2008. The selling price includes a one-year warranty on parts. Based on past experience, it is expected that 500 units (5 percent) will be defective, and that warranty repair costs will average $100 per unit.

At December 31, it is necessary to accrue the estimated warranty costs for the 2008 sales. The calculation is as follows:

Number of units sold	10,000
Estimated rate of defective units	× 5%
Total estimated defective units	500
Average warranty repair cost	× $100
Estimated product warranty liability	$50,000

The adjusting entry is:

Dec. 31	Warranty Expense	50,000	
	Warranty Liability		50,000
	To accrue estimated warranty costs.		

A	=	L	+	OE
		+50,000		−50,000

Cash flows: no effect

In 2008, warranty contracts were honoured on 300 units at a total cost of $30,000. These costs are likely recorded when they are incurred, but for our illustration they are being recorded in one summary journal entry:

Dec. 31	Warranty Liability	30,000	
	Repair Parts Inventory (and/or Wages Payable)		30,000
	To record honouring of 300 warranty contracts on 2008 sales.		

A	=	L	+	OE
−30,000		−30,000		

Cash flows: no effect

At year end, a warranty expense of $50,000 is reported as an operating expense in the income statement. The estimated warranty liability of $20,000 ($50,000 – $30,000) is classified as a current liability on the balance sheet.

In the following year, all costs incurred to honour warranty contracts on 2008 sales should be debited to the Warranty Liability account, like what was shown above for the 2008 sales. The Warranty Liability account will be carried forward from year to year, increased by the current year's estimated expense and decreased by the actual warranty costs incurred. It is quite likely that the actual expenses will not exactly equal the estimated liability amount. Every year, as is done with accounts receivable and the allowance for doubtful accounts, the warranty liability should be reviewed and adjusted if necessary.

Promotions

To attract or keep customers, many companies offer promotions or savings on the merchandise they sell. These **promotions** take varying forms, including cash rebates for returning a receipt, rebate coupon, or bar code, or coupons which can be redeemed for a cash discount at the time of purchase.

Promotions such as these are designed to increase sales and are important for many businesses. For example, the Coupon Industry Association of Canada reported that 3.5 billion coupons were distributed in 2005. Of these, 100 million coupons were redeemed and resulted in consumer savings of $129 million.

In recent years, there has been a lot of debate about whether the cost of such promotions should be recorded as an expense or as a decrease in revenue. For example, assume that a company sells software for $200, and gives a $25 rebate coupon that allows the customer to send in a proof of purchase and get $25 back. Should the company record sales revenue of $200 and promotions expense of $25, or should the company record net sales revenue of $175 and no expense? Both methods increase net income by $175, but the classification is different.

While there are a few exceptions, accountants have decided that when a promotional item results in a reduced selling price, it should be accounted for as a decrease in revenue and not as an expense. From the company's perspective, it is certainly true that selling an item with a coupon, which reduces the price to the buyer, is no different than if the company had lowered the sales price of the item. Both cases result in less revenue for the company.

Promotions, similar to product warranties, result in an estimated liability because at the time of the sale it is not known how many customers will redeem the promotional offer and when they will do this. In fact, promotions are sometimes redeemed over a very long period of time. For example, the Coupon Industry Association of Canada notes that the average period for coupons is 183 days, which can easily affect two fiscal years for a company. However, because some redemption is likely and can be reasonably estimated based on past experience, the decrease in revenue and related liability should be recorded in the period of sale to follow the revenue recognition principle.

To illustrate, assume that on January 10 Crunchy Cookies (the manufacturer) issues 60,000 store discount coupons which save customers $0.50 when they buy Crunchy Cookie Dough. The coupons expire on March 31 and the company has a January 31 year end. Based on past experience, Crunchy Cookies estimates that 10 percent of the coupons will be redeemed. The entry to record the initial liability when the promotion begins is as follows:

A	=	L	+	OE
		+3,000		−3,000

Cash flows: no effect

Jan. 10	Sales Discount for Coupon Redemptions (60,000 × 10% × $0.50)	3,000	
	Coupon Liability		3,000
	To accrue estimated coupon liability.		

The account Sales Discount for Coupon Redemptions is a contra sales account, and is deducted from sales to give net sales in the same way that sales returns and allowances are deducted from sales as we learned in Chapter 5. The coupon liability is reported as a current liability on the balance sheet.

The actual process of redeeming the coupon begins at the grocery store when the customer buys the dough and presents the coupon. The grocery store then subtracts the cash amount of the coupon ($0.50) from the customer's bill, records a receivable from Crunchy Cookies, and sends this and other coupons to Crunchy Cookies so the grocery store can be repaid for the amounts it has paid to customers. When Crunchy Cookies receives the coupons, it pays the grocery store cash for the value of the coupons redeemed.

By the end of the month, if 5,000 coupons have been redeemed, Crunchy Cookies makes the following entry to record the redemption of these coupons:

A	=	L	+	OE
−2,500		−2,500		

 Cash flows: −2,500

Jan. 31	Coupon Liability (5,000 × $0.50)	2,500	
	Cash		2,500
	To record paying grocery stores for coupons redeemed.		

Crunchy Cookies could also choose to make this entry more often, depending on when it pays the grocery stores for the coupons they submit for redemption.

The liability account should be reviewed periodically and adjusted for expired coupons. In addition, if Crunchy Cookies' original estimate of the liability is different from actual redemptions, the difference is adjusted in the period when it becomes known.

Accounting for promotional items has many additional complexities which we have not seen here. Further detail on this topic will be left to an intermediate accounting course.

ACCOUNTING IN ACTION ▶ Business Insight

Canadian Tire "Money" (CTM), first introduced in 1958, is the most successful loyalty program in Canadian retail history. The "money" resembles real currency (although the bills are considerably smaller than Bank of Canada notes), and is issued in denominations of 5 cents, 10 cents, 25 cents, 50 cents, one dollar, and two dollars with no expiry date. CTM is given out by the cashiers for purchases paid for by cash, debit card, or Canadian Tire Options MasterCard credit card. Customers can use CTM to buy anything at a Canadian Tire store. In fact, some privately owned businesses in Canada also accept CTM as payment since the owners of many of these businesses shop at Canadian Tire.

? How should Canadian Tire account for issuing and redeeming its Canadian Tire money at the point of sale?

BEFORE YOU GO ON . . .

▶Review It

1. Explain the difference between definitely determinable liabilities and estimated liabilities.
2. How does estimating a warranty liability respect the matching principle?
3. Why is the estimated cost of promotions debited to a contra revenue account rather than an expense account?

▶Do It

Hockey Gear Company sells hockey skates with a two-year warranty against defects. The company expects that 5 percent of the units sold will be returned in the first year after they are sold and 2 percent in the second year. The average cost to repair or replace a defective unit under warranty is $50. The company reported the following sales and warranty cost information:

	Units Sold	Actual Warranty Costs Incurred
2007	10,000	$20,000
2008	15,000	45,000

Calculate the balance in the Warranty Expense and Warranty Liability accounts at the end of 2008.

Action Plan

- Calculate the warranty expense by multiplying the number of units sold by the percentage that is expected to be returned and by the average warranty cost.
- Record warranty expenses in the period of the sale.
- The warranty liability is increased by the expense in each period and decreased by the actual costs of repairs and replacements.

Solution

2007: Total defective units = 5% + 2% = 7%
  10,000 × 7% = 700 × $50 = $35,000

Warranty Expense		Warranty Liability			
35,000		Actual	20,000	Estimate	35,000
				Bal. Dec. 31, 2007	15,000

2008: 15,000 × 7% = 1,050 × $50 = $52,500

Warranty Expense		Warranty Liability			
52,500		Actual	20,000	Estimate	35,000
				Bal. Dec. 31, 2007	15,000
		Actual	45,000	Estimate	52,500
				Bal. Dec. 31, 2008	22,500

Related exercise material: BE10–6, BE10–7, BE10–8, E10–6, E10–7, and E10–8.

the navigator

Contingencies

The current liabilities discussed earlier in this chapter were either **definitely determinable** or **estimable**. In both cases, there is no uncertainty about their existence. We knew when they were due and how much was owed, or we were able to reasonably estimate this. With contingencies, however, we are uncertain about everything—their existence, amount, and timing.

A **contingency** is defined as an existing condition or situation that is uncertain and it cannot be known if a gain (and a related contingent asset) or loss (and a related contingent liability) will result from the situation until one or more future events happen or do not happen. Although contingent assets exist, contingent liabilities are far more common. *Financial Reporting in Canada* reports that 82 percent of the 200 public companies that it surveyed disclosed contingent liabilities in a recent year. Less than 6 percent reported contingent assets.

Although the topic of this chapter is liabilities, we will discuss both contingent liabilities and contingent assets together since the requirements for accounting and disclosure are similar.

Contingent Liabilities

Suppose your company is involved in a dispute with the Canada Revenue Agency over the amount of the company's sales tax liability. Should you report the disputed amount as a liability on the balance sheet? Or suppose your company is involved in a lawsuit, which, if you lose, might result in bankruptcy. Liabilities such as these depend on the occurrence or non-occurrence of a future event. This event will confirm the existence of the liability, the amount payable, the payee, and/or the date payable. These types of liabilities are called **contingent liabilities**.

Recording contingent liabilities is difficult because these losses and liabilities are dependent—in other words, contingent—on some future event. The characteristic of conservatism requires that these contingencies be recorded by a debit to an expense (loss) account and a credit to a liability account if both of the following conditions are met:

1. The contingency is likely (the chance of occurrence is high).
2. The amount of the contingency can be reasonably estimated.

If you find it difficult to see the difference between a contingent liability and an estimated liability, remember that estimated liabilities are known to exist; it is only their amount or timing that is unknown. For example, a product warranty liability depends on the future failure of a product and that will definitely happen for some of the products sold. Estimates are not as uncertain as contingencies. Contingent liabilities are for unusual situations. They are not for ongoing and recurring activities such as product warranties.

When a contingent liability is likely but cannot be reasonably estimated, or if it is not determinable—neither likely nor unlikely—it is only necessary to disclose the contingency in the notes to the financial statements. Examples of contingencies that may require disclosure are pending or threatened lawsuits and threats of expropriation of property.

If a contingency is unlikely—the chance of occurrence is small—it should still be disclosed if the event could have a substantial negative effect on the company's financial position. Otherwise, it does not need to be disclosed. A loan guarantee is an example of a contingency that should be disclosed even if the chance of having to pay the loan is small. General risk contingencies that can affect anyone who is operating a business, such as the possibility of a war, strike, or recession, are not reported in the notes to the financial statements.

Forzani discloses both guarantees and lawsuits in the notes to its financial statements. Here are two selected extracts from this note:

Illustration 10-2 ◀

Disclosure of contingent
liabilities

THE FORZANI GROUP LTD.
Notes to the Consolidated Financial Statements
January 29, 2006

12. Contingencies and Guarantees

The Company has provided the following guarantees to third parties:

(a) The Company has provided guarantees to certain franchisees' banks pursuant to which it has agreed to buy back inventory from the franchisee in the event that the bank realizes on the related security ... Historically, the Company has not had to repurchase significant inventory from franchisees pursuant to these guarantees. The Company has not recognized the guarantee in its financial statements.

(d) Claims and suits have been brought against the Company in the ordinary course of business. In the opinion of management, all such claims and suits are adequately covered by insurance, or if not so covered, the results are not expected to materially affect the Company's financial policies.

Contingent Assets

Like contingent liabilities, **contingent assets** involve uncertainty that will only be resolved when a future event occurs or does not occur. This event will confirm the existence of a future cash inflow or other economic benefits that will result in an asset. Examples of contingent assets include insurance claims or potential legal actions that could favour the company.

Contingent assets, or gains, are treated even more conservatively than contingent liabilities, or losses. They are never recorded or accrued in the financial statements. They are disclosed in the notes only if it is likely that a gain will be realized.

Accounting offers many examples of losses being recognized and gains not being recognized. The rationale behind this inconsistency is **conservatism**, where the goal is to be sure that any negative effect on investors and creditors is fully disclosed. Critics of this inconsistent approach denounce the lack of symmetry in the treatment of gains and losses. Illustration 10-3 summarizes the treatment of contingent liabilities and assets:

Illustration 10-3 ◀

Accounting treatment of
contingencies

Conditions	Contingent Liability (Loss)		Contingent Asset (Gain)	
	Accrue	Disclose	Accrue	Disclose
Likely and reasonably estimable	X			X
Likely but not estimable		X		X
Neither likely nor unlikely (not determinable)		X		
Unlikely (but negative effect possible)		X		

ACCOUNTING IN ACTION ▶ Business Insight

There are many contingencies in the real world. Lawsuits are the most common type of contingency, followed by environmental contingencies. Environmental contingencies generally relate to liabilities that could be incurred in order to clean up environmental problems.

The Canadian National Railway Company discloses the following information in the notes to its financial statements: "A risk of environmental liability is inherent in railroad and related transportation operations..." The Company goes on to say, "The magnitude of such... liabilities and the costs of complying with environmental laws and containing or remediating contamination cannot be reasonably estimated... There can thus be no assurance that material liabilities or costs related to environmental matters will not be incurred in the future, or will not have a material adverse effect on the Company's financial position or results of operations in a particular quarter or fiscal year, or that the Company's liquidity will not be adversely impacted by such environmental liabilities or costs."

? Environmental contingencies are generally considered to be harder to estimate than contingencies from lawsuits. What might be the reason for this difference?

BEFORE YOU GO ON . . .

▶Review It

1. What are the accounting guidelines for contingent liabilities?
2. What is the difference between estimated liabilities and contingent liabilities?
3. When should a contingent liability be recorded? Disclosed?
4. Why are contingent assets treated differently than contingent liabilities?

▶Do It

A list of possible contingencies follows. Identify whether each of the following should be accrued, disclosed, or not reported:

1. A company risks being damaged by floods. The company is located on a flood plain but has never experienced any damage from flooding in the past.
2. The government may expropriate a company's assets so that a new highway can be built. So far, there have been no discussions about how much the government might pay the company.
3. A company is being sued for $1 million for unlawful termination of an employee.
4. A company has guaranteed other companies' loans but the guarantees are unlikely to result in any payments.
5. A reassessment of a company's income tax will likely result in a refund.

Action Plan

• Remember that contingent liabilities are accrued when they are likely and estimable. Otherwise, they are only disclosed. They are not disclosed if they are unlikely.
• Remember that contingent assets are never recorded. They are only disclosed if they are likely.

Solution

1. No disclosure required
2. Disclosure required
3. Accrual required if likely; otherwise just disclose
4. Disclosure required
5. Disclosure required

the navigator

Related exercise material: BE10–9, BE10–10, E10–9, and E10–10.

Financial Statement Presentation

study objective 4

Prepare the current liabilities section of the balance sheet.

As indicated in Chapter 4, current liabilities are the first category reported in the liabilities section of the balance sheet. Each of the main types of current liabilities is listed separately. In addition, the terms of operating lines of credit and notes payable and other information about the individual items are disclosed in the notes to the financial statements.

Current liabilities are usually listed in order of liquidity, by maturity date. Sometimes it is difficult to determine which specific obligations should be listed in which order. A more common method of presenting current liabilities is to list them by order of size, with the largest ones first. Many companies show bank loans, notes payable, and accounts payable first, regardless of the amounts.

The following is an excerpt from Tim Hortons' balance sheet:

Illustration 10-4 ◀

Presentation of current liabilities

TIM HORTONS INC. Balance Sheet (partial) April 2, 2006 (in thousands)	*Tim Hortons*	
Current assets		$1,153,671
Current liabilities		
Accounts payable	$ 82,274	
Accrued expenses	92,914	
Advertising fund restricted liabilities	34,321	
Amounts payable to Wendy's	14,851	
Notes payable to Wendy's	622,077	
Current portion of long-term obligations	208,069	
Total current liabilities		$1,054,506

Tim Hortons also discloses information about contingencies in the notes to its financial statements, as follows:

Illustration 10-5 ◀

Disclosure of contingent liabilities

TIM HORTONS INC. Notes to Consolidated Financial Statements (partial) April 2, 2006	*Tim Hortons*

Note 11 Commitments and Contingencies

The Company has guaranteed certain lease and debt payments primarily for franchisees, amounting to $0.9 million. In the event of default by a franchise owner, the Company generally retains the right to acquire possession of the related restaurants. The Company is also the guarantor on $5.0 million in letters of credit with various parties; however, management does not expect any material loss to result from these instruments because it does not believe performance will be required. The length of the lease, loan and other arrangements guaranteed by the Company or for which the Company is contingently liable varies, but generally does not exceed nine years.

In addition to the above guarantees, the Company is party to many agreements executed in the ordinary course of business that provide for indemnification of third parties, under specified circumstances, such as lessors of real property leased by the Company, distributors, service providers for various types of services (including commercial banking, investment banking, tax, actuarial and other services), software licensors, marketing and advertising firms, securities underwriters and others. Generally, these agreements obligate the Company to indemnify the third parties only if certain events occur or claims are made, as these contingent events or claims are defined in each of these agreements. The Company believes that the resolution of any claims that might arise in the future, either individually or in the aggregate, would not materially affect the earnings or financial condition of the Company. The liability recorded related to the above indemnity agreements is not material.

Companies must carefully monitor the relationship of current liabilities to current assets. This relationship is critical in evaluating a company's short-term ability to pay debt. There is usually concern when a company has more current liabilities than current assets, because it may not be able to make its payments when they become due.

In Tim Hortons' case, it has a positive current ratio. You will recall from Chapter 4 that the current ratio is calculated by dividing current assets by current liabilities. Tim Hortons' current ratio is 1.1:1 ($1,153,671 ÷ $1,054,506). It is not a high current ratio, but does indicate that Tim Hortons has enough current assets to cover its current liabilities. In addition, Tim Hortons discloses in the notes to its financial statements that it has overdraft protection of $15 million and a $300-million operating line of credit that it can draw on for additional liquidity requirements.

Recall also that the current ratio should never be interpreted without also looking at the receivables and inventory turnover ratios to ensure that all of the current assets are indeed liquid. We cannot do this for Tim Hortons as the example does not give us enough information.

BEFORE YOU GO ON . . .

▶Review It

1. Describe the reporting and disclosure requirements for current liabilities.
2. What current liabilities does The Forzani Group report and in what order? The answer to this question is at the end of the chapter.

Related exercise material: BE10–11, BE10–12, E10–4, E10–11, and E10–12.

APPENDIX 10A ▶ PAYROLL ACCOUNTING

study objective 5

Calculate the payroll for a pay period.

Payroll accounting involves more than just paying employee salaries and wages. In addition to paying salaries and wages, companies are required by law to have payroll records for each employee, to report and remit payroll deductions, and to respect provincial and federal laws on employee compensation.

As we learned in the chapter, there are two types of payroll costs—employee costs and employer costs. The first type, employee costs, involves amounts paid to employees (net pay) and amounts paid by employees (payroll deductions). The second type, employer costs, involves amounts paid by the employer on behalf of the employee (employee benefits). We will explore employee and employer payroll costs in the following sections.

Employee Payroll Costs

Determining the payroll costs for employees involves calculating (1) gross pay, (2) payroll deductions, and (3) net pay.

Gross Pay

Gross pay, or earnings, is the total compensation earned by an employee. It consists of wages or salaries, plus any bonuses and commissions.

Total wages for an employee are determined by multiplying the hours worked by the hourly rate of pay. In addition to the hourly pay rate, most companies are required by law to pay hourly workers for overtime work at the rate of at least one and one-half times the minimum hourly wage. The number of hours that need to be worked before overtime becomes payable is based on a standard work week. A 44-hour standard work week is fairly common but this will vary by industry and occupation.

Assume that Mark Jordan works for Academy Company as a shipping clerk. His authorized pay rate is $10 per hour. The calculation of Mark's gross pay (total wages) for the 48 hours shown on his time card for the weekly pay period ending June 17, 2006, is as follows:

Type of Pay	Hours	×	Rate	=	Gross Pay
Regular	44	×	$10	=	$440
Overtime	4	×	15	=	60
Total wages					$500

This calculation assumes that Jordan receives one and one-half times his regular hourly rate ($10 × 1.5) for any hours worked in excess of 44 hours per week (overtime). Overtime rates can be as much as twice the regular rates.

The salary for an employee is generally based on a weekly, biweekly, monthly, or yearly rate. If the rate is a yearly one, it is prorated over the number of payroll periods (e.g., 26, 52, etc.) that the company uses. Most executive and administrative positions are salaried and do not earn overtime pay.

Payroll Deductions

As anyone who has received a paycheque knows, gross pay is usually very different from the amount that is actually received. The difference is due to payroll deductions. These deductions do not result in an expense for the employer. The employer is only a collection agent as it later pays the deductions to the government (if they are mandatory deductions such as income tax, CPP, and EI) or to some other agency (if they are voluntary deductions such as for a union, an insurance company, or the United Way). The designated collection agency for the federal government is known as the Receiver General, a division of the Canada Revenue Agency (CRA).

Mandatory Payroll Deductions. Payroll deductions may be mandatory or voluntary. Mandatory deductions are required by law and include income tax, Canada Pension Plan contributions, and employment insurance premiums. We will discuss these in the following sections.

Personal Income Tax. In accordance with the *Income Tax Act*, employers are required to withhold income tax from employees for each pay period. The amount to be withheld is determined by three variables: (1) the employee's gross pay, (2) the number of credits claimed by the employee, and (3) the length of the pay period. To indicate to the Canada Revenue Agency (CRA) which credits he or she wants to claim, the employee must complete a Personal Tax Credits Return (known as a TD1 form). There is no limit on the amount of gross pay that is subject to income tax withholdings. The higher the pay or earnings, the higher the amount of taxes withheld.

The calculation of personal income tax withholdings is complicated and is best done using payroll deduction tables supplied by the CRA. We will discuss these payroll deduction tables in a later section. For now, assume that we been able to determine the total income tax owed for Mark Jordan using these tables. His federal income tax is $45.50 and provincial income tax, $24.50, for a total income tax owed of $70 on his gross pay of $500.

Canada Pension Plan (CPP). All employees between the ages of 18 and 70, except those employed in the province of Quebec, must contribute to the Canada Pension Plan. Quebec has its own similar program, the Quebec Pension Plan (QPP). These plans give extra disability, retirement, and death benefits to qualifying Canadians.

Contribution rates are set by the federal government and are adjusted every January if there are increases in the cost of living. At the time of writing, employee contributions under the *Canada Pension Plan Act* were 4.95 percent of pensionable earnings. Pensionable earnings are gross earnings less a basic yearly exemption (currently $3,500). A maximum ceiling or limit ($42,100 in 2006) is imposed on pensionable earnings. The exemption and ceiling are prorated to the relevant pay period (e.g., weekly, biweekly, semimonthly, or monthly).

For example, Mark Jordan's CPP contribution for the weekly pay period ending June 17 is $21.42, calculated as follows:

> Gross pay: $500
> Basic yearly CPP exemption: $3,500
> Prorated basic exemption per week: $3,500 ÷ 52 = $67.31
> Weekly deduction: $500 − $67.31 = $432.69 × 4.95% = $21.42

In addition to withholding employee deductions for remittance to the Receiver General, companies must also make contributions for their employees. We will discuss the employer's contributions later in this appendix.

Employment Insurance (EI). The Canada Pension Plan is for all employees, whether they are self-employed or employed by others. Employment insurance is paid only by people who are not self-employed. Employment insurance is designed to give income protection for a limited period of time to employees who are temporarily laid off, who are on parental leave, or who lose their jobs.

Under the provisions of the *Employment Insurance Act*, an employee is currently required to pay a premium of 1.87 percent on insurable earnings, to a maximum earnings ceiling of $39,000. In most cases, insured earnings are gross earnings plus any taxable benefits. There is no specified yearly exemption. The employment insurance premium for Mark Jordan for the June 17 payroll is $9.35 ($500 × 1.87%).

Payroll Deductions Tables. As mentioned earlier, payroll deductions tables are a useful way to determine payroll deductions. Payroll deductions tables indicate the amount of income tax that should be withheld from gross wages based on the number of credits claimed. There are separate tables for weekly, biweekly, semimonthly, and monthly pay periods. Income tax deductions vary by province. CPP and EI also vary, but by wage level. The easiest way to determine all of these payroll deductions is to use tables, rather than to try to calculate the deductions. Tables can be requested from any CRA office or downloaded from the CRA's website < http://www.cra-arc.gc.ca/tax/business/tod/ >. Simply download the file "Tables on Diskette." This program, which can also be used directly on the CRA's website, performs the lookup function and accurately calculates payroll information.

Illustration 10A-1 on the following page shows the results of payroll information entered for Mark Jordan. For a weekly wage of $500, with an assumed TD1 claim code of 1, the federal and Ontario income taxes to be withheld total $70. CPP and EI contributions are $21.42 and $9.35, respectively.

These are the same amounts shown earlier. Whether you calculate employee payroll deductions manually or by using the tables, be careful to use the correct table, as rates, exemptions, and other regulations can and do change often.

Voluntary Payroll Deductions. Unlike mandatory payroll deductions, which are required by law, voluntary payroll deductions are chosen by the employee.

Employees may choose to authorize withholdings for charitable, retirement, and other purposes. All voluntary deductions from gross pay should be authorized in writing by the employee. The authorization may be made individually or as part of a group plan. Deductions for charitable organizations such as the United Way, or for financial arrangements such as Canada Savings Bonds and the repayment of loans from company credit unions, are made individually. In contrast, deductions for union dues, extended health insurance, life insurance, and pension plans are often made on a group basis. In the calculation of net pay in the next section, we assume that Mark Jordan has voluntary deductions of $10 for the United Way and $5 for union dues.

Payroll Deductions for Salary			
Employee's name (optional)	Mark Jordan		
Employer's name (optional)	Academy Company		
Pay period ending date (optional)	2006-06-17		
Gross salary (or pension income) for the pay period			500.00
Total EI insurable earnings for the pay period			500.00
Taxable salary or pension income			500.00
Federal tax deductions	45.50		
Provincial or territorial tax deductions	24.50		
Total tax on salary or pension income	70.00	70.00	
Canada Pension Plan (CPP) deductions		21.42	
Employment Insurance (EI) deductions		9.35	
Requested additional tax deduction		0.00	
Total deductions on salary or pension income		100.77	100.77
Net amount			399.23
Total claim amount (from federal TD1)	Claim Code 1 (Minimum—8,639.00)		
Total claim amount (from provincial or territorial TD1)	Claim Code 1 (Minimum—8,377.00)		
Pay period	Weekly (52 pay periods a year)		
Province or territory of employment	Ontario		

Net Pay

Net pay is determined by subtracting payroll deductions from gross pay. For Mark Jordan, net pay for the weekly pay period ending June 17 is $384.23, calculated as follows:

Gross pay		$500.00
Payroll deductions:		
Income tax	$70.00	
CPP	21.42	
EI	9.35	
United Way	10.00	
Union dues	5.00	115.77
Net pay		$384.23

Before we learn how to record employee payroll costs and deductions, we will turn our attention to *employer* payroll costs. After this discussion, we will record the total employee and employer payroll costs for Academy Company, where Mark Jordan works.

Employer Payroll Costs

Employer payroll costs are amounts that the federal and provincial governments require employers to pay. The federal government requires CPP and EI contributions from employers. The provincial governments require employers to fund a Workplace Health, Safety, and Compensation Plan. These contributions, plus such items as paid vacations and pensions, are referred to as employee benefits.

Canada Pension Plan

We have seen that each employee must contribute to the Canada Pension Plan. The employer must also contribute to the CPP, by matching each employee's contribution. This matching contribution is an employee benefits expense for the employer and is charged at the same rate and according to the same maximum earnings that apply to the employee. Note that employer payroll costs are not debited to the Salaries and Wages Expense account, but rather to a separate Employee Benefits Expense account. The account CPP Payable is used for both the employee's and the employer's CPP contributions.

Employment Insurance

Employers are required to contribute 1.4 times an employee's EI deductions in a calendar year. The account Employee Benefits Expense is debited for this contribution and EI Payable is credited to recognize this liability.

Workplace Health, Safety, and Compensation

Helpful hint CPP and EI premiums are paid by both the employer and the employee. Workers' compensation is paid entirely by the employer.

The Workplace Health, Safety, and Compensation Plan gives benefits to workers who are injured or disabled on the job. The cost of this program is paid entirely by the employer; the employee is not required to make contributions to this plan. Employers are assessed a rate—usually between 0.25 percent and 10 percent of their gross payroll—based on the risk of injury to employees and past experience.

Additional Employee Benefits

In addition to the three employer payroll costs described above, employers have other employee benefit costs. Two of the most important are paid absences and post-employment benefits. We will describe these briefly here, but leave further detail to an intermediate accounting course.

Paid Absences. Employees have the right to receive compensation for absences under certain conditions. The compensation may be for paid vacations, sick pay benefits, and paid holidays. A liability should be estimated and accrued for future paid absences. When the amount cannot be estimated, the potential liability should be disclosed. Ordinarily, vacation pay is the only paid absence that is accrued. Other types of paid absences are only disclosed in notes to the statements.

Post-Employment Benefits. Post-employment benefits are payments by employers to retired or terminated employees. These payments are for (1) supplemental health care, dental care, and life insurance, and (2) pensions. Employers must use the accrual basis in accounting for post-employment benefits. It is important to match the cost of these benefits with the periods where the employer benefits from the services of the employee.

Recording the Payroll

Recording the payroll involves maintaining payroll records, recording payroll expenses and liabilities, paying the payroll, and filing and remitting payroll deductions.

Payroll Records

Employers must give each employee a Statement of Remuneration Paid (T4 slip) following the end of each calendar year. The employee then uses it to prepare his or her personal income tax return. This statement shows the employee's employment income and income tax, CPP contributions, and EI premiums deducted for the year, in addition to other voluntary deductions.

The record that gives this information and other essential data is called the employee earnings record. An extract from Mark Jordan's employee earnings record for the month of June is shown in Illustration 10A-2 on the following page. This record includes the pay details calculated in Illustration 10A-1 for the week ending June 17, highlighted in red.

ACADEMY COMPANY
Employee Earnings Record
Year Ended December 31, 2006

	Name	Mark Jordan		Address	162 Bowood Avenue
	Social Insurance Number	113-114-469			Toronto
	Date of Birth	December 24, 1982			Ontario, M4N 1Y6
	Date Employed	September 1, 2004		Telephone	416-486-0669
	Date Employment Ended			E-mail	jordan@sympatico.ca
	Job Title	Shipping Clerk		Claim Code	1

| 2006 Period Ending | Total Hours | Gross Pay | | | | Deductions | | | | | | Payment | |
		Regular	Overtime	Total	Cumulative	Income Tax	CPP	EI	United Way	Union Dues	Total	Net Amount	Cheque #
June 3	46	440.00	30.00	470.00	10,470.00	63.50	19.93	8.79	10.00	5.00	107.22	362.78	974
10	47	440.00	45.00	485.00	10,955.00	66.80	20.68	9.07	10.00	5.00	111.55	373.45	1028
17	48	440.00	60.00	500.00	11,455.00	70.00	21.42	9.35	10.00	5.00	115.77	384.23	1077
24	46	440.00	30.00	470.00	11,925.00	63.50	19.93	8.79	10.00	5.00	107.22	362.78	1133
Total		1,760.00	165.00	1,925.00		263.80	81.96	36.00	40.00	20.00	441.76	1,483.24	

A separate earnings record is kept for each employee and updated after each pay period. The cumulative payroll data on the earnings record are used by the employer to (1) determine when an employee has reached the maximum earnings subject to CPP and EI premiums, (2) file information returns with the CRA (as explained later in this section), and (3) give each employee a statement of gross pay and withholdings for the year.

In addition to employee earnings records, many companies find it useful to prepare a payroll register. This record accumulates the gross pay, deductions, and net pay per employee for each pay period and becomes the documentation for preparing a paycheque for each employee. Academy Company's payroll register is presented in Illustration 10A-3. It shows the data for Mark Jordan in the wages section, highlighted in red. In this example, Academy Company's total weekly payroll is $17,210, as shown in the gross pay column.

Illustration 10A-2 ▲

Employee earnings record

Illustration 10A-3 ▼

Payroll register

ACADEMY COMPANY
Payroll Register
Week Ending June 17, 2006

| Employee | Total Hours | Gross Pay | | | Deductions | | | | | | Payment | |
		Regular	Overtime	Gross	Income Tax	CPP	EI	United Way	Union Dues	Total	Net Pay	Cheque #
Office Salaries												
Aung, Ng	44	638.00		638.00	177.75	28.25	11.93	15.00		232.93	405.07	998
Canton, Mathew	44	649.00		649.00	146.40	28.79	12.14	20.00		207.33	441.67	999
Mueller, William	44	583.00		583.00	107.45	25.53	10.90	11.00		154.88	428.12	1000
Subtotal		5,200.00		5,200.00	1,750.54	226.20	97.24	120.00		2,193.98	3,006.02	
Wages												
Caron, Réjean	44	440.00	30.00	470.00	76.30	19.93	8.79	10.00	5.00	120.02	349.98	1025
Jordan, Mark	48	440.00	60.00	500.00	70.00	21.42	9.35	10.00	5.00	115.77	384.23	1077
Milroy, Lee	47	440.00	45.00	485.00	80.50	20.68	9.07	10.00	5.00	125.25	359.75	1089
Subtotal		11,000.00	1,010.00	12,010.00	3,896.36	522.44	224.59	300.00	215.00	5,158.39	6,851.61	
Total		16,200.00	1,010.00	17,210.00	5,646.90	748.64	321.83	420.00	215.00	7,352.37	9,857.63	

Note that this record is a listing of each employee's payroll data for the pay period. In some companies, the payroll register is a special journal. Postings are made directly to ledger accounts. In other companies, the payroll register is a supplementary record that gives the data for a general journal entry and later posting to the ledger accounts. At Academy Company, the second procedure is used.

In a computerized accounting system, the payroll register is automatically updated from input information on the employees' earnings records. The register also provides the supporting documentation for electronic funds transfers between the company's bank account and those of its employees. Alternatively, the register is used to generate electronically printed payroll cheques. Automatic outputs from a computerized payroll system also include monthly reports for the CRA and annual T4 slips.

Recording Payroll Expenses and Liabilities

Payroll expenses are equal to the employees' gross salaries and wages plus the employer's payroll costs. Employee payroll deductions are not an expense to the company; they are the part of an employee's gross salaries and wages that have not been paid to the employee and must instead be paid to the government or another third party. They remain a current liability to the company until they are remitted.

Employee Payroll Costs. A journal entry is made to record the employee portion of the payroll. For the week ending June 17, the entry for Academy Company, using total amounts from the company's payroll register for the period, as shown in Illustration 10A-3, is as follows:

A	=	L	+	OE
		+5,646.90		−5,200.00
		+748.64		−12,010.00
		+321.83		
		+420.00		
		+215.00		
		+9,857.63		

Cash flows: no effect

June 17	Salaries Expense	5,200.00	
	Wages Expense	12,010.00	
	Income Tax Payable		5,646.90
	CPP Payable		748.64
	EI Payable		321.83
	United Way Payable		420.00
	Union Dues Payable		215.00
	Salaries and Wages Payable		9,857.63
	To record payroll for week ending June 17.		

Specific liability accounts are credited for the required and voluntary deductions made in the pay period, as shown above. Separate expense accounts are used for gross pay because office workers are on salary and other employees are paid an hourly rate. The amount credited to Salaries and Wages Payable is the sum of the individual cheques that the employees will receive when the payroll is paid.

Employer Payroll Costs. Employer payroll costs are usually recorded when the payroll is journalized. The entire amount of gross pay is subject to four of the employer payroll costs mentioned earlier: CPP, EI, Workers' Compensation, and vacation pay. For the June 17 payroll, Academy Company's CPP is $748.64 ($748.64 × 1). Its EI premium is $450.56 ($321.83 × 1.4).

Assume that Academy Company is also assessed for Workers' Compensation at a rate of 1 percent. Its expense for the week would therefore be $172.10 [($5,200 + $12,010) × 1%]. For vacation pay, assume that Academy Company employees accrue vacation days at an average rate of 4 percent of the gross payroll (equivalent to two weeks of vacation). The accrual for vacation benefits in one pay period—one week—is therefore $688.40 [($5,200 + $12,010) × 4%].

Some provinces, including the Province of Ontario, require an additional employer payroll cost—an employer health tax to help fund health care. The maximum health tax in the Province of Ontario is 1.95 percent of payroll, but the tax rate varies by the amount of payroll and the first $400,000 of remuneration is exempt from this tax. Academy's payroll for the year has not yet reached this level so it is exempt from this health tax.

Accordingly, the entry to record the employer payroll costs or employee benefits associated with the June 17 payroll is as follows:

June 17	Employee Benefits Expense	2,059.70	
	CPP Payable		748.64
	EI Payable		450.56
	Workers' Compensation Payable		172.10
	Vacation Pay Payable		688.40
	To record employer payroll costs on June 17 payroll.		

A	=	L	+	OE
		+748.64		−2,059.70
		+450.56		
		+172.10		
		+688.40		

Cash flows: no effect

These liability accounts are classified as current liabilities since they will be paid within the next year. Employee Benefits Expense is often combined with Salaries and Wages Expense on the income statement and classified as an operating expense.

Recording Payment of the Payroll

Payment of the payroll by cheque or electronic funds transfer (EFT) is made from either the employer's regular bank account or a payroll bank account. Each paycheque or EFT is usually accompanied by a statement of earnings document. This shows the employee's gross pay, payroll deductions, and net pay for the period and for the year to date.

After the payroll has been paid, the cheque numbers are entered in the payroll register. The entry to record payment of the payroll for Academy Company follows:

June 17	Salaries and Wages Payable	9,857.63	
	Cash		9,857.63
	To record payment of payroll.		

A	=	L	+	OE
−9,857.63		−9,857.63		

↓ Cash flows: −9,857.63

Many companies use a separate bank account for payroll. Only the total amount of each period's payroll is transferred, or deposited, into that account before it is distributed. This helps the company determine if there are any unclaimed amounts. This is another example of an imprest fund, first introduced with petty cash in Chapter 7.

When they report and remit their payroll deductions, companies combine withholdings of income tax, CPP, and EI. Generally, the withholdings must be reported and remitted monthly on a Statement of Account for Current Source Deductions (PD7A remittance form), and no later than the 15th day of the month following the month's pay period. Depending on the size of the payroll deductions, however, the employer's payment deadline could be different. For example, large employers must remit more often than once a month, and small employers, with perfect payroll deduction remittance records, can remit quarterly. Workplace Health, Safety, and Compensation costs are remitted quarterly to the Workplace Health, Safety, and Compensation Commission. Remittances can be made by mail or through deposits at any Canadian financial institution. When payroll deductions are remitted, payroll liability accounts are debited and Cash is credited.

The entry to record the remittance of payroll deductions by Academy Company in the following month is as follows:

A	=	L	+	OE
−8,723.67		−5,646.90		
		−1,497.28		
		−772.39		
		−420.00		
		−215.00		
		−172.10		

⬇ Cash flows: −8,723.67

July 13	Income Tax Payable	5,646.90	
	CPP Payable ($748.64 + $ 748.64)	1,497.28	
	EI Payable ($321.83 + $450.56)	772.39	
	United Way Payable	420.00	
	Union Dues Payable	215.00	
	Workers' Compensation Payable	172.10	
	Cash		8,723.67
	To record payment of payroll deductions for June 17 payroll.		

Note that the vacation pay liability recorded on June 17 is not debited or "paid" until the employees actually take their vacation.

Other payroll information returns or forms must be filed by the employer with the government by the last day of February each year. In addition, as noted previously, employers must give employees a Statement of Remuneration Paid (T4 slip) by the same date.

Practice Tools:
Demonstration Problems

Demonstration Problem

Benoit Company has the following selected transactions:

Feb. 1 Signed a $50,000, 6-month, 9% note payable to the CIBC, receiving $50,000 in cash. Interest is payable at maturity.

   10 Cash register receipts totalled $37,565, plus 6% GST and 8% PST.

   28 The payroll for the month is salaries of $50,000. A total of $15,000 in income taxes is withheld. CPP and EI contributions are $2,475 and $935, respectively. The salaries are paid on March 1.

The following adjustment data are noted at the end of the month:

1. Interest expense should be accrued on the note.
2. Employer payroll costs include CPP of $2,475 and EI of $1,309. The company also pays a monthly cost of $500 for a dental plan for its employees.
3. Some sales were made under warranty. Of the units sold under warranty this month, 350 are expected to become defective. Repair costs are estimated to be $40 per defective unit.

Instructions

(a) Record the February transactions. Round your calculations to the nearest dollar.
(b) Record the adjusting entries at February 28.

Solution to Demonstration Problem

Action Plan
- Remember that interest rates are annual rates and must be adjusted for periods of time less than one year.
- Remember that sales taxes collected must be sent to the government and are not part of sales revenue.
- Remember that employee deductions for income tax, CPP, and EI reduce the salaries payable.
- Employer contributions to CPP, EI, and the dental plan create an additional expense.
- Warranty costs are expensed in the period when the sales occur.

(a)

Feb. 1	Cash	50,000	
	Notes Payable		50,000
	Issued 6-month, 9% note to CIBC.		
10	Cash	42,824	
	Sales		37,565
	GST Payable ($37,565 × 6%)		2,254
	PST Payable ($37,565 × 8%)		3,005
	To record sales and sales taxes payable.		
28	Salaries Expense	50,000	
	Income Taxes Payable		15,000
	CPP Payable		2,475
	EI Payable		935
	Salaries Payable		31,590
	To record February salaries.		

(b)

Feb. 28	Interest Expense ($50,000 × 9% × $\frac{1}{12}$)	375	
	Interest Payable		375
	To record accrued interest for February.		
28	Employee Benefits Expense	4,284	
	CPP Payable		2,475
	EI Payable		1,309
	Dental Plan Payable		500
	To record employee benefit costs for February.		
28	Warranty Expense (350 × $40)	14,000	
	Warranty Liability		14,000
	To record estimated product warranty liability.		

Summary of Study Objectives

1. **Account for definitely determinable liabilities.** Definitely determinable liabilities have certainty about their existence, amount, and timing—in other words, they have a known amount, payee, and due date. Examples of definitely determinable current liabilities include operating lines of credit, notes payable, accounts payable, sales taxes, unearned revenue, current maturities of long-term debt, and accrued liabilities such as property taxes, payroll, and interest.

2. **Account for estimated liabilities.** Estimated liabilities exist, but their amount or timing is uncertain. Product warranties and promotional costs are estimated and recorded either as an expense (for warranties) or as a decrease of revenue (for promotional costs) and a liability in the period where the sales occur. These liabilities are reduced when repairs under warranty or redemptions occur.

3. **Account for contingencies.** A contingency depends on a future event to confirm its existence (and possibly the amount and timing). Contingent liabilities should be recorded if it is likely that the contingency will occur and the amount is reasonably estimable. If the contingency is probable but the amount is not estimable, or if the likelihood is not determinable, then the contingency should be disclosed in the notes to the statements. Contingent assets are never recorded and are disclosed only if they are likely.

4. **Prepare the current liabilities section of the balance sheet.** The nature and amount of each current liability and contingency should be reported in the balance sheet or in the notes accompanying the financial statements.

5. **Calculate the payroll for a pay period (Appendix 10A).** In recording employee payroll costs, Salaries and Wages Expense is debited for the gross pay, individual liability accounts are credited for payroll deductions, and Salaries and Wages Payable is credited for net pay. In recording employer payroll costs, Employee Benefits Expense is debited for the employer's share of CPP, EI, Workers' Compensation, vacation pay, and any other benefits provided. Each benefit is credited to its specific current liability account.

Glossary

Study Aids: Glossary
Practice Tools: Key Term Matching Activity

Collateral Property pledged as security for a loan. (p. 519)

Contingency An existing condition or situation that is uncertain and could lead to a loss (and a related contingent liability) or gain (and a related contingent asset) and the result will only be known when one or more future events happen or do not happen. (p. 530)

Contingent asset A potential asset that may become an actual asset in the future. (p. 531)

Contingent liability A potential liability that may become an actual liability in the future. (p. 530)

Definitely determinable liability A liability whose existence, amount, and timing are known with certainty. (p. 518)

Employee benefits Payments made by an employer, in addition to wages and salaries, to give pension, insurance, medical, or other benefits to its employees. (p. 523)

Estimated liability An existing liability whose amount or timing is uncertain and must be estimated. (p. 526)

Gross pay Total compensation earned by an employee. Also known as gross earnings. (p. 522)

Net pay Gross pay less payroll deductions. (p. 522)

Notes payable Obligations in the form of written promissory notes. (p. 519)

Operating line of credit Pre-authorized approval to borrow money at a bank when it is needed, up to a pre-set limit. (p. 518)

Payroll deductions Deductions from gross pay to determine the amount of a paycheque. (p. 522)

Product warranties Promises made by the seller to a buyer to repair or replace a product if it is defective or does not perform as intended. (p. 526)

Promotions Cash rebates, coupons, or other items offered as a decrease in sales price to encourage sales. (p. 527)

Trade payables Accounts and notes payable that result from purchase transactions with suppliers. (p. 519)

Note: All questions, exercises, and problems below with an asterisk (*) relate to material in Appendix 10A.

Self-Study Questions

Practice Tools: Self-Assessment Quizzes

Answers are at the end of the chapter.

(SO 1) AP 1. Gilbert Company borrows $88,500 on September 1, 2008, from the Bank of Nova Scotia by signing an 8-month, 6% note. Interest is payable at maturity. What is the accrued interest at December 31, 2008?
(a) $1,328   (c) $1,770
(b) $3,540   (d) $5,310

(SO 1) AP 2. Rioux Company, located in Quebec, has $4,515 of sales on which it charged 6% GST and 7.5% QST. If QST is charged on the selling price plus GST, what is the amount (rounded to the nearest dollar) that should be credited to QST Payable?
(a) $271   (c) $359
(b) $339   (d) $610

(SO 1) AP 3. On March 1, Swift Current Company receives its property tax assessment of $13,200 for the 2008 calendar year. The property tax bill is due May 1. If Swift Current prepares quarterly financial statements, how much property tax expense should the company report for the quarter ended March 31, 2008?
(a) $3,300   (c) $9,900
(b) $4,400   (d) $13,200

4. Rebecca works for The Blue Company at a salary of (SO 1) $550 per week. Canada Pension Plan contributions are $23.89 for the employee and the same for the employer. Income taxes are $87.80. Employment insurance premiums are $10.29 for the employee and $14.41 for the employer. How much is Rebecca's weekly net pay (i.e., her take-home pay)?
(a) $389.72   (c) $413.61
(b) $428.02   (d) $423.90

5. Recording estimated warranty expense in the year of the (SO 2) sale best follows which accounting principle?
(a) Cost   (c) Matching
(b) Full disclosure   (d) Revenue recognition

6. Frost Cereal Company started a sales promotion at the (SO 2) beginning of the year. Each consumer who sends in five UPC symbols (bar codes) from cereal box tops receives a prize. Frost sells 300,000 boxes of cereal in the year. The company estimates that 20% of the UPC symbols of the cereal boxes sold will eventually be returned for the premium. In all, 35,000 box tops are returned and redeemed for 7,000 prizes in the current year. Each prize costs Frost $2. What is the estimated liability for this promotion at the end of the year?

(a) $10,000   (c) $16,000
(b) $14,000   (d) $24,000

(SO 3) K 7. If a contingent liability is reasonably estimable and it is likely that the contingency will occur, the contingent liability:
    (a) should be accrued in the accounts.
    (b) should be disclosed in the notes accompanying the financial statements.
    (c) should not be recorded or disclosed until the contingency actually happens.
    (d) should be paid immediately.

(SO 3) K 8. If a contingent asset is reasonably estimable and it is likely that the contingency will occur, the contingent asset:
    (a) should be accrued in the accounts.
    (b) should be disclosed in the notes accompanying the financial statements.
    (c) should not be recorded or disclosed until the contingency actually happens.
    (d) should be collected immediately.

9. Current liabilities are listed in the balance sheet: **(SO 4) K**
    (a) in order of liquidity (due date).
    (b) in order of size.
    (c) in no particular order.
    (d) All of the above

*10. During a recent week, Emilie Marquette worked 35 **(SO 5) AP** hours at an hourly wage of $10 per hour. Her weekly CPP exemption is $67.31, and the CPP contribution rate is 4.95%. Her EI premium is calculated at 1.87%. The employee's and employer's share of CPP and EI are:
    (a) employee CPP, $13.99; EI, $6.55; employer CPP, $13.99; EI, $6.55.
    (b) employee CPP, $13.99; EI, $6.55; employer CPP, $13.99; EI, $9.17.
    (c) employee CPP, $17.32; EI, $6.55; employer CPP, $17.32; EI, $9.17.
    (d) employee CPP, $13.99; EI, $6.55; employer CPP, $19.59; EI, $6.55.

Questions

(SO 1) K 1. How is a note payable similar to, and different from, (a) an account payable, and (b) an operating line of credit?

(SO 1) C 2. Your roommate says, "Sales taxes are reported as expenses in the income statement." Do you agree? Explain.

(SO 1) C 3. Explain how sales taxes would be calculated in each of the following situations: (a) GST and PST calculated on the selling price, (b) PST calculated on the selling price plus GST, and (c) HST included in the selling price.

(SO 1) C 4. Explain how property taxes should be recorded when the bill arrives sometime in the spring but covers the entire calendar year?

(SO 1) C 5. What are unearned revenues and why are they classified as a liability? Give an example of unearned revenue.

(SO 1) C 6. What is the difference between salaries and wages?

(SO 1) C 7. What is the difference between gross pay and net pay? Which amount (gross or net) should a company record as salaries and wages expense?

(SO 1) C 8. Explain the different types of employee and employer payroll deductions, and give examples of each.

(SO 2) C 9. The accountant for Amiable Appliances feels that warranty expense should not be recorded unless an appliance is returned for repair. "Otherwise, how do you know if the appliance will be returned, and if so, how much it will cost to fix?" he says. Do you agree? Explain.

(SO 2) C 10. Explain what happens if the estimated warranty liability does not agree with the actual warranty costs incurred.

11. A motion picture company recently released a DVD of a **(SO 2) C** popular movie with a $5 mail-in rebate if the customer sends proof of purchase. How should the motion picture company account for these rebates?

12. Explain the difference between the entries made by a **(SO 2) C** grocery store when it receives a $1 coupon off the price of Tide from a customer and the entries made by **Procter & Gamble**, the manufacturer of Tide, when it receives the coupon from the grocery store for redemption.

13. Why is the cost of product warranties recorded as an **(SO 2) C** expense but the cost of promotions is recorded as a decrease in revenue?

14. What are the differences between definitely determinable, estimated, and contingent liabilities? **(SO 1, 2, 3) K**

15. What is a contingent liability? Give an example of a con- **(SO 3) C** tingent liability that is likely but not estimable, and an example of a contingent liability that is not determinable.

16. Under what circumstances is a contingent liability re- **(SO 3) C** corded in the accounts? Under what circumstances is a contingent liability disclosed only in the notes to the financial statements?

17. What is a debt guarantee? Why is a debt guarantee an **(SO 3) C** example of a contingent liability?

18. What is the difference between a contingent liability **(SO 3) C** and a contingent asset? Give an example of each.

19. What is the accounting treatment for (a) contingent liabil- **(SO 3) C** ities and (b) contingent assets? Why is it not the same?

(SO 4) K 20. In what order should current liabilities be listed on the balance sheet?

(SO 4) K 21. How is an operating line of credit reported or disclosed in the financial statements?

(SO 4) C 22. Anwar Company incurred a long-term liability of $100,000 on January 1, 2007. Of this debt, $20,000 must be repaid annually, each January 1. Explain how Anwar should classify this liability on its balance sheet at (a) December 31, 2007, and (b) December 31, 2008.

(SO 4) K 23. Where in the financial statements should a company report employee payroll deductions? Employer payroll costs?

24. How can a company determine if its current liabilities are too high? (SO 4

*25. Explain how CPP and EI are each calculated. (SO 5

*26. How is the amount deducted from an employee's wages for income tax determined? (SO 5

*27. What are an employee earnings record and a payroll register? (SO 5

*28. To whom, and how often, are payroll deductions remitted? (SO 5

*29. What are some additional employee benefits paid by employers? How are they accounted for? (SO 5

Brief Exercises

Record note payable.
(SO 1) AP

BE10–1 Bourque Company borrows $60,000 from First Bank on July 1, 2007, signing a 9-month, 6% note payable. Interest is payable the first of each month, starting August 1. Prepare journal entries for Bourque Company to record: (a) the receipt of the proceeds of the note on July 1, 2007; (b) the first interest payment on August 1, 2007; (c) the accrual of interest at Bourque's year end, December 31, 2007; and (d) the payment of the note at maturity, April 1, 2008.

Record sales taxes.
(SO 1) AP

BE10–2 Auto Supply Company reports cash sales of $8,550 on March 16. All sales are subject to 6% GST and 8% PST. Record the sales assuming the sales amount of $8,550 (a) does not include the GST and PST, and (b) does include the GST and PST.

Record unearned revenue and prepaid rent.
(SO 1) AP

BE10–3 Centennial Property Company collects $4,400 cash for four months' rent in advance from Rikard's Menswear on October 1, 2008. Both companies have a December 31 fiscal year end. Prepare journal entries for both companies on October 1 and December 31, 2008.

Record property tax.
(SO 1) AP

BE10–4 Dresner Company has a December 31 fiscal year end. It receives a $7,500 property tax bill for the 2008 calendar year on March 31, 2008. The bill is payable on May 31. Prepare entries for March 31, May 31, and December 31, assuming the company adjusts its accounts annually.

Record payroll.
(SO 1) AP

BE10–5 Zerbe Consulting Company's gross salaries for the week ended August 22 were $15,000. Deductions included $730 for CPP, $280 for EI, and $4,305 for income taxes. The company's payroll costs were $730 for CPP and $392 for EI. Prepare journal entries to record (a) the employee payroll costs, assuming salaries were paid August 22, and (b) the employer payroll costs, assuming these will not be paid until September.

Record warranty.
(SO 2) AP

BE10–6 On December 1, Ng Company introduces a new product that includes a one-year warranty on parts. In December, 1,000 units are sold. Management believes that 5% of the units will be defective and that the average warranty cost will be $75 per unit. (a) Prepare the adjusting entry at December 31 to accrue the estimated warranty cost. (b) The following year, the cost of defective parts replaced under the warranty was $3,500. Prepare an entry to record the replacement of the parts.

Record cash rebate.
(SO 2) AP

BE10–7 In August, Mega-Big Motion Picture Company sells 100,000 copies of a recently released DVD of a popular movie. Each DVD contains a $4 rebate if the consumer sends in proof of purchase with the completed rebate form. Mega-Big estimates that 15% of the purchasers will claim the rebate. Prepare an adjusting entry at August 31 to accrue the estimated rebate liability. What will be the entry to record each rebate when it is redeemed?

BE10–8 One-Stop Department Store has a loyalty program where customers are given One-Stop "Money" for cash or debit card purchases. The amount they receive is equal to 2% of the pre-tax sales total. Customers can use the One-Stop Money to pay for part or all of their next purchase at One-Stop Department Store. On July 3, 2008, Judy Wishloff purchases merchandise for $100. She uses $5 of One-Stop Money that she has from an earlier purchase, and pays for the rest of the purchase with cash. What entry or entries will One-Stop Department Store record for this transaction? Ignore taxes.

Record loyalty rewards issued and redeemed. (SO 2) AP

BE10–9 For each of the following independent situations, indicate whether it should be (1) recorded, (2) disclosed, or (3) neither recorded nor disclosed. Explain your reasoning.

Account for contingencies. (SO 3) C

(a) A customer has sued a company for $1 million. Currently the company is unable to determine if it will win or lose the lawsuit.

(b) A customer has sued a company for $1 million. The company will likely lose the lawsuit.

(c) A company has been audited by the CRA, resulting in additional income tax payable of $250,000. The company has appealed the decision, and believes it will likely win the appeal.

(d) A company has appealed an income tax assessment by the CRA. If the company's appeal is successful, it will recover $100,000 of income tax. The company's accountant has advised management that the company has a good chance of winning the appeal.

(e) A company has guaranteed a $300,000 loan for one of its key suppliers. The supplier has a good credit rating and is not expected to default on the loan.

BE10–10 Athabasca Toil & Oil Company is a defendant in a lawsuit for improper discharge of pollutants and waste into the Athabasca River. Athabasca's lawyers have advised that the company will likely lose this lawsuit and that it could settle out of court for $50,000. How should Athabasca record this current liability? What are the arguments for and against recording this contingent liability?

Record contingent liability. (SO 3) AP

BE10–11 Identify which of the following items should be classified as a current liability. For those that are not current liabilities, identify where they should be classified.

Identify current liabilities. (SO 1, 2, 3, 4) K

1. A product warranty
2. Cash received in advance for airline tickets
3. HST collected on sales
4. Bank indebtedness
5. Interest owing on an overdue account payable
6. Interest due on an overdue account receivable
7. A lawsuit pending against a company. The company is not sure of the likely outcome.
8. Amounts withheld from the employees' weekly pay
9. Prepaid property tax
10. A $75,000 mortgage payable, of which $5,000 is due in the next year

BE10–12 Sleeman Breweries Ltd. reported the following current assets and current liabilities (in thousands) at December 31, 2005:

Prepare current liabilities section and calculate current ratio. (SO 4) AP

Accounts payable and		Current portion of long-term debt	$ 16,794
accrued liabilities	$45,349	Income taxes recoverable	1,114
Accounts receivable	45,825	Inventories	44,788
Bank indebtedness	9,744	Prepaid expenses	6,271

(a) Prepare the current liabilities section of the balance sheet.
(b) Calculate the current ratio.

*****BE10–13** Becky Sherrick's regular hourly wage rate is $16, and she receives an hourly rate of $24 for work over 40 hours per week. In the pay period ended January 15, Becky worked 45 hours. Becky's income tax withholding is $143.70, her CPP deductions total $34.29, and her EI deductions total $14.21. Calculate Becky's gross and net pay for the pay period.

Calculate gross and net pay. (SO 5) AP

*****BE10–14** Data for Becky Sherrick are given in BE10–13. Prepare the journal entries to record Becky's pay for the period, assuming she was paid on January 15.

Record payroll. (SO 5) AP

Record payroll.
(SO 5) AP

*BE10–15   In January, the gross pay in Bri Company totalled $70,000, from which $3,330 was deducted for the Canada Pension Plan, $1,310 for employment insurance, and $19,360 for income tax. Prepare the entries to record the January payroll, including the employee benefit costs.

Exercises

Record note payable and note receivable.
(SO 1) AP

E10–1   Briffet Construction borrows $200,000 from TD Bank on October 1, 2007. It signs a 1-year, 6% note payable. Interest is payable the first of each month, starting November 1.

Instructions

(a) Record for Briffet Construction (1) the transaction on October 1, 2007, (2) the first interest payment on November 1, 2007, and (3) the payment of the note on October 1, 2008.
(b) Record for TD Bank (1) the transaction on October 1, 2007, (2) the first interest receipt on November 1, 2007, and (3) the collection of the note on October 1, 2008.

Record sales taxes.
(SO 1) AP

E10–2   In providing accounting services to small businesses, you encounter the following independent situations:

1. Sainsbury Company rang up $26,500 of sales, plus GST of 6% and PST of 7%, on its cash register on April 10.
2. Hockenstein Company prices its merchandise with sales taxes included. Its register total for April 15 is $19,549, which includes 6% GST and 7% PST.
3. Habib Company rang up $30,000 of sales on its cash register on April 21. The company charges 6% GST and 7.5% PST on all sales. PST is charged on sales plus GST.

Instructions

Record the sales transactions and related taxes for each client.

Record unearned subscription revenue.
(SO 1) AP

E10–3   Westwood Company publishes a monthly skateboard magazine, *Adventure Time*. Subscriptions to the magazine cost $48 per year. In November 2007, Westwood sells 7,000 subscriptions which begin with the December issue. Westwood prepares financial statements quarterly and recognizes subscription revenue earned at the end of each quarter. Westwood's year end is December 31.

Instructions

(a) Prepare the entry in November for the receipt of the subscriptions.
(b) Prepare the adjusting entry at December 31, 2007, to record subscription revenue earned in December.
(c) Prepare the adjusting entry at March 31, 2008, to record subscription revenue earned in the first quarter of 2008.

Record property tax; determine financial statement impact.
(SO 1, 4) AP

E10–4   Seaboard Company receives its annual property tax bill of $25,800 for the 2008 calendar year on April 30, 2008, and it is payable on June 30, 2008. Seaboard has a May 31 fiscal year end.

Instructions

(a) Prepare the journal entries for Seaboard on April 30, May 31, and June 30, 2008, assuming that the company makes monthly adjusting entries.
(b) What is recorded on Seaboard's May 31, 2008 balance sheet and income statement for the year ended May 31, 2008 in regard to property taxes? (Assume property tax expense for the period June 1 to December 31, 2007 was $15,050.)

Record payroll.
(SO 1) AP

E10–5   Hidden Dragon Restaurant's gross payroll for August is $40,500. The company deducted $1,715 for CPP, $757 for EI, and $8,010 for income taxes from the employees' cheques. Employees are paid monthly at the end of each month. Hidden Dragon's related payroll costs for August are $1,715 for CPP and $1,060 for EI.

Instructions

(a) Prepare a journal entry for Hidden Dragon on August 31 to record the payment of the August payroll to employees.

(b) Prepare a journal entry on August 31 to accrue Hidden Dragon's employer payroll costs.

(c) On September 15, Hidden Dragon pays the government the correct amounts for August's payroll. Prepare a journal entry to record this remittance.

E10–6 Sinclair Company sells automatic can openers under a 90-day warranty for defective merchandise. Based on past experience, Sinclair estimates that 3% of the units sold will become defective in the warranty period. Management estimates that the average cost of replacing or repairing a defective unit is $15. The units sold and actual units defective in the last two months of 2008 are as follows:

Record warranty costs.
(SO 2) AP

Month	Units Sold	Units Defective
November	30,000	300
December	32,000	620
	62,000	920

Instructions

(a) Calculate the estimated warranty liability at December 31 for the units sold in November and December.

(b) Prepare the journal entries to record (1) the estimated liability for warranties, and (2) the costs incurred in honouring the 920 warranty claims as at December 31 (assume an actual cost of $13,800).

E10–7 The CopyCat Company manufactures and sells photocopiers, with a two-year service warranty. The company estimates that on average it will make 10 service calls a year for each unit sold over the two-year warranty period, at an average cost of $50 per service call.

Calculate warranty costs for multiple years.
(SO 2) AP

The company reports the following sales and service call information:

	Year 1	Year 2	Year 3
Sales (units)	1,000	1,100	1,200
Actual service calls	10,000	20,000	25,000

Instructions

(a) Calculate the warranty expense for each year.

(b) Calculate the warranty liability at the end of each year.

E10–8 Crispy Cookies sells cookies for $3 a package. Starting in 2007 as a way to boost sales, the company included inside each box a 50-cent rebate coupon that can be returned and redeemed, along with proof of purchase. There is no expiry date on these coupons. Crispy Cookies estimates that 15% of these coupons will eventually be redeemed. Crispy Cookies has a December 31 year end. Sales are 150,000 boxes of cookies in 2007 and 190,000 in 2008. Redemptions total 20,000 coupons in 2007 and 23,000 in 2008.

Calculate coupon liability.
(SO 2) AP

Instructions

(a) What amount should be recorded as contra revenue (sales discounts for coupon redemptions) in 2007? In 2008?

(b) How much cash was paid out by Crispy Cookies for the coupons in 2007? In 2008?

(c) What is the coupon liability that should be reported at December 31, 2007? At December 31, 2008?

(d) Was the cash paid for redemptions the same amount as what was recorded for the sales discount for coupon redemptions? Explain why or why not.

E10–9 A list of possible liabilities follows:

Identify type of liability.
(SO 1, 2, 3) C

1. An automobile company recalled a particular car model because of a possible problem with the brakes. The company will pay to replace the brakes.

2. A large retail store has a policy of refunding purchases to dissatisfied customers under a widely advertised "money-back, no questions asked" guarantee.
3. A manufacturer offers a three-year warranty at the time of sale.
4. To promote sales, a company offers prizes (e.g., a chance to win a trip) in return for a specific type of bottle cap.
5. A local community has filed suit against a chemical company for contamination of drinking water. The community is demanding compensation, and the amount is uncertain. The company is vigorously defending itself.

Instructions

(a) State whether you believe each of the above liabilities is definitely determinable, estimable, or contingent, and explain why.
(b) If you identify the liability as contingent in part (a), state whether it should be recorded, disclosed, or neither recorded nor disclosed in the financial statements.

Analyze contingent liability.
(SO 3) AP

E10–10 Sleep-a-Bye Baby Company is the defendant in a lawsuit alleging that its portable baby cribs are unsafe. The company has offered to replace the crib free of charge for any concerned parent. Nonetheless, it has been sued for damages and distress amounting to $500,000. The company plans to vigorously defend its product safety record in court.

Instructions

(a) What should the company record or report in its financial statements for this situation? Explain why.
(b) What if Sleep-a-Bye Baby Company's lawyers advise that it is very likely the company will have to pay damages of $100,000? Does this change what should be recorded or reported in the financial statements? Explain.

Determine financial statement impact of transactions.
(SO 1, 2, 3, 4) AP

E10–11 Here is a list of transactions:

1. Purchased inventory (perpetual system) on account.
2. Extended the payment terms of the account payable in item 1 above by issuing a 6-month, 5% note payable.
3. Recorded accrued interest on the note payable from item 2 above.
4. Recorded cash sales of $74,100, plus HST of 14%.
5. Recorded wage expense of $35,000. Paid employees $25,000; the difference was for various payroll deductions withheld.
6. Recorded employer's share of employee benefits.
7. Accrued property taxes payable when bill received.
8. Disclosed a contingent liability on a lawsuit whose likely outcome the company cannot determine.
9. Recorded the estimated liability for product rebates outstanding.
10. Paid product rebate claims that were accrued in item 9 above.

Instructions

Set up a table using the format shown below. Indicate the effect ("+" for increase, "–" for decrease, and "NE" for no effect) of each of the above transactions on the financial statement categories indicated. The first one has been done for you as an example.

	Assets	Liabilities	Owner's Equity	Revenues	Expenses	Net Income
1.	+	+	NE	NE	NE	NE

Prepare current liabilities section of balance sheet. Calculate current ratio.
(SO 4) AP

E10–12 Larkin Company has the following liability accounts at August 31, 2008, after posting adjusting entries:

Accounts payable	$67,000	Mortgage payable	$120,000
Bank indebtedness	50,000	Note payable	80,000
Coupon liability	4,000	Property taxes payable	8,000
GST payable	12,000	PST payable	16,000
Income tax payable	28,000	Unearned revenue	24,000
Interest payable	8,000	Warranty liability	18,000

Additional information:

1. Bank indebtedness is from an operating line of credit which is due on demand.
2. On August 31, 2008, the unused operating line of credit is $25,000.
3. Coupon and warranty costs are expected to be incurred within one year.
4. Of the mortgage, $10,000 is due each year.
5. The note payable matures in three years.

Instructions

(a) Prepare the current liabilities section of the balance sheet.
(b) Calculate Larkin's current ratio, assuming total current assets are $367,500.

*E10–13   Kate Gough's regular hourly wage rate is $13, and she receives a wage of 1.5 times the regular hourly rate for work over 40 hours per week. In a September weekly pay period, Kate worked 43 hours. Kate lives in Alberta and has a claim code of 1 for tax deductions. After this information is input, the following information is generated:

Record payroll.
(SO 5) AP

Payroll Deductions for Salary			
Employee's name (optional) Employer's name (optional) Pay period ending date (optional)	Kate Gough 2006-09-16		
Gross salary (or pension income) for the pay period			578.50
Total EI insurable earnings for the pay period			578.50
Taxable salary or pension income			578.50
Federal tax deductions	57.35		
Provincial or territorial tax deductions	25.25		
Total tax on salary or pension income	82.60	82.60	
Canada Pension Plan (CPP) deductions		25.30	
Employment Insurance (EI) deductions		10.82	
Requested additional tax deduction		0.00	
Total deductions on salary or pension income		118.72	118.72
Net amount			459.78
Total claim amount (from federal TD1)	Claim Code 1 (Minimum—8,639.00)		
Total claim amount (from provincial or territorial TD1)	Claim Code 1 (Minimum—8,377.00)		
Pay period	Weekly (52 pay periods a year)		
Province or territory of employment	Alberta		

Instructions

(a) Record Kate's salary on September 16, assuming it was also paid on this date.
(b) Record the employer's related payroll costs on September 16, assuming they were not paid on this date.

*E10–14   Ahmad Company has the following data for the weekly payroll ending January 31:

Record payroll.
(SO 5) AP

	Hours Worked						Hourly Rate	Income Tax Withheld	Health Insurance
Employee	M	Tu	W	Th	F	S			
A. Kassam	8	8	9	8	10	3	$11	$ 81	$10
H. Faas	8	8	8	8	8	2	13	87	15
G. Labute	9	10	8	8	9	0	14	107	15

Employees are paid 1.5 times the regular hourly rate for all hours worked over 40 hours per week. CPP is deducted at a rate of 4.95% on earnings over the $67.31 weekly exemption, and EI is deducted at a rate of 1.76% of gross pay. Ahmad Company must make payments to the Worker's Compensation Plan equal to 2% of the gross payroll. In addition, Ahmad matches the employees' health insurance contributions.

Instructions

(a) Prepare the payroll register for the weekly payroll.
(b) Record the payroll and Ahmad Company's employee benefits.

Calculate missing payroll amounts. Record payroll. (SO 5) AP

*E10–15 Selected data from the February 28 payroll register for Yue Company follow, with some amounts missing:

Gross pay:		Deductions:	
Regular	$ (a)	Canada Pension Plan	$ (c)
Overtime	1,050	Employment insurance	243
Total	(b)	Income tax	3,389
		Union dues	139
		United Way	225
		Total deductions	(d)
		Net pay	(e)
		Accounts debited:	
		Warehouse wages expense	5,070
		Store wages expense	(f)

Pensionable earnings are $11,800. CPP premiums are 4.95% of pensionable earnings. EI premiums are 1.87% of gross pay.

Instructions

(a) Fill in the missing amounts. Round all answers to the nearest dollar.
(b) Calculate the company's contributions to the Canada Pension Plan and employment insurance.
(c) Record all aspects of the February 28 payroll and its payment.
(d) Record the payment of amounts withheld, assuming they were paid on March 10.

Problems: Set A

Identify liabilities. (SO 1, 2, 3, 4) AP

P10–1A The following transactions occurred in Iqaluit Company in the year ended April 30:

1. Iqaluit purchased goods for $12,000 on April 29, terms n/30, FOB destination. The goods arrived on May 3.
2. Weekly salaries of $10,000 are paid every Friday for a five-day (Monday to Friday) work week. This year, April 30 is a Thursday. Payroll deductions include income tax withholdings of $3,000, and CPP of 4.95% and EI of 1.87% of gross pay.
3. Property taxes of $40,000 were assessed on March 1 for the calendar year. They are payable on May 1.
4. The company purchased equipment for $35,000 on April 1. It issued a 6-month, 5% note in payment. Interest is payable monthly on the first of each month.
5. Iqaluit offered a two-year warranty on one of its new products. It estimated it would cost $45 to honour each warranty and that 5% of the units sold would be returned for replacement within the warranty period. By April 30, 10,000 units of the product had been sold and customers had returned 100 units under the warranty.
6. The company has a $225,000, 20-year mortgage payable, of which $10,000 is currently due.
7. Iqaluit was named in a lawsuit alleging negligence for an oil spill that leaked into the neighbouring company's water system. Iqaluit's legal counsel estimates that the company will likely lose the suit. Restoration costs are expected to total $250,000.

Instructions

(a) Identify which transactions above should be presented in the current liabilities section and which in the long-term liabilities section of Iqaluit's balance sheet on April 30. Identify the account title(s) and amount(s) for each reported liability.
(b) Indicate any information that should be disclosed in the notes to Iqaluit's financial statements.

P10–2A MileHi Mountain Bikes markets mountain-bike tours to clients vacationing in various locations in the mountains of British Columbia. On February 29, 2008, the company had one 6-month, 6% note, with the principal and interest payable to Eifert Company on March 31. It had a balance of $15,000 in Notes Payable, $375 in Interest Payable, and $1,115 in Interest Expense.

> *Record note transactions; show financial statement presentation.*
> *(SO 1, 4) AP*

To prepare for the upcoming summer biking season, MileHi had the following transactions related to notes payable:

Mar. 2 Purchased Mongoose bikes to use as rentals by issuing an $8,000, 3-month, 7% note payable. Interest is payable at maturity.
31 Paid the $15,000 Eifert note, plus interest.
Apr. 1 Issued a $25,000, 9-month, 7% note to Mountain Real Estate for the purchase of mountain property on which to build bike trails. Interest is payable the first of each month.
May 1 Paid interest on the Mountain Real Estate note (see April 1 transaction).
2 Borrowed $18,000 from Western Bank by issuing a 4-month, 6% note. The funds will be used for working capital for the beginning of the season. Interest is payable at maturity.
June 1 Paid interest on the Mountain Real Estate note (see April 1 transaction).
2 Paid the Mongoose note, plus interest (see March 2 transaction).
30 Accrued interest for the Mountain Real Estate and Western Bank notes at the company's year end.

Instructions

(a) Record the transactions.
(b) Show the balance sheet presentation of notes payable and interest payable at June 30.
(c) Show the income statement presentation of interest expense for the year.

P10–3A On January 1, 2008, Zaur Company's general ledger had these liability accounts:

> *Record current liability transactions; prepare current liabilities section.*
> *(SO 1, 2, 4) AP*

Accounts payable	$52,000	Income tax payable	$ 4,640
Coupon liability	2,150	PST payable	6,430
CPP payable	1,905	Unearned service revenue	16,000
EI payable	1,058	Warranty liability	5,750
GST payable	7,500		

In January, the following selected transactions occurred:

Jan. 2 Issued 50,000 coupons for $1 each with an expiry date of April 30, 2008. Based on past experience, 10% of these coupons are expected to be redeemed.
5 Sold merchandise for $15,800 cash, plus 6% GST and 7% PST. Zaur uses a periodic inventory system.
12 Provided services for customers who had previously made advance payments of $7,000.
14 Paid $7,500 to the Receiver General (federal government) and $6,430 to the Provincial Treasurer (provincial government) for sales taxes collected in December 2007.
15 Paid $7,603 to the Receiver General for amounts owing from the December payroll for CPP, EI, and income tax ($1,905 + $1,058 + $4,640).
17 Paid $32,000 to creditors on account.
20 Sold 500 units of a new product on account for $60 per unit, plus 6% GST and 7% PST. The cost of the unit sold is $25 per unit. This new product has a two-year warranty. It is expected that 6% of the units sold will be returned for repair at an average cost of $10 per unit.
21 Borrowed $18,000 from HSBC Bank on a 3-month, 6% note. Interest is payable monthly on the fifteenth day of the month.
30 Paid $2,400 for coupons redeemed in the month (see January 2 transaction).

Jan. 31 Determined that the company had used $875 of parts inventory in January to honour warranty contracts (see January 20 transaction).

31 Recorded and paid the monthly payroll. Gross salaries were $22,500. Amounts withheld include income tax of $5,135, CPP of $1,027, and EI of $421.

Instructions

(a) Record the transactions.
(b) Record adjusting entries for the following:
  1. Interest on the note payable for half a month
  2. The estimated warranty liability
  3. Employee benefits, which include CPP of $1,027 and EI of $589
(c) Prepare the current liabilities section of the balance sheet at January 31.

Record warranty transactions.
(SO 2) AP

P10–4A On January 1, 2006, Logue Company began a warranty program to stimulate sales. It is estimated that 5% of the units sold will be returned for repair at an estimated cost of $25 per unit. Sales and warranty figures for the three years ended December 31 are as follows:

	2006	2007	2008
Sales (units)	600	660	720
Sales price per unit	$100	$105	$110
Units returned for repair under warranty	30	35	35
Actual warranty costs	$750	$800	$850

Instructions

(a) Calculate the warranty expense for each year and warranty liability at the end of each year.
(b) Record the warranty transactions for each year. Credit Repair Parts Inventory for the actual warranty costs.

Record coupon transactions.
(SO 2) AP

P10–5A The Easy Tax Company produces and sells a personal income tax software program to retail stores for $15. The retail stores sell the software to consumers for $25. In January 2008, Easy Tax promoted the software in Office Supply Mart's advertising flyer and included a $3 coupon that consumers can use to reduce the price of the software. The coupon has an expiry date of April 30, 2008. Stores must submit all redeemed coupons to Easy Tax by the tenth day of the month following the sale. Based on past experience, Easy Tax estimates that 15,000 of these coupons will be redeemed before the expiry date.

Instructions

(a) Record the following transactions for Office Supply Mart:
  1. In the month of January, Office Supply Mart sells 100 software packages for cash. Forty-five customers pay the full price and 55 present the $3 coupon and pay the reduced price. Assume that all branches of Office Supply Mart use a perpetual inventory system.
  2. On January 31, Office Supply Mart sends Easy Tax the coupons redeemed to date and requests a refund.
  3. On February 10, Office Supply Mart receives the requested refund from Easy Tax.
(b) Record the following transactions for Easy Tax:
  1. The estimated coupon liability in January
  2. Receipt of the 55 coupons presented for redemption by Office Supply Mart on January 31
  3. The payment to Office Supply Mart on February 10 for the redeemed coupons
(c) On May 15, 2008, Easy Tax determines that in total 15,750 coupons have been redeemed. What entry, if any, should Easy Tax prepare?

Discuss reporting of contingent liability.
(SO 3, 4) AP

P10–6A On September 20, 2008, White-Wall Tire Co. recalls 10 million defective White-Wall tires. The White-Wall tires have been linked to numerous deaths, injuries, and incidents of tire separation and blowouts. White-Wall offers to provide free tire inspections and replace suspect tires through its dealership network. When a dealer replaces the recalled tires with a White-Wall brand, the company reimburses the dealer for the wholesale price of the tires, plus $20 per tire to cover mounting and balancing and the extra paperwork involved. When other competing brands are used to replace the recalled tire, White-Wall reimburses the dealer up to $100 per tire, which gives the dealer the usual profit margin.

Instructions

What should White-Wall Tire Co. record or disclose in its December 31, 2008, financial statements for this situation? Explain why.

P10–7A   On March 4, a fire destroyed the chemistry building on the University of Learning's campus. The University has filed a claim with its insurance company. At March 31, the University's year end, the claim has not been settled.

Discuss reporting of contingent asset.
(SO 3, 4) AP

Instructions

Under each of the following independent assumptions, explain what the university should record or disclose in its March 31 financial statements:

(a) The insurance claim is likely to be successful.
(b) The insurance claim is unlikely to be successful because the insurance company believes the fire is suspicious.
(c) The university receives written confirmation from the insurance company that the claim will be paid in full, but not before the financial statements are issued.

P10–8A   Telesat Canada reports the following current assets and current liabilities (in thousands) at December 31, 2005:

Prepare current liabilities section; calculate and comment on ratios.
(SO 4) AP

Accounts payable and		Dividends payable	$	449
accrued liabilities	$ 38,905	Income taxes payable		16,895
Cash and cash equivalents	113,477	Other current assets		36,177
Current future tax asset	3,737	Other current liabilities		63,586
Debt due within one year	152,838	Receivables		59,380
Deferred revenues and deposits	30,314	Short-term investments		51,058

Instructions

(a) Prepare the current liabilities section of the balance sheet.
(b) Calculate the current ratio.
(c) On December 31, 2004, Telesat had current assets of $263,176 thousand and current liabilities of $148,295 thousand. Did the current ratio improve or weaken in 2005?

*P10–9A   Scoot Scooters has four employees who are paid on an hourly basis, plus time-and-a-half for hours in excess of 40 a week. Payroll data for the week ended March 15, 2008, follow:

Prepare payroll register and record payroll.
(SO 5) AP

Employee	Total Hours	Hourly Rate	Income Tax	CPP	EI	United Way
P. Kilchyk	40	$ 9.50	$35.05	$15.48	$7.11	$0.00
B. Quon	42	10.00	47.10	17.95	8.04	5.00
C. Pospisil	40	11.50	54.15	19.44	8.60	7.50
B. Verwey	44	10.50	55.10	19.59	8.66	5.00

Instructions

(a) Prepare a payroll register for the weekly payroll.
(b) Record the payroll on February 15, and the accrual of employee benefits expense.
(c) Record the payment of the payroll on February 15.
(d) Record the payment of the employee benefits on March 15.

*P10–10A   The following payroll liability accounts are included in the ledger of Amora Company on January 1, 2008:

Record and post payroll transactions.
(SO 5) AP

Canada Pension Plan payable	$ 8,788	Union dues payable	$ 1,200
Canada Savings Bonds payable	2,420	United Way donations payable	750
Employment insurance payable	4,768	Vacation pay payable	10,704
Income tax payable	25,510	Workers' compensation payable	5,676

In January, the following transactions occurred:

Jan. 10 Sent a cheque to the union treasurer for union dues.
12 Issued a cheque to the Receiver General for the amounts due for CPP, EI, and income tax.
17 Issued a cheque to United Way.
20 Paid the Workers' Compensation Plan.
31 Prepared the monthly payroll register, which showed office salaries $40,800; store wages $48,400; income tax withheld $23,400; CPP withheld $4,127; EI withheld $1,668; union dues withheld $1,250; United Way contributions $750; and Canada Savings Bonds deductions $1,210.
31 Prepared payroll cheques for the net pay and distributed them to employees.

At January 31, the company also made the following adjusting entries for employee benefits:

1. The employer's share of CPP and EI
2. Workers' Compensation Plan at 6% of gross pay
3. Vacation pay at 4% of gross pay

Instructions

(a) Enter the beginning balances in general ledger accounts.
(b) Record and post the January transactions and adjustments.

Calculate missing payroll amounts and record.
(SO 5) AN

*P10–11A Selected data follow from a payroll register for the week ended June 30 for Slovac Company, with some amounts missing:

Store wages expense	$ (a)	United Way	$ 600
Warehouse wages expense	9,800	Income tax	(c)
CPP deductions	1,165	Net pay	11,410
EI deductions	(b)	Overtime earnings	1,490
Group insurance plan	400	Regular earnings	23,150
Union dues	260	Total gross pay	(d)

Instructions

(a) Fill in the missing amounts.
(b) Record the payroll, including the employer's portion of CPP and EI, for the week ended June 30.
(c) Record the payment of the payroll to the employees on June 30, and the remittance of the amounts due to the Receiver General on July 15.

Problems: Set B

Identify liabilities.
(SO 1, 2, 3, 4) AP

P10–1B The following transactions occurred in Wendell Company in the year ended December 31:

1. Wendell purchased goods for $120,000 on December 23, terms n/30, FOB shipping point. The goods were shipped on December 27.
2. Weekly salaries of $6,000 are paid every Friday for a five-day (Monday to Friday) work week. This year, December 31 is a Wednesday. Payroll deductions include income tax withholdings of $1,800, and CPP of 4.95% and EI of 1.87% of gross pay.
3. Wendell is the defendant in a negligence suit. Wendell's legal counsel estimates that Wendell may suffer a $75,000 loss if it loses the suit. In legal counsel's opinion, the likelihood of success in the case cannot be determined at this time.
4. Wendell issued a $500,000, 5-year, 6% note payable on July 1. The note requires payment of the principal in instalments of $100,000 each June 30 for the next five years. Interest is due monthly on the first of each month.
5. The company received $25,000 from customers in December for services to be performed in January.

6. Wendell issued a mail-in purchase rebate on one of its specialty inventory items sold between September 1 and November 30. Each item was sold for $45 and had a $4 rebate attached to it. A total of 4,500 items were sold in that period. Wendell estimates that 25% of the customers will request a rebate. By December 31, Wendell had issued $3,900 in rebates.

7. The company has a $100,000 operating line of credit. No money is owed on this line of credit to date.

Instructions

(a) Identify which transactions above should be presented in the current liabilities section and which in the long-term liabilities section of Wendell's balance sheet on December 31. Identify the account title(s) and amount(s) for each reported liability.

(b) Indicate any information that should be disclosed in the notes to Wendell's financial statements.

P10–2B The current liabilities section of the December 31, 2007, balance sheet of Learnstream Company included notes payable $12,000 and interest payable $420. The note payable was issued to Tanner Company on June 30, 2007. Interest of 7% is payable at maturity, February 29, 2008.

Record note transactions; show financial statement presentation.
(SO 1, 4) AP

The following selected transactions occurred in the year ended December 31, 2008:

Jan. 12 Purchased merchandise on account from McCoy Company for $20,000, terms n/30. Learnstream uses a perpetual inventory system.

  31 Issued a $20,000, 3-month, 5% note to McCoy Company in payment of an account. Interest is payable monthly.

Feb. 29 Paid interest on the McCoy note (see January 31 transaction).

  29 Paid the Tanner note, plus interest.

Mar. 31 Paid interest on the McCoy note (see January 31 transaction).

Apr. 30 Paid the McCoy note, plus one month's interest (see January 31 transaction).

July 1 Purchased equipment from Scottie Equipment by paying $11,000 cash and signing a $30,000, 1-year, 6% note. Interest is payable at maturity.

Dec. 31 Accrued interest for the Scottie note at the company's year end.

Instructions

(a) Record the transactions.
(b) Show the balance sheet presentation of notes payable and interest payable at December 31.
(c) Show the income statement presentation of interest expense for the year.

P10–3B On January 1, 2008, Shumway Software Company's general ledger contained these liability accounts:

Record current liability transactions; prepare current liabilities section.
(SO 1, 2, 4) AP

Accounts payable	$42,500	GST payable	$ 5,800
Coupon liability	4,500	Income tax payable	2,515
CPP payable	1,340	PST payable	6,600
EI payable	756	Unearned service revenue	15,000

In January, the following selected transactions occurred:

Jan. 2 Issued a $50,000, 4-month, 7% note. Interest is payable at maturity.

   5 Sold merchandise for $8,800 cash, plus 6% GST and 7.5% PST. PST is charged on the selling price plus GST. The cost of this sale was $4,600. Shumway Software uses a perpetual inventory system.

  12 Provided services for customers who had made advance payments of $8,500.

  14 Paid $5,800 to the Receiver General (federal government) and $6,600 to the Minister of Finance (provincial government) for sales taxes collected in December 2007.

  15 Paid $4,611 to the Receiver General for amounts owing from the December payroll for CPP, EI, and income tax ($1,340 + $756 + $2,515).

  20 Sold 500 units of a new product on account for $55 per unit, plus 6% GST and 7.5% PST. This new product has a one-year warranty. It is estimated that 9% of the units sold will be returned for repair at an average cost of $10 per unit. The cost of this sale was $25 per unit.

Jan. 29 Paid $2,900 for coupons redeemed in the month.

31 Recorded and paid the monthly payroll. Gross salaries were $16,000. Amounts withheld included income tax of $3,215, CPP of $720, and EI of $299.

Instructions

(a) Record the transactions.
(b) Record adjusting entries for the following:
1. Interest on the note payable
2. The estimated warranty liability
3. Employee benefits, which include CPP of $720 and EI of $419
(c) Prepare the current liabilities section of the balance sheet at January 31.

Record warranty transactions.
(SO 2) AP

P10–4B On January 1, 2006, Hopewell Company began a warranty program to stimulate sales. It is estimated that 5% of the units sold will be returned for repair at an estimated cost of $30 per unit. Sales and warranty figures for the three years ended December 31 are as follows:

	2006	2007	2008
Sales (units)	500	550	600
Sales price per unit	$150	$120	$125
Units returned for repair under warranty	25	30	35
Actual warranty costs	$750	$800	$850

Instructions

(a) Calculate the warranty expense for each year and warranty liability at the end of each year.
(b) Record the warranty transactions for each year. Credit Repair Parts Inventory for the actual warranty costs.

Record coupon transactions.
(SO 2) AP

P10–5B The Safe Computing Company produces and sells an anti-spam software program to retail stores for $30. The retail stores sell the software to consumers for $40. In March 2008, Safe Computing advertised the software in *PC Magazine* and included a $3 coupon that consumers can use to reduce the price of the software. The coupon has an expiry date of September 30, 2008. Retail stores must submit all redeemed coupons to Safe Computing by the tenth day of the month following the sale. Based on past experience, Safe Computing estimates that 10,000 of these coupons will be redeemed before the expiry date.

Instructions

(a) Record the following transactions for Collegiate Computer Store—one of Safe Computing Company's customers:
1. In the month of April, Collegiate Computer Store sells 50 software packages for cash. Twenty customers pay the full price and 30 present the $3 coupon and pay the reduced price. Assume Collegiate uses a perpetual inventory system.
2. On April 30, Collegiate sends Safe Computing the coupons redeemed to date and requests a refund.
3. On May 10, Collegiate receives the requested refund from Safe Computing.
(b) Record the following transactions for Safe Computing:
1. The estimated coupon liability in March
2. Receipt of the 30 coupons presented for redemption by Collegiate Computer Store on April 30
3. The payment to Collegiate Computer Store on May 10 for the redeemed coupons
(c) On October 15, 2008, Safe Computing determines that in total 10,250 coupons have been redeemed. What entry, if any, should Safe Computing prepare?

Discuss reporting of
contingent liability.
(SO 3, 4) AP

P10–6B The **Northern Affairs Program** of the Government of Canada manages waste and contaminated sites in Nunavut, the Northwest Territories, and Yukon. There are currently 1,826 contaminated waste sites in northern Canada. At 984 sites, cleanup has already been completed.

A total of 370 sites are receiving active attention. The cost to clean up these sites is estimated at $914 million. The remaining 472 sites have been assessed and are of low risk.

Instructions

What should the Government of Canada record or disclose in its financial statements for this situation? Explain why.

P10–7B   Atom Construction Company is in the second year of a three-year construction schedule to build a nuclear plant in the province of Ontario. The province has agreed to pay the company a bonus if the plant is completed on time and on budget. Atom Construction Company has never missed a deadline and also has a history of completing projects on budget.

Discuss reporting of contingent liability and asset. (SO 3, 4) AP

Instructions

(a) What should the Province of Ontario record or disclose in its financial statements in this situation? Explain why.
(b) What should Atom Construction Company record or disclose in its financial statements in this situation? Explain why.

P10–8B   Kangaroo Media Inc. reports the following current assets and current liabilities at December 31, 2005:

Prepare current liabilities section; calculate and comment on ratios. (SO 4) AP

Accounts payable and		Short-term investments	$2,865,992
accrued liabilities	$2,492,031	Current portion of long-term debt	178,763
Accounts receivable	1,932,999	Deferred revenues	1,260,035
Bank loan payable	193,190	Inventories	1,966,481
Cash and cash equivalents	3,908,887	Prepaid expenses	174,478

Instructions

(a) Prepare the current liabilities section of the balance sheet.
(b) Calculate the current ratio.
(c) At December 31, 2004, Kangaroo Media Inc. had current assets of $3,879,375 and current liabilities of $674,260. Did the current ratio improve or weaken in 2005?

*P10–9B   Sure Value Hardware has four employees who are paid on an hourly basis, plus time-and-a-half for hours worked in excess of 40 hours a week. Payroll data for the week ended March 14, 2008, follow:

Prepare payroll register and record payroll. (SO 5) AP

Employee	Total Hours	Hourly Rate	Income Tax	CPP	EI	United Way
I. Dahl	40	$15.00	$ 89.70	$26.37	$11.22	$5.00
F. Gualtieri	42	15.00	99.35	28.60	12.06	5.00
G. Ho	44	14.50	108.00	30.68	12.85	8.00
A. Israeli	46	14.50	122.75	32.83	13.66	5.00

The first three employees are sales clerks (store wages expense) and the other employee does administrative duties (office wages expense).

Instructions

(a) Prepare a payroll register for the weekly payroll.
(b) Record the payroll on March 14, and the accrual of employee benefits expense.
(c) Record the payment of the payroll on March 14.
(d) Record the payment of employee benefits on April 15.

*P10–10B   The following payroll liability accounts are included in the ledger of Drumheller Company on January 1, 2008:

Record and post payroll transactions. (SO 5) AP

Canada Pension Plan payable	$5,454	Income tax payable	$18,600
Canada Savings Bonds payable	2,500	Union dues payable	1,250
Disability insurance payable	1,050	Vacation pay payable	6,450
Employment insurance payable	2,923	Workers' compensation payable	5,263

In January, the following transactions occurred:

Jan. 8 Sent a cheque to the insurance company for the disability insurance.
10 Sent a cheque for $1,250 to the union treasurer for union dues.
12 Issued a cheque to the Receiver General for the amounts due for CPP, EI, and income tax.
15 Purchased Canada Savings Bonds for employees by writing a cheque for $2,500.
20 Paid the amount due to the Workers' Compensation Plan.
31 Completed the monthly payroll register, which shows office salaries $26,400; store wages $37,400; income tax withheld $16,760; CPP withheld $3,014; EI withheld $1,193; union dues withheld $950; Canada Savings Bond deductions $1,200; and long-term disability insurance premiums $1,100.
31 Prepared payroll cheques for the net pay and distributed the cheques to the employees.

At January 31, the company also made the following adjusting entries for employee benefits:

1. The employer's share of CPP and EI
2. Workers' Compensation Plan at 7% of gross pay
3. Vacation pay at 4% of gross pay

Instructions

(a) Enter the beginning balances in general ledger accounts.
(b) Journalize and post the January transactions and adjustments.

Calculate missing payroll amounts and record.
(SO 5) AP

*P10–11B   Selected data follow from a payroll register for the week ended December 31 for Western Electric Company, with some amounts missing:

Administrative salaries	$ (a)	Long-term disability insurance	$ 1,500
CPP deductions	28,710	Net pay	457,235
Dental insurance premiums	2,400	Total deductions	(b)
EI deductions	12,155	Total gross pay	(c)
Electricians' wages	470,000	United Way contributions	5,000
Income tax	143,000		

In addition to CPP and EI, Western Electric Company's employee benefits include matching the employees' contributions to the dental and long-term disability insurance plans and paying workers' compensation of $26,000.

Instructions

(a) Fill in the missing amounts.
(b) Record the payroll, including employee benefits, for the week ended December 31.
(c) Record the payment of the payroll to the employees on December 31, and the remittance of the amounts due to third parties on January 15.

Continuing Cookie Chronicle

(*Note*: This is a continuation of the Cookie Chronicle from Chapters 1 through 9.)

As you may remember, Cookie Creations sells fine European mixers that it purchases from Kzinski Supply Co. Kzinski's warranty terms are as follows:

Kzinski warrants the fine European mixer to be free of defects in material and workmanship for a period of one year from the date of original purchase. If the mixer has such a defect, Kzinski will repair or replace the mixer free of charge for parts and labour. The product must be shipped prepaid to an authorized Kzinski service centre. The cost to ship the mixer is paid by the consumer. The cost to return the product to the consumer is paid by Kzinski.

Based on past experience, Kzinski has found that approximately 10% of mixers sold are returned for repair or replacement. The authorized service centre for Canada is located in Toronto.

Natalie is considering assuming the responsibility of paying for the costs of shipping to Toronto any mixer sold by Cookie Creations needing repair. Before doing so, she has come to you for advice on accounting for this type of transaction and asks the following questions:

1. Because I value my customers, I am willing to assume the cost of shipping any mixer I have sold needing repair. I imagine that some years I won't have to pay anything and other years I may have to pay a lot. Is this what you would call a contingent liability? Explain to me what a contingent liability is and why this is or is not considered one.

2. I estimate that I am going to sell 30 mixers in 2008 and that it will cost approximately $50 to ship a mixer needing repair to Toronto. If I assume that Kzinski's estimates are correct, what will be recorded on my balance sheet in 2008? What will be recorded on my income statement in 2008?

3. What if, during 2009, only two mixers sold in 2008 are returned for repair and it costs me $75 in total to ship them to Toronto? What if, during 2009, four mixers sold in 2008 are returned for repair and it costs me $175 to ship them to Toronto? What will the impact be on my income statement and balance sheet in 2009 based on what I previously recorded using the information in (2) above?

4. Why go through all of the calculations in 2008 when you do not know for sure what is going to happen in 2009? Why not just wait until 2009? Is there a reason for doing all of this work?

Instructions

(a) Answer Natalie's questions.

(b) Prepare the journal entries required for 2008 and 2009 using the information provided in questions 2 and 3 above.

Cumulative Coverage—Chapters 3 to 10

The unadjusted trial balance of LeBrun Company at its year end, July 31, 2008, is as follows:

LEBRUN COMPANY
Trial Balance
July 31, 2008

	Debit	Credit
Cash	$ 18,300	
Petty cash	200	
Accounts receivable	35,000	
Allowance for doubtful accounts		$ 2,000
Note receivable (due December 31, 2008)	10,000	
Merchandise inventory	59,500	
Prepaid expenses	16,000	
Land	50,000	
Building	155,000	
Accumulated amortization—building		10,800
Equipment	25,000	
Accumulated amortization—equipment		12,200
Patent	75,000	
Accumulated amortization—patent		15,000
Accounts payable		81,000
Mortgage payable (due August 1, 2026)		121,190
S. LeBrun, capital		127,690
S. LeBrun, drawings	65,000	
Sales		750,000
Cost of goods sold	500,000	
Operating expenses	100,000	
Interest revenue		300
Interest expense	11,180	
Totals	$1,120,180	$1,120,180

Adjustment data:

1. The July 31 bank statement reported debit memos for service charges of $30 and an NSF cheque received from a customer on account of $450.
2. Estimated uncollectible accounts receivable at July 31 are $3,500.
3. The note receivable has interest of 6% and was issued on December 31, 2007. Interest is payable the first of each month.
4. A physical count of inventory determined that $57,000 of inventory was actually on hand.
5. Prepaid expenses of $5,500 expired in the year (use the account Operating Expenses).
6. Amortization is calculated on the long-lived assets using the following methods and useful lives:
   Building: straight-line, 25 years, $15,000 residual value
   Equipment: double declining-balance, five years, $2,000 residual value
   Patent: straight-line, 15 years, no residual value
7. The 8% mortgage payable was issued on August 1, 2001. Interest is paid monthly at the beginning of each month for the previous month's interest. Of the mortgage principal, $1,680 is currently due.
8. Accrued liabilities at July 31 are $1,350.

Instructions

(a) Prepare the adjusting journal entries required at July 31. (Round your calculations to the nearest dollar.)
(b) Prepare an adjusted trial balance at July 31.
(c) Prepare a multiple-step income statement and statement of owner's equity for the year, and a balance sheet at July 31.

BROADENING YOUR PERSPECTIVE

Financial Reporting and Analysis

Financial Reporting Problem

BPY10–1 Refer to the financial statements of **The Forzani Group Ltd.** and the Notes to Consolidated Financial Statements in Appendix A.

Instructions

Answer the following questions about the company's current and contingent liabilities:

(a) What were Forzani's total current liabilities at January 29, 2006? What was the increase (decrease) in total current liabilities from the previous year?
(b) Which specific current liabilities did Forzani present on the January 29 balance sheet?
(c) Calculate Forzani's current ratio, receivables turnover, and inventory turnover ratios for 2006. Comment on Forzani's overall liquidity.
(d) Does Forzani report any contingent liabilities? If so, where are they disclosed? Explain the nature, amount, and significance of Forzani's contingent liabilities, if any.

Interpreting Financial Statements

BYP10–2 Saputo Inc. reported the following information about contingencies in the notes to its March 31, 2006, financial statements:

SAPUTO INC.
Notes to the Consolidated Financial Statements
March 31, 2006

The company is defendant to certain claims arising from the normal conduct of its business. The Company believes that the final resolution of these claims will not have a material adverse effect on its earnings or financial position. Subsequent to March 31, 2006 there has been a proposed change to the income tax legislation that would likely have an impact on the consolidated financial statements. The Company is currently evaluating the impact and alternatives to reduce it.

The Company from time to time offers indemnifications to third parties in the normal course of its business, in connection with business or asset acquisitions or dispositions. These indemnification provisions may be in connection with breach of representations and warranties and for future claims for certain liabilities, including liabilities related to tax and environmental matters. The terms of these indemnification provisions vary in duration. At March 31, 2006, given that the nature and amount of such indemnifications depend on future events, the Company is unable to reasonably estimate its maximum potential liability under these agreements. The Company has not made any significant payments in the past, and as at March 31, 2006 and 2005, had not recorded a liability associated with these indemnifications.

Source: Saputo's annual report, 2006, p. 55

Instructions

(a) Why would Saputo Inc. disclose information about these legal disputes in the notes to the financial statements instead of accruing these as liabilities in its accounting records?
(b) Where should Saputo Inc. record the legal costs incurred to date on the disputes (i.e., the costs before going to trial)?
(c) Why would Saputo Inc. disclose the proposed change to the income tax legislation?

Critical Thinking

Collaborative Learning Activity

Note to instructors: Additional instructions and material for this group activity can be found on the Instructor Resource Site.

BYP10–3 In this group activity, you will work in pairs to review the accounting for notes payable and its relationship to notes receivable (Chapter 8). On September 30, 2007, a borrower signs a 6-month, 5.5% note payable in exchange for $10,000 cash. Interest is payable at maturity. Both the borrower and lender have a December 31 year end and adjustments are made only annually.

Instructions

(a) In your pair, decide who will play the roles of lender and borrower.
(b) Based on your role, record the journal entries for:
    1. issue of the note
    2. year-end adjustments
    3. maturity of the note
(c) Compare your answer to that of your partner. If they are different, explain how you decided on your journal entries.
(d) You may be asked by your instructor to write a short quiz on this topic.

Study Aids:
Working in Groups

Communication Activity

Study Aids:
Writing Handbook

BYP10–4 The Show Time movie theatre sells thousands of gift certificates every year. The certificates can be redeemed at any time since they have no expiry date. Some of them may never be redeemed (because they are lost or forgotten, for example). The owner of the theatre has raised some questions about the accounting for these gift certificates.

Instructions

Write a memo to answer the following questions from the owner:

(a) Why is a liability recorded when these certificates are sold? After all, they bring customers into the theatre, where they spend money on snacks and drinks, etc. Why should something which helps generate additional revenue be treated as a liability?

(b) How should the gift certificates which are never redeemed be treated? At some point in the future, can the liability related to them be eliminated? If so, what type of journal entry would be made?

Ethics Case

Study Aids:
Ethics in Accounting

BYP10–5 Nice Nuke Company, which owns and operates a nuclear plant, recently received notice from the provincial government that it has to find a new disposal site for its radioactive waste. The company was also told that it is responsible for the environmental cleanup of the old site. The vice-president of engineering and the vice-president of finance meet to discuss the situation. The engineer says that it could take many years to clean up the site and that the cost could be considerable—a minimum of $50 million and perhaps as much as $100 million.

The vice-president of finance says that there is no way that the company can afford to record this liability. He says he is not even sure that he wants to disclose the potential liability, because of how this could affect the company's share price.

Instructions

(a) Who are the stakeholders in this situation?

(b) What are the alternative reporting options that the company can use?

(c) What is the likely impact of each alternative on the company's financial position?

(d) Is there anything unethical in what the vice-president of finance suggests doing about this potential liability?

(e) What do you recommend the company do?

ANSWERS TO CHAPTER QUESTIONS

Answers to Accounting in Action Insight Questions

Across the Organization Insight, p. 524

Q: Why is it important for a company to offer its employees a meaningful benefit plan? What can a company do to avoid paying unreasonable costs?

A: Companies need to ensure that they encourage employee health and well-being if they want to have a safe, healthy, and productive workforce. They can keep the costs reasonable by identifying and controlling the main reasons for the increases in benefit plan costs and using the latest measures to control these costs. In addition, companies may find it helpful to become partners with others, including their employees, in order to make benefit and wellness programs more efficient.

Business Insight, p. 529

Q: How should Canadian Tire account for issuing and redeeming its Canadian Tire money at the point of sale?

A: At the point of sale when the money is issued to its customers, Canadian Tire should debit a contra revenue account, such as Sales Discount for CTM Issued, and credit a liability account, such as CTM Liability. If a customer also redeems previously acquired CTM to pay for part (or all) of a purchase, Canadian Tire should do the following: (1) debit the CTM liability account for the CTM redeemed; (2) debit Cash for the rest of the purchase cost; and (3) credit Sales for the total purchase amount.

Business Insight, p. 531

Q: Environmental contingencies are generally considered to be harder to estimate than contingencies from lawsuits. What might be the reason for this difference?

A: The requirement to account for environmental contingencies is relatively new compared to the requirement to account for contingencies from lawsuits. Although it is difficult to predict if the company will win or lose a lawsuit and what type of settlement may be involved, there is a vast history of case law that can be used to help a company form an opinion. Environmental regulations, in contrast, are still evolving and there is often no system (e.g., regulatory compliance audits, environmental site assessment data, etc.) that would help a company estimate the possible cost, or even the existence, of environmental contingencies for many years.

Answer to Forzani Review It Question 2, p. 534

The Forzani Group reports only two current liabilities: (1) accounts payable and accrued liabilities and (2) the current portion of long-term debt. These two liabilities are listed in order of size. They may also be listed in order of maturity but we don't have enough information to determine this.

Answers to Self-Study Questions

1. c   2. c   3. a   4. b   5. c   6. a   7. a   8. b   9. d   *10. b

Remember to go back to the Navigator Box at the beginning of the chapter to check off your completed work.

appendix A
Specimen Financial Statements:

The Forzani Group Ltd.

In this appendix we illustrate current financial reporting with a comprehensive set of corporate financial statements that are prepared in accordance with generally accepted accounting principles. We are grateful for permission to use the actual financial statements of The Forzani Group Ltd.—Canada's largest sporting goods retailer.

Forzani's financial statement package features a balance sheet, combined statement of operations (or income statement as we know it) and retained earnings, cash flow statement, and notes to the financial statements. The financial statements are preceded by two reports: a statement of management's responsibilities for financial reporting and the auditors' report.

We encourage students to use these financial statements in conjunction with relevant material in the textbook. As well, these statements can be used to solve the Review It questions in the Before You Go On section within the chapter and the Financial Reporting Problem in the Broadening Your Perspective section of the end-of-chapter material.

Annual reports, including the financial statements, are reviewed in detail on the companion website to this textbook.

Annual Report
Walkthrough

THE FORZANI GROUP LTD.

MANAGEMENT'S RESPONSIBILITIES FOR FINANCIAL REPORTING

The Annual Report, including the consolidated financial statements, is the responsibility of the management of the Company. The consolidated financial statements were prepared by management in accordance with generally accepted accounting principles. The significant accounting policies used are described in Note 2 to the consolidated financial statements. The integrity of the information presented in the financial statements, including estimates and judgments relating to matters not concluded by year-end, is the responsibility of management. Financial information presented elsewhere in this Annual Report has been prepared by management and is consistent with the information in the consolidated financial statements.

Management is responsible for the development and maintenance of systems of internal accounting and administrative controls. Such systems are designed to provide reasonable assurance that the financial information is accurate, relevant and reliable, and that the Company's assets are appropriately accounted for and adequately safeguarded. The Board of Directors is responsible for ensuring that management fulfills its responsibilities for final approval of the annual consolidated financial statements. The Board appoints an Audit Committee consisting of three directors, none of whom is an officer or employee of the Company or its subsidiaries. The Audit Committee meets at least four times each year to discharge its responsibilities under a written mandate from the Board of Directors. The Audit Committee meets with management and with the independent auditors to satisfy itself that they are properly discharging their responsibilities, reviews the consolidated financial statements and the Auditors' Report, and examines other auditing, accounting and financial reporting matters. The consolidated financial statements have been reviewed by the Audit Committee and approved by the Board of Directors of The Forzani Group Ltd. The consolidated financial statements have been examined by the shareholders' auditors, Ernst & Young, LLP, Chartered Accountants. The Auditors' Report outlines the nature of their examination and their opinion on the consolidated financial statements of the Company. The independent auditors have full and unrestricted access to the Audit Committee, with and without management present.

Bob Sartor
Chief Executive Officer

Richard Burnet, CA
Vice-President & Chief Financial Officer

F2006 ANNUAL REPORT

AUDITORS' REPORT

To the Shareholders of
The Forzani Group Ltd.

We have audited the consolidated balance sheet of The Forzani Group Ltd. as at January 29, 2006 and the consolidated statements of operations and retained earnings and cash flows for the 52 weeks then ended. These financial statements are the responsibility of the Company's management. Our responsibility is to express an opinion on these financial statements based on our audit.

We conducted our audit in accordance with Canadian generally accepted auditing standards. Those standards require that we plan and perform an audit to obtain reasonable assurance whether the financial statements are free of material misstatement. An audit includes examining, on a test basis, evidence supporting the amounts and disclosures in the financial statements. An audit also includes assessing the accounting principles used and significant estimates made by management, as well as evaluating the overall financial statement presentation.

In our opinion, these consolidated financial statements present fairly, in all material respects, the financial position of the Company as at January 29, 2006 and the results of its operations and its cash flows for the 52 weeks then ended in accordance with Canadian generally accepted accounting principles.

The consolidated balance sheet as at January 30, 2005 and the consolidated statements of operations and retained earnings and cash flows for the 52 weeks then ended were audited by other auditors who expressed an opinion without reservation on those statements in their report dated March 21, 2005.

Calgary, Canada
March 23, 2006

Ernst & Young LLP

Ernst & Young LLP
Chartered Accountants

THE FORZANI GROUP LTD.

THE FORZANI GROUP LTD.
Consolidated Balance Sheets
(in thousands)

As at	January 29, 2006	January 30, 2005
ASSETS (note 6)		
Current		
Cash	$ 19,266	$ 26,018
Accounts receivable	68,927	58,576
Inventory	278,002	278,631
Prepaid expenses	2,647	3,022
	368,842	366,247
Capital assets (note 3)	193,594	179,702
Goodwill and other intangibles (note 4)	75,805	52,790
Other assets (note 5)	10,080	9,415
Future income tax asset (note 9)	4,885	-
	$ 653,206	$ 608,154
LIABILITIES		
Current		
Accounts payable and accrued liabilities	$ 244,293	$ 238,239
Current portion of long-term debt (note 6)	5,135	1,580
	249,428	239,819
Long-term debt (note 6)	58,805	40,278
Deferred lease inducements	62,883	62,613
Deferred rent liability	3,810	2,213
Future income tax liability (note 9)	-	384
	374,926	345,307
SHAREHOLDERS' EQUITY		
Share capital (note 8)	138,131	137,811
Contributed surplus	4,271	2,915
Retained earnings	135,878	122,121
	278,280	262,847
	$ 653,206	$ 608,154

See accompanying notes to the consolidated financial statements.

Approved on behalf of the Board:

Roman Doroniuk, CA

John M. Forzani

[38]

THE FORZANI GROUP LTD.
Consolidated Statements of Operations and Retained Earnings
(in thousands, except share data)

	For the 52 weeks ended January 29, 2006	For the 52 weeks ended January 30, 2005
Revenue		
Retail	$ 856,149	$718,820
Wholesale	273,255	266,234
	1,129,404	985,054
Cost of sales	746,313	651,158
Gross margin	383,091	333,896
Operating and administrative expenses		
Store operating	225,218	190,891
General and administrative	88,720	66,536
	313,938	257,427
Operating earnings before undernoted items	69,153	76,469
Amortization	41,343	35,885
Interest	6,145	4,447
Loss on write-down of investment (note 14)	-	2,208
	47,488	42,540
Earnings before income taxes	21,665	33,929
Provision for income taxes (note 9)		
Current	8,784	10,207
Future	(876)	2,177
	7,908	12,384
Net earnings	13,757	21,545
Retained earnings, opening	122,121	101,528
Adjustment arising from normal course issuer bid (note 8(b))	-	(952)
Retained earnings, closing	$ 135,878	$ 122,121
Earnings per share (note 8(c))	$ 0.42	$ 0.66
Diluted earnings per share (note 8(c))	$ 0.42	$ 0.66

See accompanying notes to the consolidated financial statements.

THE FORZANI GROUP LTD.

THE FORZANI GROUP LTD.
Consolidated Statements of Cash Flows
(in thousands)

	For the 52 weeks ended January 29, 2006	For the 52 weeks ended January 30, 2005
Cash provided by (used in) operating activities		
Net earnings	$ 13,757	$ 21,545
Items not involving cash		
Amortization	41,343	35,885
Amortization of deferred finance charges	637	828
Amortization of deferred lease inducements	(10,661)	(10,459)
Rent expense (note 7)	2,281	4,565
Stock-based compensation (note 8(d))	1,356	27
Write-down of investment and other assets	-	2,213
Future income tax expense	(876)	2,177
	47,837	56,781
Changes in non-cash elements of working capital (note 7)	(1,979)	(6,545)
	45,858	50,236
Cash provided by (used in) financing activities		
Net proceeds from issuance of share capital	320	967
Increase in long-term debt	23,573	3,563
Decrease in revolving credit facility	-	-
Debt assumed on acquisition (note 15(c))	(17,922)	-
Proceeds from deferred lease inducements	9,368	13,402
	15,339	17,932
Changes in non-cash elements of financing activities (note 7)	(2,450)	(4,375)
	12,889	13,557
Cash provided by (used in) investing activities		
Net addition of capital assets	(50,837)	(45,726)
Net addition of other assets	(3,751)	(7,112)
Acquisition of wholly-owned subsidiary (note 15)	(12,428)	(9,589)
	(67,016)	(62,427)
Changes in non-cash elements of investing activities (note 7)	1,517	1,337
	(65,499)	(61,090)
Increase (decrease) in cash	(6,752)	2,703
Net cash position, opening	26,018	23,315
Net cash position, closing	$ 19,266	$ 26,018

See accompanying notes to the consolidated financial statements.

The Forzani Group Ltd.
Notes to Consolidated Financial Statements
(Tabular amounts in thousands)

1. Nature of Operations

The Forzani Group Ltd. "FGL" or "the Company" is Canada's largest sporting goods retailer. FGL currently operates 260 corporate stores under the banners: Sport Chek, Sport Mart, Coast Mountain Sports and National Sports. The Company is also the franchisor/licensor of 204 stores under the banners: Sports Experts, Intersport, RnR, Econosports, Atmosphere, Tech Shop/Pegasus, Nevada Bob's Golf, and Hockey Experts. FGL operates four websites, dedicated to the Canadian online sporting goods market, www.sportchek.ca, www.sportmart.ca, www.sportsexperts.ca and www.nationalsports.com.

2. Significant Accounting Policies

The consolidated financial statements have been prepared by management in accordance with Canadian generally accepted accounting principles ("GAAP"). The financial statements have, in management's opinion, been prepared within reasonable limits of materiality and within the framework of the accounting policies summarized below:

(a) Organization

The consolidated financial statements include the accounts of The Forzani Group Ltd. and its subsidiaries, all of which are wholly owned.

(b) Inventory

Inventory is valued at the lower of laid-down cost and net realizable value. Laid-down cost is determined using the weighted average cost method and includes invoice cost, duties, freight, and distribution costs. Net realizable value is defined as the expected selling price.

Volume rebates and other supplier discounts are included in income when earned. Volume rebates are accounted for as a reduction of the cost of the related inventory and are "earned" when the inventory is sold. All other rebates and discounts are "earned" when the related expense is incurred.

(c) Capital assets

Capital assets are recorded at cost and are amortized using the following methods and rates:

Building	- 4% declining-balance basis
Building on leased land	- straight-line basis over the lesser of the length of the lease and estimated useful life of the building, not exceeding 20 years
Furniture, fixtures, equipment and automotive	- straight-line basis over 3-5 years
Leasehold improvements	- straight-line basis over the lesser of the length of the lease and estimated useful life of the improvements, not exceeding 10 years

The carrying value of long-lived assets are reviewed at least annually or whenever events indicate a potential impairment has occurred. An impairment loss is recorded when a long-lived asset's carrying value exceeds the sum of the undiscounted cash flows expected from its use and eventual disposition. The impairment loss is measured as the amount by which the carrying value exceeds its fair value.

(d) Variable Interest Entities

Variable interest entities ("VIE") are consolidated by the Company if and when the Company is the primary beneficiary of the VIE, as described in CICA Accounting Guideline 15 "Consolidation of Variable Interest Entities".

(e) Goodwill and other intangibles

Goodwill represents the excess of the purchase price of entities acquired over the fair market value of the identifiable net assets acquired.

Goodwill and other intangible assets with indefinite lives are not amortized, but tested for impairment at year end and, if required, asset values reduced accordingly. The method used to assess impairment is a review of the fair value of the asset based on its earnings and a market earnings multiple.

Non-competition agreement costs are amortized, on a straight-line basis, over the life of the agreements, not exceeding five years.

THE FORZANI GROUP LTD.

The Forzani Group Ltd.
Notes to Consolidated Financial Statements
(Tabular amounts in thousands)

(f) Other assets

Other assets include deferred financing charges, system and interactive development costs, long-term receivables and a long-term investment in a trademark licensing company.

Financing charges represent fees incurred in establishing and renegotiating the Company's credit facilities. These costs are being amortized over the term of the facilities.

System development costs relate to the implementation of computer software. Upon activation, costs are amortized over the estimated useful lives of the systems (3 – 8 years).

Interactive development costs relate to the development of the sportchek.ca interactive web site, designed as a part of the Company's multi-channel retailing and branding strategy. These costs are being amortized over five years following the commencement of the web site's operations in June, 2001.

Long-term receivables are carried at cost less a valuation allowance, if applicable.

Long-term investments are carried at cost and periodically reviewed for impairment based on the market value of the shares.

(g) Deferred lease inducements and property leases

Deferred lease inducements represent cash and non-cash benefits that the Company has received from landlords pursuant to store lease agreements. These lease inducements are amortized against rent expense over the term of the lease.

The Company capitalizes any rent expense during the fixturing period as a cost of leasehold improvements. Such expense is recognized on a straight-line basis over the life of the lease.

(h) Revenue recognition

Revenue includes sales to customers through corporate stores operated by the Company and sales to, and service fees from, franchise stores and others. Sales to customers through corporate stores operated by the Company are recognized at the point of sale, net of an estimated allowance for sales returns. Sales of merchandise to franchise stores and others are recognized at the time of shipment. Royalties and administration fees are recognized when earned, in accordance with the terms of the franchise/license agreements.

(i) Store opening expenses

Operating costs incurred prior to the opening of new stores, other than rent incurred during the fixturing period, are expensed as incurred.

(j) Fiscal year

The Company's fiscal year follows a retail calendar. The fiscal years for the consolidated financial statements presented are the 52-week periods ended January 29, 2006 and January 30, 2005.

(k) Foreign currency translation

Foreign currency accounts are translated to Canadian dollars. At the transaction date, each asset, liability, revenue or expense is translated into Canadian dollars using the exchange rate in effect at that date. At the year-end date, monetary assets and liabilities are translated into Canadian dollars using the exchange rate in effect at that date, or by rates fixed by forward exchange contracts, and the resulting foreign exchange gains and losses are included in income in the current period, to the extent that the amount is not hedged.

(l) Financial instruments

Accounts receivable, accounts payable and accrued liabilities, long-term debt and derivative transactions, constitute financial instruments. In the normal course of business the Company also enters into leases in respect of real estate and certain point-of-sale equipment.

The Company enters into forward foreign currency contracts and options, with financial institutions, as hedges of other financial transactions and not for speculative purposes. The Company's policies do not allow leveraged transactions and are designed to minimize foreign currency risk. The Company's policies require that all hedges be linked with specific liabilities on the balance sheet and be formally assessed, both at inception, and on an ongoing basis, as to their effectiveness in offsetting changes in the fair values of the hedged liabilities.

(m) Measurement uncertainty

The preparation of the financial statements, in conformity with GAAP, requires management to make estimates and assumptions that affect the reported amounts of assets and liabilities and disclosures of contingent assets and liabilities at the date of the consolidated financial statements and the reported amounts of revenue and expenses during the reporting period. Actual results could differ from these estimates. Estimates are used when accounting for items such as product warranties, inventory provisions, amortization, uncollectible receivables and the liability for the Company's loyalty program.

F2006 ANNUAL REPORT

The Forzani Group Ltd.
Notes to Consolidated Financial Statements
(Tabular amounts in thousands)

(n) Stock-based compensation

The Company accounts for stock-based compensation using the fair value method. The fair value of the options granted are estimated at the date of grant using the Black-Scholes valuation model and recognized as an expense over the option-vesting period.

(o) Income taxes

The Company follows the liability method under which future income tax assets and obligations are determined based on differences between the financial reporting and tax basis of assets and liabilities, measured using tax rates substantively enacted at the balance sheet date.

Changes in tax rates are reflected in the consolidated statement of operations in the period in which they are substantively enacted.

(p) Asset retirement obligations

The Company recognizes asset retirement obligations in the period in which a reasonable estimate of the fair value can be determined. The liability is measured at fair value and is adjusted to its present value in subsequent periods through accretion expense. The associated asset retirement costs are capitalized as part of the carrying value of the related asset and amortized over its useful life.

(q) Comparative figures

Certain 2005 comparative figures have been reclassified to conform with the presentation adopted for the current year ending January 29, 2006.

3. Capital Assets

| | | 2006 | | | 2005 | |
	Cost	Accumulated Amortization	Net Book Value	Cost	Accumulated Amortization	Net Book Value
Land	$ 3,173	$ -	$ 3,173	$ 3,173	$ -	$ 3,173
Buildings	20,007	3,197	16,810	17,637	2,498	15,139
Building on leased land	4,564	2,330	2,234	3,159	1,898	1,261
Furniture, fixtures, equipment and automotive	176,670	104,254	72,416	145,838	84,042	61,796
Leasehold improvements	205,519	106,595	98,924	187,141	89,177	97,964
Construction in progress	37	-	37	369	-	369
	$ 409,970	$ 216,376	$193,594	$ 357,317	$ 177,615	$179,702

4. Goodwill and Other Intangibles

| | | 2006 | | | 2005 | |
	Cost	Accumulated Amortization	Net Book Value	Cost	Accumulated Amortization	Net Book Value
Goodwill	$ 47,818	$ 1,187	$46,631	$ 25,243	$ 1,187	$ 24,056
Trademarks/Tradenames	28,693	626	28,067	25,715	561	25,154
Non-competition agreements	4,000	2,893	1,107	5,680	2,100	3,580
	$ 80,511	$ 4,706	$75,805	$ 56,638	$ 3,848	$ 52,790

THE FORZANI GROUP LTD.

The Forzani Group Ltd.
Notes to Consolidated Financial Statements
(Tabular amounts in thousands)

5. Other Assets

| | | 2006 | | | 2005 | |
	Cost	Accumulated Amortization	Net Book Value	Cost	Accumulated Amortization	Net Book Value
Interactive development	$ 2,649	$ 2,649	$ -	$ 2,649	$ 2,133	$ 516
Deferred financing charges	1,660	286	1,374	3,598	2,284	1,314
System development	1,569	1,407	162	1,569	1,277	292
Other deferred charges	3,030	853	2,177	1,808	704	1,104
	$ 8,908	$ 5,195	$ 3,713	$ 9,624	$ 6,398	$ 3,226

	2006	2005
Depreciable other assets net book value (see above)	$ 3,713	$ 3,226
Long-term receivables (at interest rates of prime plus 1% and expiring between September 2009 and July 2010)	3,279	2,973
Investment in a trademark licensing company	3,088	3,088
Other	-	128
	$ 10,080	$ 9,415

6. Long-term Debt

	2006	2005
G.E. term loan	$ 50,000	$ 25,000
Vendor take-back, unsecured with interest rate of prime plus 1% due August 1, 2006	4,606	4,428
Mortgages, with monthly blended payments of $79,625, including interest at rates from approximately 4.9% to 6.2%, compounded semi-annually, secured by land and buildings, expiring between September 2006 and October 2009 (each with a fifteen year amortization).	9,078	9,658
Amounts due under non-competition agreements, (payment negotiated and retired in 2006)	-	2,680
Asset retirement obligation	97	92
Other	159	-
	63,940	41,858
Less current portion	5,135	1,580
	$ 58,805	$ 40,278

Principal payments on the above, due in the next five years, are as follows:

2007	$ 3,810
2008	$ 523
2009	$ 50,519
2010	$ 529
2011	$ 557

Effective June 30, 2005, the Company extended its existing credit agreement to June 30, 2008. The amended and restated agreement with GE Canada Finance Holding Company, National Bank of Canada and Royal Bank of Canada increased the $175 million credit facility to $235 million, comprised of a $185 million revolving loan (2005 - $150 million), and a $50 million term loan (2005 - $25 million) repayable at maturity. Under the terms of the credit agreement, the interest rate payable on both the revolving and term loans is based on the Company's financial performance as determined by its interest coverage ratio. As at January 29, 2006, the average interest rate paid was 4.80% (January 30, 2005 - 4.05%). The facility is collateralized by general security agreements against all existing and future acquired assets of the Company. As at January 29, 2006, the Company is in compliance with all covenants.

F2006 ANNUAL REPORT

The Forzani Group Ltd.
Notes to Consolidated Financial Statements
(Tabular amounts in thousands)

Based on estimated interest rates currently available to the Company for mortgages with similar terms and maturities, the fair value of the mortgages at January 29, 2006 amounted to approximately $8,553,000 (2005 - $9,658,000). Interest costs incurred for the 52-week period ended January 29, 2006 on long-term debt amounted to $2,318,000 (2005 - $1,358,000). The fair value of the other long-term debt components above approximates book value given their short terms to maturity and floating interest rates.

7. Supplementary Cash Flow Information

	2006	2005
Rent expense		
Straight-line rent expense	$ 1,484	$ 2,213
Non-cash free rent	797	2,352
	$ 2,281	$ 4,565
Changes in non-cash elements of working capital		
Accounts receivable	$ (10,038)	$ (22,257)
Inventory	24,544	(13,607)
Prepaid and other expenses	1,140	8,270
Accounts payable and accrued liabilities	(17,761)	20,363
Non-cash free rent	136	686
	$ (1,979)	$ (6,545)
Changes in non-cash elements of financing activities		
Non-cash lease inducements	$ (2,450)	$ (4,375)
Changes in non-cash elements of investing activities		
Non-cash capital asset additions	$ 1,517	$ 1,337
Cash interest paid	$ 6,183	$ 4,685
Cash taxes paid	$ 7,285	$ 20,613

8. Share Capital

(a) Authorized

An unlimited number of Class A shares (no par value)
An unlimited number of Preferred shares, issuable in series

(b) Issued
    Class A shares

	Number	Consideration
Balance, February 1, 2004	31,791	$ 128,880
Shares issued upon employees exercising stock options	634	2,477
Shares issued to acquire businesses (note 15)	585	7,012
Shares redeemed pursuant to normal course issuer bid	(135)	(558)
Balance, January 30, 2005	32,875	$ 137,811
Shares issued upon employees exercising stock options	47	320
Balance, January 29, 2006	32,922	$ 138,131

During 2005, 135,100 Class A shares were purchased pursuant to the Company's Normal Course Issuer Bid for a total expenditure of $1,510,000. The price in excess of carrying value was charged to retained earnings.

THE FORZANI GROUP LTD.

The Forzani Group Ltd.
Notes to Consolidated Financial Statements
(Tabular amounts in thousands)

(c)   Earnings Per Share

	2006	2005
Basic	$ 0.42	$ 0.66
Diluted	$ 0.42	$ 0.66

The Company uses the treasury stock method to calculate diluted earnings per share. Under the treasury stock method, the numerator remains unchanged from the basic earnings per share calculation, as the assumed exercise of the Company's stock options does not result in an adjustment to earnings. Diluted calculations assume that options under the stock option plan have been exercised at the later of the beginning of the year or date of issuance, and that the funds derived therefrom would have been used to repurchase shares at the average market value of the Company's stock, 2006 - $12.41 (2005 - $12.83). Anti-dilutive options, 2006 - 749,000 (2005 – 1,740,000) are excluded from the effect of dilutive securities. The reconciliation of the denominator in calculating diluted earnings per share is as follows:

	2006	2005
Weighted average number of class A shares outstanding (basic)	32,899	32,572
Effect of dilutive options	248	155
Weighted average number of common shares outstanding (diluted)	33,147	32,727

(d)   Stock Option Plan

The Company has granted stock options to directors, officers and employees to purchase Class A shares at prices between $9.39 and $19.19 per share. These options expire on dates between August 22, 2006 and December 2, 2010.

The Company has two stock option plans. The first plan has the following general terms: options vest over a period ranging from 2 to 5 years and the maximum term of the options granted is 5 years. During the year, 250,000 options (2005 – 205,000 options) were issued under this plan. The related stock based compensation was $1,356,000 (2005 - $27,000). The second plan has the following general terms: options vest over a period ranging from 3 to 5 years dependent on the Company achieving certain performance targets, and the maximum term of the options granted is 5 years. During the year, 525,000 options (2005 – 950,000 options) were issued under this plan. There was no related stock based compensation in either 2006 or 2005 as the Company has deemed the targets may not be met. The total number of shares authorized for option grants under both option plans is 3,262,833.

During the 52-weeks ended January 29, 2006, the following options were granted:

Options issued	Weighted average fair value per option	Weighted average risk-free rate	Weighted average expected option life	Weighted average expected volatility	Weighted average expected dividend yield
775,000	$5.52	3.64%	4.08 years	46.55%	0.00%

A summary of the status of the Company's stock option plans as of January 29, 2006 and January 30, 2005, and any changes during the year ending on those dates is presented below:

Stock Options	2006		2005	
	Options	Weighted Average Exercise Price	Options	Weighted Average Exercise Price
Outstanding, beginning of year	2,159	$ 12.13	2,809	$ 13.34
Granted	775	$ 12.15	1,156	$ 10.71
Exercised	47	$ 6.85	634	$ 3.91
Forfeited	100	$ 19.19	1,172	$ 18.12
Outstanding, end of year	2,787	$ 11.88	2,159	$ 12.13
Options exercisable at year end	755		742	

The Forzani Group Ltd.
Notes to Consolidated Financial Statements
(Tabular amounts in thousands)

The following table summarizes information about stock options outstanding at January 29, 2006:

Range of Exercise Prices	Number Outstanding	Options Outstanding Weighted Average Remaining Contractual Life	Weighted Average Exercise Price	Options Exercisable Number of Shares Exercisable	Weighted Average Exercise Price
$9.39 - $10.25	1,160	3.91	$10.24	20	$ 9.39
$11.36 - $12.66	982	2.58	$11.78	497	$11.36
$13.05 - $19.19	645	2.69	$15.01	238	$16.68
	2,787	3.16	$11.88	755	$12.99

9. Income Taxes

The components of the future income tax liability (asset) amounts as at January 29, 2006 and January 30, 2005, are as follows:

	2006	2005
Current assets	$ 3,353	$ 4,342
Capital and other assets	15,842	19,141
Tax benefit of share issuance and financing costs	(166)	(314)
Deferred lease inducements	(22,122)	(22,785)
Non-capital loss carry forward	(1,792)	-
Future income tax liability (asset)	$ (4,885)	$ 384

A reconciliation of income taxes, at the combined statutory federal and provincial tax rate to the actual income tax rate, is as follows:

	2006		2005	
Federal and provincial income taxes	$8,044	37.1%	$11,743	34.6%
Increase (decrease) resulting from:				
Effect of substantively enacted tax rate changes	(68)	(0.3%)	663	2.0%
Other, net	(68)	(0.3%)	(22)	(0.1%)
Provision for income taxes	$7,908	36.5%	$12,384	36.5%

Federal Part I.3 tax and provincial capital tax expense in the amount of $952,000 (2005 - $1,053,000) is included in operating expenses.

The Company has non-capital losses being carried forward of $1,489,000 which expire in 2011 and $2,551,000 which expire in 2015.

10. Commitments

(a) The Company is committed, at January 29, 2006 to minimum payments under long-term real property and data processing hardware and software equipment leases, for the next five years, as follows:

	Gross
2007	$ 75,904
2008	$ 73,146
2009	$ 70,366
2010	$ 63,921
2011	$ 54,517

In addition, the Company may be obligated to pay percentage rent under certain of the leases.

(b) As at January 29, 2006, the Company has open letters of credit for purchases of inventory of approximately $4,579,000 (2005 - $3,108,000).

THE FORZANI GROUP LTD.

11. Employee Benefit Plans

The Company has a defined contribution plan and a deferred profit sharing plan. Deferred profit sharing contributions are paid to a Trustee for the purchase of shares of the Company and are distributed to participating employees on a predetermined basis, upon retirement from the Company. Contributions are subject to board approval and recognized as an expense when incurred. Defined contributions are paid to employee retirement savings plans and are expensed when incurred.

The Company has accrued $100,000 (2005 - $36,000) to the employee deferred profit sharing plan and $807,000 (2005 - $666,000) to the defined contribution plan.

12. Contingencies and Guarantees

In the normal course of business, the Company enters into numerous agreements that may contain features that meet the Accounting Guideline ("AG")14 definition of a guarantee. AG-14 defines a guarantee to be a contract (including an indemnity) that contingently requires the Company to make payments to the guaranteed party based on (i) changes in an underlying interest rate, foreign exchange rate, equity or commodity instrument, index or other variable, that is related to an asset, a liability or an equity security of the counterparty, (ii) failure of another party to perform under an obligating agreement or (iii) failure of a third party to pay its indebtedness when due.

The Company has provided the following guarantees to third parties:

(a) The Company has provided guarantees to certain franchisees' banks pursuant to which it has agreed to buy back inventory from the franchisee in the event that the bank realizes on the related security. The Company has provided securitization guarantees for certain franchisees to repay equity loans in the event of franchisee default. The terms of the guarantees range from less than a year to the lifetime of the particular underlying franchise agreement, with an average guarantee term of 5 years. Should a franchisee default on its bank loan, the Company would be required to purchase between 50% – 100%, with a weighted average of 65%, of the franchisee's inventory up to the value of the franchisee's bank indebtedness. As at January 29, 2006, the Company's maximum exposure is $32,034,000 (2005 - $31,506,000). Should the Company be required to purchase the inventory, it is expected that the full value of the inventory would be recovered. Historically, the Company has not had to repurchase significant inventory from franchisees pursuant to these guarantees. The Company has not recognized the guarantee in its financial statements.

(b) In the ordinary course of business, the Company has agreed to indemnify its lenders under its credit facilities against certain costs or losses resulting from changes in laws and regulations and from any legal action brought against the lenders related to the use, by the Company, of the loan proceeds, or to the lenders having extended credit thereunder. These indemnifications extend for the term of the credit facilities and do not provide any limit on the maximum potential liability. Historically, the Company has not made any indemnification payments under such agreements and no amount has been accrued in the financial statements with respect to these indemnification agreements.

(c) In the ordinary course of business, the Company has provided indemnification commitments to certain counterparties in matters such as real estate leasing transactions, securitization agreements, director and officer indemnification agreements and certain purchases of assets (not inventory in the normal course). These indemnification agreements generally require the Company to compensate the counterparties for costs or losses resulting from any legal action brought against the counterparties related to the actions of the Company or any of the obligors under any of the aforementioned matters or failure of the obligors under any of the aforementioned matters to fulfill contractual obligations thereunder. The terms of these indemnification agreements will vary based on the contract and generally do not provide any limit on the maximum potential liability. Historically, the Company has not made any payments under such indemnifications and no amount has been accrued in the financial statements with respect to these indemnification commitments.

(d) Claims and suits have been brought against the Company in the ordinary course of business. In the opinion of management, all such claims and suits are adequately covered by insurance, or if not so covered, the results are not expected to materially affect the Company's financial position.

13. Financial Instruments

The Company is exposed to credit risk on its accounts receivable from franchisees. The accounts receivable are net of applicable allowance for doubtful accounts, which are established based on the specific credit risks associated with individual franchisees and other relevant information. Concentration of credit risk with respect to receivables is limited, due to the large number of franchisees.

F2006 ANNUAL REPORT

The Forzani Group Ltd.
Notes to Consolidated Financial Statements
(Tabular amounts in thousands)

The Company purchases a portion of its inventory from foreign vendors with payment terms in foreign currencies. To manage the foreign exchange risk associated with these purchases, the Company hedges its exposure to foreign currency by purchasing foreign exchange options and forward contracts to fix exchange rates and protect planned margins. The Company has the following derivative instruments outstanding at January 29, 2006 and January 30, 2005:

	Notional amounts maturing in		2006	2005
	Less than 1 year	Over 1 year	Total	Total
Foreign exchange contracts ($CAD)				
United States dollar contracts	$2,386	-	$2,386	$2,751
EURO contracts	-	-	-	507
Total	$2,386	-	$2,386	$3,258

The Company has included $359,000 (2005 - $320,000) of exchange losses in general and administrative expenses. No other amounts have been recognized in the consolidated financial statements. As at January 29, 2006, these instruments had $37,000 of unrealized losses (2005 - $38,000 unrealized gains).

The Company is exposed to interest rate risk on its credit facility and the term loan. Interest rate risk reflects the sensitivity of the Company's financial condition to movements in interest rates. For fiscal year 2006, a 1% change in interest rates would change interest expense by $1,449,000 (2005 - $1,108,000).

14. Write-down of Investment

During the year ended January 30, 2005, the Company reviewed the carrying value of its investment in a wholesale distribution company. As a result of this review, the Company determined that a decline in the value of this investment that was other than temporary had occurred and recorded a write-down in the amount of $2,207,952 to bring the carrying value of the investment to $26,000, this investment was subsequently disposed of in 2006.

15. Acquisitions

(a) Effective March 19, 2004, the Company acquired 100% of the outstanding shares of Gen-X Sports Inc. The acquisition was accounted for using the purchase method and accordingly the consolidated financial statements include the results of operations since the date of the acquisition.

The consideration for the transaction was $13,513,000 for all the outstanding Class A and Class B common shares. The purchase consideration consisted of $9,589,000 cash and the remainder in the form of a vendor take-back loan, payable over four years. The loan payments are in the form of 300,000 escrowed Company Class A shares distributed over the four-year period.

The assigned fair values of the underlying assets and liabilities acquired by the Company as at March 19, 2004, are summarized as follows:

Inventory	$ 6,208
Trademarks	3,280
Fixed assets	200
Goodwill	3,924
Total assets acquired	13,612
Current liabilities	(99)
Total liabilities acquired	(99)
Consideration	$13,513

(b) Effective December 17, 2004, the Company acquired a 14.29% interest in a trademark licensing company in exchange for 285,160 Class A shares of the Company, with a fair market value of $3,088,283. This acquisition was accounted for using the cost method and the investment is recorded in Other assets.

(c) Effective January 31, 2005, the Company acquired 100% of the outstanding shares of National Gym Clothing Ltd. The acquisition was accounted for using the purchase method and accordingly the consolidated financial statements include the results of operations since the date of the acquisition.

THE FORZANI GROUP LTD.

The consideration for the transaction was $13,026,000 in cash for all the outstanding common shares.

The assigned fair values of the underlying assets and liabilities acquired by the Company as at January 31, 2005, are summarized as follows:

Cash	$ 598
Accounts receivable	313
Inventory	23,915
Prepaid expenses	765
Trademarks	2,535
Fixed assets	2,261
Goodwill	21,848
Future income tax asset	4,393
Total assets acquired	**56,628**
Secured indebtedness	17,922
Accounts payable	23,815
Long-term debt	189
Deferred rent liability	113
Deferred lease inducements	1,563
Total liabilities acquired	**43,602**
Cash consideration	**$13,026**

16. Segmented Financial Information

The Company operates principally in two business segments: corporately-owned and operated retail stores and as a wholesale business selling to franchisees and others. Identifiable assets, depreciation and amortization and interest expense are not disclosed by segment as they are substantially retail in nature, with the exception of accounts receivable of $58.9 million (2005 - $48.1 million), capital assets of $16.8 million (2005 – $13.4 million) and goodwill/other assets of $8.1 million (2005 - $6.9 million) which are wholesale in nature.

In determining the reportable segments, the Company considered the distinct business models of the Retail and Wholesale operations, the division of responsibilities, and the reporting to the Board of Directors.

	2006	2005
Revenues:		
Retail	$ 856,149	$718,820
Wholesale	273,255	266,234
	1,129,404	985,054
Operating Profit:		
Retail	78,236	68,433
Wholesale	23,547	27,583
	101,783	96,016
Non-segment specific administrative expenses	32,630	19,547
Operating activities before under-noted items	69,153	76,469
Amortization	41,343	35,885
Interest expense	6,145	4,447
Loss on write-down of investments	-	2,208
	47,488	42,540
Earnings before income taxes	21,665	33,929
Income tax expense	7,908	12,384
Net earnings	$ 13,757	$ 21,545

F2006 ANNUAL REPORT

The Forzani Group Ltd.
Notes to Consolidated Financial Statements
(Tabular amounts in thousands)

---

17. Related Party Transactions

(a) An officer of the Company holds an interest in a franchise store operation. During the year, that franchise operation transacted business, in the normal course and at fair market value, with the Company, purchasing product in the amount of $5,608,000 (2005 - $5,492,000). At the end of the year, accounts receivable from the franchise operation were $888,000 (2005 – $993,000). During the year, that franchise operation opened a prototype store in Kirkland Quebec in which, in the normal course of opening prototype stores, the Company owns equipment and fixtures in the amount of $330,000.

(b) The Company has an interest in a trademark licensing company in which an employee, employed by a subsidiary, holds a partial interest. During the year, the Company, in the normal course of operations on similar terms and conditions to transactions entered into with unrelated parties, paid royalties of $346,000 (2005 – $303,000).

(c) During the year the company purchased real estate valued at $215,000 from an officer of the company in the normal course of operations and on similar terms and conditions to transactions entered into with unrelated parties.

(d) During the year the Company entered into a contract to obtain services and paid $44,000 (2005 - $nil) to a company owned by a director of the Company in the normal course of operations and on similar terms and conditions to transactions entered into with unrelated parties.

---

18. Variable Interest Entities

At January 29, 2006, the Company had a long-term receivable due from an entity which is considered a variable interest entity (VIE) under CICA Accounting Guideline 15. The entity operates several franchise stores. The long-term receivable has been outstanding since July 2003 and the Company has received guarantees for the full amount of the receivable from the shareholders of the entity. The Company has concluded that it is not the primary beneficiary of the VIE and that it is not required to consolidate this VIE in its consolidated financial statements. The Company has no exposure to loss related to the long-term receivable.

---

19. Subsequent Event

Effective January 31, 2006 the Company has acquired 100% of the outstanding common shares of Fitness Source Inc. for $6.5 million.

appendix B
Sales Taxes

All businesses operating in Canada need to understand how sales taxes apply to their particular business in their particular province or territory. Sales taxes may take the form of the **Goods and Services Tax (GST)**, **Provincial Sales Tax (PST)**, or **Harmonized Sales Tax (HST)**. GST is levied by the federal government. PST is levied by the provinces and territories, with the exception of Alberta, the Northwest Territories, Nunavut, and Yukon, where no provincial sales tax is charged. Nova Scotia, New Brunswick, and Newfoundland and Labrador have combined the GST and PST into one harmonized sales tax, known as the HST.

As an agent of the federal and provincial governments, a business is required to collect sales taxes on the sale of certain goods and services. In addition, businesses pay sales taxes on most disbursements. We will discuss the collection, payment, recording, and remittance of each of these types of sales taxes in the following sections.

Types of Sales Taxes

Goods and Services Tax

The GST is a federal sales tax on most goods and services provided in Canada. A business must register for the GST if it provides taxable goods or services in Canada and if it has revenues of more than $30,000 in any year. Businesses that have to, or decide to, voluntarily register for the GST are called registrants. Registrants can claim a credit—called an **input tax credit (ITC)**—to offset the GST they pay or owe on purchases of goods or services against the GST they collect or are owed. GST returns are submitted quarterly for most registrants (monthly for large registrants) to the Canada Revenue Agency (CRA). The taxes are payable to the Receiver General, who is the collection agent for the federal government.

The GST applies at a rate of 6% on most transactions. Transactions subject to GST are called **taxable supplies**. There are two other categories of goods and services with respect to the GST:

- zero-rated supplies, such as basic groceries and prescription drugs
- exempt supplies, such as educational services, health-care services, and financial services

No GST applies to zero-rated or exempt supplies. However, zero-rated suppliers can claim input tax credits.

Illustration B-1 provides the GST status of some typical goods and services.

Taxable Supplies	Zero-Rated Supplies	Exempt Supplies
Building materials	Prescription drugs	Used house
Ready-to-eat pizza	Uncooked pizza	Dental services
Two doughnuts	Six or more doughnuts	Insurance policy

The reason ready-to-eat pizza and two doughnuts have GST added to the purchase price is because they are considered convenience items and not basic groceries.

Provincial Sales Tax

Provincial sales taxes are charged on retail sales of certain goods and services. In the provinces charging sales tax, except Quebec and Prince Edward Island, this tax is applied to the selling price of the item before GST is applied. Similarly, GST is charged on the selling price of the item before PST is applied, thus avoiding GST being charged on PST. In Quebec and Prince Edward Island, however, the provincial sales tax is cascaded—that is, applied to the total of the selling price plus GST. Quebec's sales tax is also known as the QST (Quebec Sales Tax).

The following example shows the calculation of cascaded sales tax, using a taxable item sold in Quebec for $100:

Selling price	$100.00
GST ($100 × 6%)	6.00
QST [($100 + $6) × 7.5%]	7.95
Total	$113.95

Provincial sales taxes are remitted periodically to the Minister of Finance or Provincial Treasurer in each province.

PST rates vary by province and can change with each provincial budget. It is important to understand that the PST may not be applied at the same rate to all taxable goods and services. For example, in Ontario, the rates vary for insurance premiums and alcoholic beverages. Certain goods are exempt, such as children's clothing, textbooks, and residential rent, and may be purchased with no PST. Examples of exempt services that are not taxable include personal services such as dental and medical services. Because rates and exemptions vary by province, it is important, when starting a business, to check with provincial officials for details on how to calculate the provincial tax that must be applied to sales.

Harmonized Sales Tax

The provinces of Newfoundland and Labrador, Nova Scotia, and New Brunswick charge Harmonized Sales Tax, or HST. Instead of charging GST and PST separately, only the HST is charged at a combined rate of 14%. Similar to GST, HST returns are submitted quarterly for most registrants (monthly for large registrants) to the CRA. The federal government then gives the provincial portion of the tax to the province.

To summarize, four provinces—British Columbia, Manitoba, Ontario, and Saskatchewan—apply PST and GST to the selling price of a taxable good or service. Two provinces—Prince Edward Island and Quebec—apply PST to the total of the purchase price and the GST. Three provinces—New Brunswick, Newfoundland and Labrador, and Nova Scotia—charge a combined GST and PST (harmonized) rate of 14% on the selling price. Four provinces and territories do not charge PST—Alberta, the Northwest Territories, Nunavut, and Yukon. In addition to the different ways of applying sales taxes, the rates of sales tax differ in each province and territory, as shown on the following page:

Province/Territory	GST (HST) Rate	PST Rate	Combined Rate[1]
Alberta	6.0%	0.0%	6.0%
British Columbia	6.0%	7.0%	13.0%
Manitoba	6.0%	7.0%	13.0%
New Brunswick	14.0%	N/A	14.0%
Newfoundland and Labrador	14.0%	N/A	14.0%
Northwest Territories	6.0%	0.0%	6.0%
Nova Scotia	14.0%	N/A	14.0%
Nunavut	6.0%	0.0%	6.0%
Ontario	6.0%	8.0%	14.0%
Prince Edward Island	6.0%	10.0%	16.6%[2]
Quebec	6.0%	7.5%	13.95%[2]
Saskatchewan	6.0%	5.0%	11.0%
Yukon	6.0%	0.0%	6.0%

[1] All of these rates are in effect as of November 30, 2006 and are subject to change.
[2] In Prince Edward Island and Quebec only, the GST is included in the provincial sales tax base.

Sales Taxes Collected on Receipts

Sales taxes are collected by businesses from consumers on taxable goods and services. It is important to understand that sales taxes are not a source of revenue for a company. Sales taxes are collected by a company on behalf of the federal and provincial governments. Consequently, collected sales tax is a current liability to the company until remitted to the respective government at regular intervals.

Services

Now let's look at how service companies record sales taxes on the services they provide. Assume that a law firm bills a client for legal services. Some service providers, such as law firms, do not have to charge PST in some provinces. In these provinces, the law firm would only charge 6% GST on the legal services provided.

The following entry would be made to record the billing of a client for $500 of services provided by a law firm in Ontario on May 28. In Ontario, legal services are exempt from PST, so only 6% GST would be charged on these services.

May 28	Accounts Receivable	530	
	Legal Fees Earned		500
	GST Payable ($500 × 6%)		30
	To record revenue earned from legal fees.		

A	=	L	+	OE
+530		+30		+500

Cash flows: no effect

Note that the revenue recorded is $500, and not $530. The legal fees earned are exclusive of the GST amount collected, which is recorded as a current liability.

Assume instead that $250 of cleaning services were provided by a company in Saskatchewan for cash on July 24. These services are subject to both PST (5%) and GST (6%), and would be recorded as follows:

July 24	Cash	277.50	
	Cleaning Service Revenue		250.00
	PST Payable ($250 × 5%)		12.50
	GST Payable ($250 × 6%)		15.00
	To record cleaning service revenue.		

A	=	L	+	OE
+277.50		+12.50		+250
		+15.00		

↑ Cash flows: +277.50

If these same services were provided by a company in New Brunswick, where HST is 14%, the entry would be as follows:

A	=	L	+	OE
+285		+35		+250

↑ Cash flows: +285

July 24	Cash	285	
	Cleaning Service Revenue		250
	HST Payable ($250 × 14%)		35
	To record cleaning service revenue.		

Merchandise

Entries are needed to record the sales taxes owed when merchandise inventory (goods) is sold, or to reduce sales taxes payable when merchandise inventory is returned.

Sales

Assume that Staples sells $1,000 of office furniture, on account, in the province of Ontario, where PST is 8%. GST is 6%. Staples uses a perpetual inventory system and the cost of the furniture to Staples was $800. The following two entries are required to record the sale and the cost of the sale on May 20:

A	=	L	+	OE
+1,140		+60		+1,000
		+80		

Cash flows: no effect

A	=	L	+	OE
−800				−800

Cash flows: no effect

May 20	Accounts Receivable	1,140	
	Sales		1,000
	GST Payable ($1,000 × 6%)		60
	PST Payable ($1,000 × 8%)		80
	To record sale of merchandise on account.		
20	Cost of Goods Sold	800	
	Merchandise Inventory		800
	To record cost of merchandise sold.		

Under the periodic inventory system, the second entry would not be recorded.

Sales Returns and Allowances

If a $300 sales return and allowance were granted by Staples on May 25 for returned merchandise from the above sale, the entry to record the credit memorandum would appear as follows:

A	=	L	+	OE
−342		−18		−300
		−24		

Cash flows: no effect

A	=	L	+	OE
+240				+240

Cash flows: no effect

May 25	Sales Returns and Allowances	300	
	GST Payable ($300 × 6%)	18	
	PST Payable ($300 × 8%)	24	
	Accounts Receivable		342
	To record credit for returned merchandise.		
25	Merchandise Inventory ($300 ÷ $1,000 × $800)	240	
	Cost of Goods Sold		240
	To record cost of merchandise returned.		

Note that the GST and PST payable accounts are debited, rather than debiting a receivable account, to indicate that this is a return of previously collected sales tax. This entry assumes that the merchandise was in good condition and returned to inventory. Note also that the GST and PST did not form part of the original cost of the merchandise, and therefore are not considered in restoring the cost of the merchandise to the inventory account.

Under the periodic inventory system, the second entry would not be recorded.

Sales Taxes Paid on Disbursements

As a consumer of goods and services, a business must pay the applicable PST and GST charged by its suppliers on taxable goods and services.

Purchase of Merchandise for Resale

When purchasing merchandise for resale, the treatment of the PST is different than that of the GST. PST is a single-stage tax collected from the final consumers of taxable goods and services. Consequently, wholesalers do not charge the tax to the retailer who will in turn resell the merchandise, at a higher price, to the final consumer. By presenting a vendor registration number, retailers are able to buy merchandise for resale, exempt of the PST.

Businesses must pay GST on the purchase of merchandise but can then offset the GST paid against any GST collected. Consequently, **when merchandise is purchased, the GST paid by a business is** *not* **part of the inventory cost.** The GST paid on purchases is debited to an account called GST Recoverable and is called an input tax credit.

In Quebec, the QST works somewhat like the GST. Businesses can offset QST paid against any QST collected. The QST paid on purchases is debited to an account called QST Recoverable and is called an input tax refund. Other differences also exist in the treatment of QST. This appendix will focus on PST and does not discuss the QST in any detail.

Purchases

The following is an entry to record the purchase of merchandise for resale on May 4 at a price of $4,000, on account, using a perpetual inventory system:

May 4	Merchandise Inventory	4,000	
	GST Recoverable ($4,000 × 6%)	240	
	Accounts Payable		4,240
	To record merchandise purchased on account.		

A = L + OE
+4,000   +4,240
+240
Cash flows: no effect

The cost of the merchandise, $4,000, is not affected by the GST, which is recorded as a receivable.

Under a periodic inventory system, the $4,000 debit would have been recorded to the Purchases account.

Purchase Returns and Allowances

The entry to record a $300 return of merchandise on May 8 is as follows:

May 8	Accounts Payable	318	
	GST Recoverable ($300 × 6%)		18
	Merchandise Inventory		300
	To record the return of merchandise.		

A = L + OE
−18   −318
−300
Cash flows: no effect

Note that the GST Recoverable account is credited instead of the GST Payable account because this is a return of previously recorded GST.

Under the periodic inventory system, the credit of $300 would have been recorded to the Purchase Returns and Allowances account.

To summarize, PST is not paid on purchases of merchandise for resale. GST paid on purchases is normally recoverable and recorded as a current asset in the GST Recoverable account. Purchase returns and allowances require an adjustment of GST only, since PST was not paid on the original purchase.

Operating Expenses

Although PST is not charged on goods purchased for resale, it is charged to businesses that use taxable goods and services in their operations. For example, a business must pay GST and PST when it buys office supplies. As with all purchases made by a registered business, the GST is recoverable (can be offset as an input tax credit against GST collected). Because the PST is not recoverable, the PST forms part of the cost of the asset or expense that is being acquired.

The following is the entry for a cash purchase of office supplies on May 18 in the amount of $200 in the province of Ontario where PST is 8% and GST is 6%:

May 18	Office Supplies ($200 + $16[1] PST)	216
	GST Recoverable ($200 × 6%)	12
	Cash		228
	To record purchase of office supplies.	
[1] $200 × 8% = $16		

In this situation, the cost of the supplies includes both the supplies and the PST. Because GST is recoverable, it does not form part of the asset cost.

This same purchase would be recorded as follows if it occurred in the province of Prince Edward Island, where GST is 6% and PST is charged on GST at 10%:

May 18	Office Supplies ($200 + $21.20[2] PST)	221.20
	GST Recoverable ($200 × 6%)	12.00
	Cash		233.20
	To record purchase of office supplies.	
[2] $200 + $12 = $212 × 10% = $21.20		

Remember that in Prince Edward Island the provincial sales tax base includes both the cost of the item and the GST. That is, the PST of $21.20 is determined by multiplying 10% by $212 ($200 + $12).

When HST is applied, it is treated in the same manner as GST. HST is recoverable and does not form part of the cost of the item purchased. The purchase of office supplies would be recorded as follows if it had occurred in the province of Newfoundland and Labrador where HST is 14%:

May 18	Office Supplies	200
	HST Recoverable ($200 × 14%)	28
	Cash		228
	To record purchase of office supplies.	

Note that the same amount is paid for the supplies in Ontario and Newfoundland and Labrador, $228, but the amount recorded as the cost of the office supplies differs ($216 and $200).

Property, Plant, and Equipment

Businesses incur costs other than those for merchandise and operating expenses, such as for the purchase of property, plant, and equipment. The PST and GST apply to these purchases in the same manner as described in the operating expenses section above. All GST (or HST) paid is recoverable and is not part of the cost of the asset. The PST, however, is part of the cost of the asset being purchased as it is not recoverable.

The following is the entry for the purchase of office furniture on May 20 from Staples, on account, for $1,000 plus applicable sales taxes in Ontario. PST is 8% and GST is 6%.

May 20	Office Furniture ($1,000 + $80¹ PST)	1,080	
	GST Recoverable ($1,000 × 6%)	60	
	Accounts Payable		1,140
	To record purchase of office furniture.		

¹ $1,000 × 8% = $80

A	=	L	+	OE
+1,080		+1,140		
+60				

Cash flows: no effect

Because the PST is not recoverable, the cost of the furniture is $1,080, inclusive of the PST.

Compare this entry made by the buyer to record the purchase, to the entry made by the seller to record the sale on page B4. Both companies record accounts payable and accounts receivable in the same amount, $1,140. However, the seller records both GST and PST payable while the buyer records only GST recoverable. The PST paid by the buyer is not recoverable, so it becomes part of the cost of the office furniture, $1,080.

In Prince Edward Island, where GST is 6% and PST is charged on GST at 10%, the same entry would be recorded as follows:

May 20	Office Furniture ($1,000 + $106² PST)	1,106	
	GST Recoverable ($1,000 × 6%)	60	
	Accounts Payable		1,166
	To record purchase of office furniture.		

² $1,000 + $60 = $1,060 × 10% = $106

A	=	L	+	OE
+1,106		+1,166		
+60				

Cash flows: no effect

In P.E.I., PST is calculated on a cost base which includes the GST. Therefore, the PST of $106 is calculated on $1,060 ($1,000 + $60).

In Nova Scotia, where HST is 14%, the entry would be recorded as follows:

May 20	Office Furniture	1,000	
	HST Recoverable ($1,000 × 14%)	140	
	Accounts Payable		1,140
	To record purchase of office furniture.		

A	=	L	+	OE
+1,000		+1,140		
+140				

Cash flows: no effect

As we have noted before, the amount paid for the PST changes the amount recorded as the cost of the office furniture in each province: $1,080 in Ontario, $1,106 in Prince Edward Island, and $1,000 in Nova Scotia.

Remittance of Sales Taxes

As mentioned in the introduction, businesses act as agents of the federal and provincial governments in charging and later remitting taxes charged on sales and services. For example, Staples, the seller of office furniture illustrated on page B4, must remit GST to the CRA and PST to the Treasurer of Ontario. Notice that even if Staples has not received payment from a customer buying on account before the due date for the remittance, the tax must still be paid to the government authorities. As a registrant, however, Staples will also benefit from claiming input tax credits and recording a reduction in amounts payable from applying GST on sales.

GST (HST)

When remitting the amount owed to the federal government at the end of a reporting period for GST (or HST), the amount of GST payable is reduced by any amount in the GST Recoverable account. Any difference is remitted, as shown in the following journal entry, using assumed amounts payable and recoverable:

June 30	GST Payable	6,250	
	GST Recoverable		2,500
	Cash		3,750
	To record remittance of GST.		

The GST (HST) remittance form requires the registrant to report at specified dates, depending on the business's volume of sales. The amount of the sales and other revenue as well as the amount of GST charged on these sales, whether collected or not, is reported on the remittance form. The amount of the input tax credits claimed is also entered on the form to reduce the amount owing to CRA. If the GST recoverable exceeds the GST payable, the remittance form should be sent as soon as possible in order to ask for a refund. The entry to record the cash receipt from a GST refund will be similar to the entry shown above, except that there will be a debit to Cash, instead of a credit.

The above discussion of the remittance of GST explains why all registrants need two general ledger accounts. One account, GST Payable, is used to keep track of all GST charged on sales and revenues. The second account, GST Recoverable, is used to keep track of the GST input tax credits that have been paid on all of the business's purchases. Failure by a business to capture the proper amounts of input tax credits has a significant impact on income and on cash flows.

PST

The remittance of PST to the Treasurer or Minister of Finance of the applicable province or territory is similar to that of GST except that, since no credit can be claimed, the amount paid at the end of each reporting period is the amount of the balance in the PST Payable account.

Consequently, the entry to record a remittance of PST, using an assumed amount payable, would appear as follows:

June 30	PST Payable	7,400	
	Cash		7,400
	To record remittance of PST.		

Conclusion

Be careful when you record the amounts of taxes charged or claimed in the business accounts. Numbers must be rounded carefully. If the amount of the tax calculated is less then half a cent, the amount should be rounded down. If the amount of the tax as calculated comes to more than half a cent, the amount should be rounded up. For example, applying 6% GST on an amount of $49.20 would give you $2.952. The tax amount to be recorded can be rounded down to $2.95. Rounding might seem insignificant, but with many transactions the amounts can add up and the registrant is responsible to the government authorities for any shortfall created in error.

Sales tax law is intricate. It has added a lot of complexity to the accounting for most transactions flowing through today's businesses. Fortunately, computers that are programmed to automatically determine and record the correct sales tax rate for each good or service provided have simplified matters somewhat. Before recording sales tax transactions, however, it is important to understand all of the relevant sales tax regulations. Check the federal and provincial laws in your jurisdiction.

Brief Exercises

BEB–1   Record the purchase on account of $7,000 of merchandise for resale in the province of Manitoba. The company uses a perpetual inventory system and the purchase is PST exempt.

Record inventory purchase—perpetual inventory system.

BEB–2   Record the return of $1,000 of the merchandise purchased in BEB–1.

Record purchase return—perpetual inventory system.

BEB–3   Record the cash purchase of $500 of office supplies in the province of Saskatchewan, where PST is 5%.

Record purchase of supplies.

BEB–4   Record the purchase on account of a $15,000 delivery truck in the province of Nova Scotia, where HST is 14%.

Record truck purchase.

BEB–5   Record the purchase on account of $100 of office supplies and $4,000 of merchandise for resale in the province of Ontario. The company uses a perpetual inventory system and the purchase of merchandise is PST exempt. The PST rate is 8%.

Record purchase of supplies and inventory—perpetual inventory system.

BEB–6   Record the sale on account, for $1,800, of merchandise costing $1,200 in the province of Prince Edward Island. Assume the company uses a perpetual inventory system. The PST is 10% and the GST is included in the provincial sales tax base.

Record sales—perpetual inventory system.

BEB–7   Half of the shipment described in BEB–6 is returned as the incorrect sizes have been shipped. Record the return of merchandise on the seller's books.

Record sales return—perpetual inventory system.

BEB–8   Record the sale in BEB–6 and the credit memorandum in BEB–7 assuming the business uses a periodic inventory system.

Record sales and sales return—periodic inventory system.

BEB–9   Record the billing for $250 of services by R. R. Dennis, dentist, in the province of British Columbia. Dental services are exempt from GST and PST.

Record exempt services.

BEB–10   Record the billing of accounting fee revenue of $600 for the preparation of personal income tax returns in the province of Alberta. GST is applicable on this service. Alberta does not charge PST.

Record fees.

BEB–11   Record two payments: one cheque to the Receiver General for GST and one to the Treasurer of Ontario for PST. The balances in the accounts are as follows: GST Payable $4,450, GST Recoverable $1,900, and PST Payable $4,870.

Record the remittance of GST and PST.

BEB–12   Record the deposit of a cheque from the Receiver General for a refund of $690 following the filing of an HST return. The balances in the accounts are as follows: HST Payable $2,920 and HST Recoverable $3,610.

Record HST refund.

Exercises

EB–1   Stratton Company is a merchant operating in the province of Ontario where the PST rate is 8%. Stratton uses a perpetual inventory system. Transactions for the business are shown below:

Record sales transactions—perpetual inventory system.

Mar. 1 Paid March rent to the landlord for the rental of a warehouse. The lease calls for monthly payments of $5,500 plus 6% GST.

Mar. 3 Sold merchandise on account and shipped merchandise to Marvin Ltd. for $20,000, terms n/30, FOB shipping point. This merchandise cost Stratton $11,000.

5 Granted Marvin a sales allowance of $700 for defective merchandise purchased on March 3. No merchandise was returned.

7 Purchased on account from Tiller Ltd. merchandise for resale at a list price of $14,000, plus applicable tax.

12 Made a cash purchase at Home Depot of a desk for the shipping clerk. The price of the desk was $600 before applicable taxes.

31 Paid the monthly remittance of GST to the Receiver General. The balances in the accounts were as follows: GST Payable $4,280 and GST Recoverable $1,917.

Instructions

(a) Prepare the journal entries to record these transactions on the books of Stratton Company.

(b) Assume instead that Stratton operates in the province of Alberta, where PST is not applicable. Prepare the journal entries to record these transactions on the books of Stratton.

(c) Assume instead that Stratton operates in the province of Prince Edward Island, where PST is charged on GST at 10%. Prepare the journal entries to record these transactions on the books of Stratton.

(d) Assume instead that Stratton operates in the province of New Brunswick, where HST is 14%. Prepare the journal entries to record these transactions on the books of Stratton. Assume that the GST balances on March 31 are the balances in the HST accounts.

Record sales transactions—periodic inventory system.

EB–2 Using the information for the transactions of Stratton Company in EB–1, assume now that Stratton uses a periodic inventory system.

Instructions

(a) Prepare the journal entries to record these transactions on the books of Stratton Company.

(b) Assume now that Stratton operates in the province of Alberta, where PST is not applicable. Prepare the journal entries to record these transactions on the books of Stratton.

(c) Assume now that Stratton operates in the province of Prince Edward Island, where PST is charged on GST at 10%. Prepare the journal entries to record these transactions on the books of Stratton.

(d) Assume now that Stratton operates in the province of New Brunswick, where HST is 14%. Prepare the journal entries to record these transactions on the books of Stratton. Assume that the GST balances on March 31 provided in EB–1 are the balances in the HST accounts.

Record service transactions.

EB–3 Tom LeBrun is a sole practitioner providing accounting services in the province of Manitoba. The provincial sales tax rate in Manitoba is 7%, but accounting services are exempt of provincial sales tax. Transactions for the business are shown below:

June 8 Purchased a printer on account at a cost of $1,500. The appropriate sales taxes were added to this purchase price.

10 Purchased toner for the printer for $50 cash from a local stationery store. The store added the appropriate sales taxes to the purchase price.

12 Billed a client for accounting services provided. The fee charged was $750 and GST was added to the fee billed.

15 Collected $106 on account. The original fee was $100 and the GST charged was $6.

30 Paid the monthly remittance of GST to the Receiver General. The balances in the accounts were as follows: GST Payable $1,520.60 and GST Recoverable $820.45.

Instructions

Prepare the journal entries to record these transactions on the books of Tom LeBrun's accounting business.

Problems

PB–1   Mark's Music is a store that buys and sells musical instruments in Ontario, where the provincial sales tax is charged at a rate of 8%. Mark's Music uses a perpetual inventory system. Transactions for the business are shown below:

Record purchase and sales transactions—perpetual inventory system.

Nov. 2 Purchased two electric guitars from Fender Supply Limited, on account, at a cost of $700 each.

4 Made a cash sale of two keyboards for a total invoice price of $2,200, plus applicable taxes. The cost of each keyboard was $950.

5 Received a credit memorandum from Western Acoustic Inc. for the return of an acoustic guitar which was defective. The original invoice price before taxes was $400 and the guitar had been purchased on account.

7 One of the keyboards from the cash sale of Nov. 4 was returned to the store for a full cash refund because the customer was not satisfied with the instrument.

8 Purchased store supplies from a stationery store. The price of the supplies is $100 before all applicable taxes.

10 Sold one Omega trumpet to the Toronto Regional Band, on account, for an invoice price of $2,700 before applicable taxes. The trumpet had cost Mark's Music $1,420.

13 Purchased two saxophones from Yamaha Canada Inc. on account. The invoice price was $2,100 for each saxophone, excluding applicable taxes.

14 Collected $3,990 on account. The payment included GST of $210 and PST of $280.

16 Returned to Yamaha Canada Inc. one of the saxophones purchased on Nov. 13, as it was the wrong model. Received a credit memorandum from Yamaha for the full purchase price.

20 Made a payment on account for the amount owing to Fender Supply Limited for the purchase of Nov. 2.

30 Paid the monthly remittance of GST to the Receiver General. The balances in the accounts were as follows: GST Payable $5,540 and GST Recoverable $1,860.

30 Paid the monthly remittance of PST to the Treasurer of Ontario. The balance in PST Payable is $5,920.

Instructions

Prepare the journal entries to record the Mark's Music transactions.

PB–2   Transaction data for Mark's Music are available in PB–1. Assume Mark's Music uses a periodic inventory system instead of a perpetual inventory system.

Record purchase and sales transactions—periodic inventory system.

Instructions

Prepare the journal entries to record the Mark's Music transactions.

PB–3   David Simmons, L.L.B., is a lawyer operating as a sole practitioner in Nunavut. Nunavut does not charge provincial sales taxes. Transactions for the business are shown below:

Record service transactions.

May 1 Signed a two-year lease for the office space and immediately paid the first and last months' rent. The lease calls for the monthly rent of $1,700 plus applicable taxes.

4 Purchased an office suite of furniture, on account, from Leon's at a cost of $3,400. The appropriate sales taxes were added to this purchase price.

5 Returned one chair to Leon's due to a defect. The cost of the chair before taxes was 400.

6 Billed a client for the preparation of a will. The client was very pleased with the product and immediately paid David's invoice for fees of $1,000 plus taxes.

10 Purchased paper for the photocopier for $300 cash from a local stationery store. The store added the appropriate sales taxes to the purchase price.

13 Billed Manson Ltd. for legal services rendered connected with the purchase of land. The fee charged is $900 plus applicable taxes.

18 Paid Leon's for the furniture purchase of May 4, net of returned items.

May 19 Paid $8 cash to a local grocery store for coffee for the office coffee machine. Groceries are GST exempt.

21 In accordance with the lease agreement with the landlord, David must pay for water supplied by the municipality. The water invoice was received and the services amounted to $100 plus GST.

25 Collected a full payment from Manson Ltd. for the May 13 bill.

27 Completed the preparation of a purchase and sale agreement for Edwards Inc. and billed fees of $1,200.

June 20 Deposited a cheque from the Receiver General for a refund of $270 following the filing of the May GST return. The balances in the accounts were as follows: GST Payable $990 and GST Recoverable $1,260.

Instructions

Prepare the journal entries to record these transactions on the books of David Simmons' law practice.

appendix C

Subsidiary Ledgers and Special Journals

In the textbook, we learned how to record accounting transactions in a general journal. Each journal entry was then individually posted to its respective general ledger account. However, such a practice is only useful in a company where the volume of transactions is low. In most companies, it is necessary to use additional journals (called special journals) and ledgers (called subsidiary ledgers) to record transaction data.

We will look at subsidiary ledgers and special journals in the next sections. Both subsidiary ledgers and special journals can be used in either a manual accounting system or a computerized accounting system.

Subsidiary Ledgers

Imagine a business that has several thousand customers who purchase merchandise from it on account. It records the transactions with these customers in only one general ledger account—Accounts Receivable. It would be virtually impossible to determine the balance owed by an individual customer at any specific time. Similarly, the amount payable to one creditor would be difficult to locate quickly from a single accounts payable account in the general ledger.

Instead, companies use subsidiary ledgers to keep track of individual balances. A subsidiary ledger is a group of accounts that share a common characteristic (for example, all accounts receivable). The subsidiary ledger frees the general ledger from the details of individual balances. A subsidiary ledger is an addition to, and an expansion of, the general ledger.

Two common subsidiary ledgers are:

1. The accounts receivable (or customers') ledger, which collects transaction data for individual customers
2. The accounts payable (or creditors') ledger, which collects transaction data for individual creditors

Other subsidiary ledgers include an inventory ledger, which collects transaction data for each inventory item purchased and sold, as was described in Chapter 5. Some companies also use a payroll ledger, detailing individual employee pay records. In each of these subsidiary ledgers, individual accounts are arranged in alphabetical, numerical, or alphanumerical order.

The detailed data from a subsidiary ledger are summarized in a general ledger account. For example, the detailed data from the accounts receivable subsidiary ledger are summarized in Accounts

Receivable in the general ledger. The general ledger account that summarizes subsidiary ledger data is called a control account.

Each general ledger control account balance must equal the total balance of the individual accounts in the related subsidiary ledger. This is an important internal control function.

Example

An example of an accounts receivable control account and subsidiary ledger is shown in Illustration C-1 for Mercier Enterprises.

Illustration C-1 ▶

Accounts receivable general ledger control account and subsidiary ledger

GENERAL LEDGER

Accounts Receivable is a control account.

Accounts Receivable   No. 112

Date	Explanation	Ref.	Debit	Credit	Balance
2008					
Jan. 31			12,000		12,000
31				8,000	4,000

ACCOUNTS RECEIVABLE SUBSIDIARY LEDGER

The subsidiary ledger is separate from the general ledger.

Aaron Co.   No. 112-172

Date	Explanation	Ref.	Debit	Credit	Balance
2008					
Jan. 11	Invoice 336		6,000		6,000
19	Payment			4,000	2,000

Branden Inc.   No. 112-173

Date	Explanation	Ref.	Debit	Credit	Balance
2008					
Jan. 12	Invoice 337		3,000		3,000
21	Payment			3,000	0

Caron Co.   No. 112-174

Date	Explanation	Ref.	Debit	Credit	Balance
2008					
Jan. 20	Invoice 339		3,000		3,000
29	Payment			1,000	2,000

The example is based on the following transactions:

Credit Sales			Collections on Account		
Jan. 11	Aaron Co.	$ 6,000	Jan. 19	Aaron Co.	$4,000
12	Branden Inc.	3,000	21	Branden Inc.	3,000
20	Caron Co.	3,000	29	Caron Co.	1,000
		$12,000			$8,000

The total debits ($12,000) and credits ($8,000) in Accounts Receivable in the general ledger match the detailed debits and credits in the subsidiary accounts. The balance of $4,000 in the control account agrees with the total of the balances in the individual accounts receivable accounts (Aaron $2,000 + Branden $0 + Caron $2,000) in the subsidiary ledger.

Rather than relying on customer or creditor names in a subsidiary ledger, a computer system expands the account number of the control account. For example, if the general ledger control account Accounts Receivable was numbered 112, the first customer account in the accounts receivable subsidiary ledger might be numbered 112-001, the second 112-002, and so on. Most systems allow inquiries about specific customer accounts in the subsidiary ledger (by account number) or about the control account.

As shown, postings are made monthly to the control account in the general ledger. We will learn, in the next section, how special journals facilitate monthly postings. We will also learn how to fill in the posting references (in the Ref. column) in both the general ledger and subsidiary ledger accounts. Postings to the individual accounts in the subsidiary ledger are made daily. The rationale for posting daily is to ensure that account information is current. This enables Mercier Enterprises to monitor credit limits, send statements to customers, and answer inquiries from customers about their account balances. In a computerized accounting system, transactions are simultaneously recorded in journals and posted to both the general and subsidiary ledgers.

Advantages of Subsidiary Ledgers

Subsidiary ledgers have several advantages:

1. **They show transactions that affect one customer or one creditor in a single account.** They provide up-to-date information on specific account balances.
2. **They free the general ledger of excessive details.** A trial balance of the general ledger does not contain vast numbers of individual customer account balances.
3. **They help locate errors in individual accounts.** The potential for errors is minimized by reducing the number of accounts in one ledger and by using control accounts.
4. **They make possible a division of labour in posting.** One employee can post to the general ledger while different employees post to the subsidiary ledgers. This strengthens internal control, since one employee verifies the work of the other.

In a computerized accounting system, the last two advantages don't apply. Computerized accounting systems do not make errors such as calculation errors and posting errors. Other errors, such as entry errors, can and do still occur. Internal control must be done using different means in computerized systems since account transactions are posted automatically.

Special Journals

As mentioned earlier, journalizing transactions in a two-column (debit and credit) general journal is satisfactory only when there are few transactions. To help with the journalizing and posting of multiple transactions, most companies use special journals in addition to the general journal.

A special journal is used to record similar types of transactions. Examples include all sales of merchandise on account, or all cash receipts. The types of special journals used depend largely on the types of transactions that occur frequently. While the form, type, and number of special journals used will vary among organizations, many merchandising companies use the journals shown in Illustration C-2 to record daily transactions. The letters that appear in parentheses following the journal name represent the posting reference used for each journal.

Illustration C-2 ▶

Use of special journals and the general journal

Sales Journal (S)	Cash Receipts Journal (CR)	Purchases Journal (P)	Cash Payments Journal (CP)	General Journal (J)
All sales of merchandise on account	All cash received (including cash sales)	All purchases of merchandise on account	All cash paid (including cash purchases of merchandise)	Transactions that cannot be entered in a special journal, including correcting, adjusting, and closing entries

If a transaction cannot be recorded in a special journal, it is recorded in the general journal. For example, if you have four special journals as listed in Illustration C-2, sales returns and allowances are recorded in the general journal. Similarly, correcting, adjusting, and closing entries are recorded in the general journal. Other types of special journals may sometimes be used in certain situations. For example, when sales returns and allowances are frequent, an additional special journal may be used to record these transactions. A payroll journal is another example of a special journal. It organizes and summarizes payroll details for companies with many employees.

The use of special journals reduces the time needed for the recording and posting process. In addition, special journals permit greater division of labour because different employees can record entries in different journals. For example, one employee may journalize all cash receipts. Another may journalize credit sales. The division of responsibilities ensures that one person does not have control over all aspects of a transaction. In this instance, recording the sale has been separated from recording the collection of cash from that sale. This may reduce the opportunity for intentional or unintentional error, and is one aspect of a good internal control system.

For a merchandising company, the same special journals are used whether a company uses the periodic or perpetual system to account for its inventory. The only distinction is the number of, and title for, the columns each journal uses. We will use Karns Wholesale Supply to show the use of special journals in the following sections. Karns uses a perpetual inventory system. The variations between the periodic and perpetual inventory systems are highlighted in helpful hints for your information. In addition, special journals under a periodic inventory system are shown more fully at the end of this appendix.

Sales Journal

The sales journal is used to record sales of merchandise on account. Cash sales of merchandise are entered in the cash receipts journal. Credit sales of assets other than merchandise are entered in the general journal.

Journalizing Credit Sales

Under the perpetual inventory system, each entry in the sales journal results in one entry at selling price and another entry at cost. The entry at selling price is a debit to Accounts Receivable (a control account supported by a subsidiary ledger) and a credit of an equal amount to Sales. The entry at cost is a debit to Cost of Goods Sold and a credit of an equal amount to Merchandise Inventory. Some companies also set up Merchandise Inventory as a control account supported by a subsidiary ledger.

A sales journal with two amount columns can show a sales transaction recognized at both selling price and cost on only one line. The two-column sales journal of Karns Wholesale Supply is shown in Illustration C-3, using assumed credit sales transactions.

Illustration C-3

Sales journal—perpetual inventory system

	KARNS WHOLESALE SUPPLY Sales Journal				S1
Date	Account Debited	Invoice No.	Ref.	Accts. Receivable Dr. Sales Cr.	Cost of Goods Sold Dr. Merchandise Inventory Cr.
2008					
May 3	Abbot Sisters	101		10,600	6,360
7	Babson Co.	102		11,350	7,370
14	Carson Bros.	103		7,800	5,070
19	Deli Co.	104		9,300	6,510
21	Abbot Sisters	105		15,400	10,780
24	Deli Co.	106		21,210	15,900
27	Babson Co.	107		14,570	10,200
				90,230	62,190

Helpful hint In a periodic inventory system, the sales journal would have only one column to record the sale at selling price (Accounts Receivable Dr., Sales Cr.). The cost of goods sold is not recorded. It is calculated at the end of the period.

The reference (Ref.) column is not used in journalizing. It is used in posting the sales journal, as explained in the next section. Also, note that, unlike in the general journal, an explanation is not required for each entry in a special journal. Finally, note that each invoice is prenumbered to ensure that all invoices are journalized.

If management wishes to record its sales by department, additional columns may be provided in the sales journal. For example, a department store may have columns for home furnishings, sporting goods, shoes, etc. In addition, the federal government, and practically all provinces, require that sales taxes be charged on items sold. If sales taxes are collected, it is necessary to add more credit columns to the sales journal for GST Payable and PST Payable (or HST Payable).

Posting the Sales Journal

Postings from the sales journal are made **daily to the individual accounts receivable accounts** in the subsidiary ledger. Posting **to the general ledger is done monthly**. Illustration C-4 shows both the daily postings to the accounts receivable subsidiary ledger and the monthly postings to the general ledger accounts. We have assumed that Karns Wholesale Supply does not maintain an inventory subsidiary ledger. However, if it did, the procedure is similar to that illustrated for the accounts receivable subsidiary ledger.

A check mark (√) is inserted in the reference posting column to indicate that the daily posting to the customer's account has been made. A check mark is used when the subsidiary ledger accounts are not individually numbered. If the subsidiary ledger accounts are numbered, the account number is used instead of the check mark in the reference posting column. At the end of the month, the column totals of the sales journal are posted to the general ledger. Here, the column totals are posted as a debit of $90,230 to Accounts Receivable (account no. 112), a credit of $90,230 to Sales (account no. 401), a debit of $62,190 to Cost of Goods Sold (account no. 505), and a credit of $62,190 to Merchandise Inventory (account no. 120). Inserting the account numbers below the column totals indicates that the postings have been made. In both the general ledger and subsidiary ledger accounts, the reference S1 indicates that the posting came from page 1 of the sales journal.

Illustration C-4 ▶

Sales journal—perpetual
inventory system

				KARNS WHOLESALE SUPPLY	
				Sales Journal	S1
Date	Account Debited	Invoice No.	Ref.	Accts. Receivable Dr. Sales Cr.	Cost of Goods Sold Dr. Merchandise Inventory Cr.
2008					
May 3	Abbot Sisters	101	√	10,600	6,360
7	Babson Co.	102	√	11,350	7,370
14	Carson Bros.	103	√	7,800	5,070
19	Deli Co.	104	√	9,300	6,510
21	Abbot Sisters	105	√	15,400	10,780
24	Deli Co.	106	√	21,210	15,900
27	Babson Co.	107	√	14,570	10,200
				90,230	62,190
				(112)/(401)	(505)/(120)

Individual amounts are posted daily to the subsidiary ledger.

Totals are posted at the end of the accounting period to the general ledger.

ACCOUNTS RECEIVABLE SUBSIDIARY LEDGER

Abbot Sisters

Date	Ref.	Debit	Credit	Balance
2008				
May 3	S1	10,600		10,600
21	S1	15,400		26,000

Babson Co.

Date	Ref.	Debit	Credit	Balance
2008				
May 7	S1	11,350		11,350
27	S1	14,570		25,920

Carson Bros.

Date	Ref.	Debit	Credit	Balance
2008				
May 14	S1	7,800		7,800

Deli Co.

Date	Ref.	Debit	Credit	Balance
2008				
May 19	S1	9,300		9,300
24	S1	21,210		30,510

GENERAL LEDGER

Accounts Receivable   No. 112

Date	Ref.	Debit	Credit	Balance
2008				
May 31	S1	90,230		90,230

Merchandise Inventory   No. 120

Date	Ref.	Debit	Credit	Balance
2008				
May 31	S1		62,190	62,190cr[1]

Sales   No. 401

Date	Ref.	Debit	Credit	Balance
2008				
May 31	S1		90,230	90,230

Cost of Goods Sold   No. 505

Date	Ref.	Debit	Credit	Balance
2008				
May 31	S1	62,190		62,190

The subsidiary ledger is separate from the general ledger.

Accounts Receivable is a control account.

[1] The normal balance for Merchandise Inventory is a debit. But, because of the sequence in which we have posted the special journals, with the sales journal first, the credits to Merchandise Inventory are posted before the debits. This posting sequence explains the credit balance in Merchandise Inventory, which exists only until the other journals are posted.

Proving the Ledgers

The next step is to "prove" the ledgers. To do so, we must determine two things: (1) The sum of the subsidiary ledger balances must equal the balance in the control account. (2) The total of the general ledger debit balances must equal the total of the general ledger credit balances. The proof of the postings from the sales journal to the general and subsidiary ledgers follows:

Accounts Receivable Subsidiary Ledger		General Ledger	
		Debits	
Abbot Sisters	$26,000	Accounts Receivable	$ 90,230
Babson Co.	25,920	Cost of Goods Sold	62,190
Carson Bros.	7,800		$152,420
Deli Co.	30,510		
	$90,230	**Credits**	
		Merchandise Inventory	$ 62,190
		Sales	90,230
			$152,420

Advantages of the Sales Journal

The use of a special journal to record sales on account has a number of advantages. First, the one-line–two-column entry for each sales transaction saves time. In the sales journal, it is not necessary to write out the four account titles for the two transactions. Second, only totals, rather than individual entries, are posted to the general ledger. This saves posting time and reduces the possibility of errors in posting. Third, the prenumbering of sales invoices helps to ensure that all sales are recorded and that no sale is recorded more than once. Finally, a division of labour results, because one individual can take responsibility for the sales journal alone. These last two advantages help internal control.

Cash Receipts Journal

All receipts of cash are recorded in the cash receipts journal. The most common types of cash receipts are cash sales of merchandise and collections of accounts receivable. Many other possibilities exist, such as a receipt of money from a bank loan and cash proceeds from disposals of equipment. A one- or two-column cash receipts journal would not have enough space for all possible cash receipt transactions. A multiple-column cash receipts journal is therefore used.

Generally, a cash receipts journal includes the following columns: a debit column for cash, and credit columns for accounts receivable, sales, and other accounts. The Other Accounts column is used when the cash receipt does not involve a cash sale or a collection of accounts receivable. Under a perpetual inventory system, each sales entry is accompanied by another entry that debits Cost of Goods Sold and credits Merchandise Inventory. A separate column is added for this purpose. A five-column cash receipts journal is shown in Illustration C-5.

Additional credit columns may be used if they significantly reduce postings to a specific account. For example, cash receipts from cash sales normally include the collection of sales taxes, which are later remitted to the federal and provincial governments. Most cash receipts journals have a separate credit column for sales tax collections. Other examples include the cash receipts of a loan company, such as Household Financial Centre, which cover thousands of collections from customers. These collections are credited to Loans Receivable and Interest Revenue. A significant saving in posting time would result from using separate credit columns for Loans Receivable and Interest Revenue, rather than using the Other Accounts credit column. In contrast, a retailer that has only one interest collection a month would not find it useful to have a separate column for Interest Revenue.

Illustration C-5 ▶

Cash receipts journal—
perpetual inventory system

Helpful hint In a periodic inventory system, the Cash Receipts journal would have one column fewer. The Cost of Goods Sold Dr. and Merchandise Inventory Cr. would not be recorded.

KARNS WHOLESALE SUPPLY
Cash Receipts Journal
CR1

Date	Account Credited	Ref.	Cash Dr.	Accounts Receivable Cr.	Sales Cr.	Cost of Goods Sold Dr. Mdse. Inv. Cr.	Other Accounts Cr.
2008							
May 1	D. Karns, Capital	301	5,000				5,000
7			1,900		1,900	1,240	
10	Abbot Sisters	√	10,600	10,600			
12			2,600		2,600	1,690	
17	Babson Co.	√	11,350	11,350			
22	Notes Payable	200	6,000				6,000
23	Carson Bros.	√	7,800	7,800			
28	Deli Co.	√	9,300	9,300			
			54,550	39,050	4,500	2,930	11,000
			(101)	(112)	(401)	(505)/(120)	(X)

Individual amounts are posted daily to the subsidiary ledger.

Totals are posted at the end of the accounting period to the general ledger.

ACCOUNTS RECEIVABLE SUBSIDIARY LEDGER

Abbot Sisters

Date	Ref.	Debit	Credit	Balance
2008				
May 3	S1	10,600		10,600
10	CR1		10,600	0
21	S1	15,400		15,400

Babson Co.

Date	Ref.	Debit	Credit	Balance
2008				
May 7	S1	11,350		11,350
17	CR1		11,350	0
27	S1	14,570		14,570

Carson Bros.

Date	Ref.	Debit	Credit	Balance
2008				
May 14	S1	7,800		7,800
23	CR1		7,800	0

Deli Co.

Date	Ref.	Debit	Credit	Balance
2008				
May 19	S1	9,300		9,300
24	S1	21,210		30,510
28	CR1		9,300	21,210

The subsidiary ledger is separate from the general ledger.

Accounts Receivable is a control account.

GENERAL LEDGER

Cash   No. 101

Date	Ref.	Debit	Credit	Balance
2008				
May 31	CR1	54,550		54,550

Accounts Receivable   No. 112

Date	Ref.	Debit	Credit	Balance
2008				
May 31	S1	90,230		90,230
31	CR1		39,050	51,180

Merchandise Inventory   No. 120

Date	Ref.	Debit	Credit	Balance
2008				
May 31	S1		62,190	62,190Cr.
31	CR1		2,930	65,120Cr.

Notes Payable   No. 200

Date	Ref.	Debit	Credit	Balance
2008				
May 22	CR1		6,000	6,000

D. Karns, Capital   No. 301

Date	Ref.	Debit	Credit	Balance
2008				
May 1	CR1		5,000	5,000

Sales   No. 401

Date	Ref.	Debit	Credit	Balance
2008				
May 31	S1		90,230	90,230
31	CR1		4,500	94,730

Cost of Goods Sold   No. 505

Date	Ref.	Debit	Credit	Balance
2008				
May 31	S1	62,190		62,190
31	CR1	2,930		65,120

Journalizing Cash Receipt Transactions

To illustrate the journalizing of cash receipts transactions, we will continue with the May transactions of Karns Wholesale Supply. Collections from customers are for the entries recorded in the sales journal in Illustration C-3. The entries in the cash receipts journal are based on the following cash receipts:

> May 1 D. Karns makes an investment of $5,000 in the business.
> 7 Cash receipts for merchandise sales total $1,900. The cost of goods sold is $1,240.
> 10 A cheque for $10,600 is received from Abbot Sisters in full payment of invoice No. 101.
> 12 Cash receipts for merchandise sales total $2,600. The cost of goods sold is $1,690.
> 17 A cheque for $11,350 is received from Babson Co. in full payment of invoice No. 102.
> 22 Cash is received by signing a 4% note for $6,000, payable September 22 to the National Bank.
> 23 A cheque for $7,800 is received from Carson Bros. in full payment of invoice No. 103.
> 28 A cheque for $9,300 is received from Deli Co. in full payment of invoice No. 104.

Further information about the columns in the cash receipts journal follows:

Debit Columns:

1. **Cash.** The amount of cash actually received in each transaction is entered in this column. The column total indicates the total cash receipts for the month. The total of this column is posted to the cash account in the general ledger.

2. **Cost of Goods Sold.** The Cost of Goods Sold Dr./Merchandise Inventory Cr. column is used to record the cost of the merchandise sold. (The sales column records the selling price of the merchandise.) The cost of goods sold column is similar to the one found in the sales journal. The amount debited to Cost of Goods Sold is the same amount credited to Merchandise Inventory. One column total is posted to both accounts at the end of the month.

Credit Columns:

3. **Accounts Receivable.** The Accounts Receivable column is used to record cash collections on account. The amount entered here is the amount to be credited to the individual customer's account.

4. **Sales.** The Sales column is used to record all cash sales of merchandise. Cash sales of other assets (property, plant, and equipment, for example) are not reported in this column. The total of this column is posted to the account Sales.

5. **Merchandise Inventory.** As noted above, the Cost of Goods Sold Dr./Merchandise Inventory Cr. column is used to record the reduction in the merchandise available for future sale. The amount credited to Merchandise Inventory is the same amount debited to Cost of Goods Sold. One column total is posted to both accounts at the end of the month.

6. **Other Accounts.** The Other Accounts column is used whenever the credit is not to Accounts Receivable, Sales, or Merchandise Inventory. For example, in the first entry, $5,000 is entered as a credit to D. Karns, Capital. This column is often referred to as the sundry accounts column.

In a multi-column journal, only one line is generally needed for each entry. In some cases, it is useful to add explanatory information, such as the details of the note payable, or to reference supporting documentation, such as invoice numbers if cash sales are invoiced. Note also that the Account Credited column is used to identify both general ledger and subsidiary ledger account titles. The former is shown in the May 1 entry for Karns' investment. The latter is shown in the May 10 entry for the collection from Abbot Sisters.

Debit and credit amounts for each line must be equal. When the journalizing has been completed, the amount columns are totalled. The totals are then compared to prove the equality of debits and credits in the cash receipts journal. Don't forget that the Cost of Goods Sold Dr./Merchandise Inventory Cr. column total represents both a debit and a credit amount. Totalling the columns of a journal and proving the equality of the totals is called footing (adding down) and cross-footing (adding across) a journal.

The proof of the equality of Karns' cash receipts journal is on the following page:

Debit		Credits	
Cash	$54,550	Accounts Receivable	$39,050
Cost of Goods Sold	2,930	Merchandise Inventory	2,930
	$57,480	Sales	4,500
		Other Accounts	11,000
			$57,480

Posting the Cash Receipts Journal

Posting a multi-column journal involves the following steps:

1. All column totals, except for the Other Accounts total, are posted once at the end of the month to the account title specified in the column heading, such as Cash, Accounts Receivable, Sales, Cost of Goods Sold, and Merchandise Inventory. Account numbers are entered below the column totals to show that the amounts have been posted.
2. The total of the Other Accounts column is not posted. Individual amounts that make up the Other Accounts total are posted separately to the general ledger accounts specified in the Account Credited column. See, for example, the credit posting to D. Karns, Capital. The symbol X is inserted below the total for this column to indicate that the amount has not been posted.
3. The individual amounts in a column (Accounts Receivable, in this case) are posted daily to the subsidiary ledger account name specified in the Account Credited column. See, for example, the credit posting of $10,600 to Abbot Sisters.

The abbreviation CR is used in both the subsidiary and general ledgers to identify postings from the cash receipts journal.

Proving the Ledgers

After the posting of the cash receipts journal is completed, it is necessary to prove the ledgers. As shown below, the sum of the subsidiary ledger account balances equals the control account balance. The general ledger totals are also in agreement.

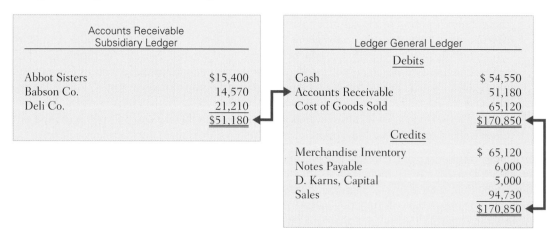

Accounts Receivable Subsidiary Ledger		Ledger General Ledger	
		Debits	
Abbot Sisters	$15,400	Cash	$ 54,550
Babson Co.	14,570	Accounts Receivable	51,180
Deli Co.	21,210	Cost of Goods Sold	65,120
	$51,180		$170,850
		Credits	
		Merchandise Inventory	$ 65,120
		Notes Payable	6,000
		D. Karns, Capital	5,000
		Sales	94,730
			$170,850

Purchases Journal

All purchases of merchandise on account are recorded in the purchases journal. Each entry in this journal results in a debit to Merchandise Inventory and a credit to Accounts Payable. When a one-column purchases journal is used, other types of purchases on account and cash purchases cannot be journalized in it. For example, credit purchases of equipment or supplies must be recorded in the general journal. Likewise, all cash purchases are entered in the cash payments journal. If there are many credit purchases for items other than merchandise, the purchases journal can be expanded to a multi-column format.

The purchases journal for Karns Wholesale Supply is shown in Illustration C-6, with assumed credit purchases.

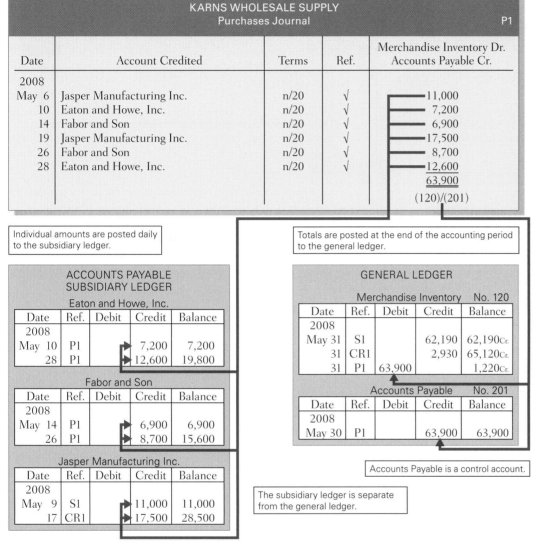

KARNS WHOLESALE SUPPLY
Purchases Journal — P1

Date	Account Credited	Terms	Ref.	Merchandise Inventory Dr. Accounts Payable Cr.
2008				
May 6	Jasper Manufacturing Inc.	n/20	√	11,000
10	Eaton and Howe, Inc.	n/20	√	7,200
14	Fabor and Son	n/20	√	6,900
19	Jasper Manufacturing Inc.	n/20	√	17,500
26	Fabor and Son	n/20	√	8,700
28	Eaton and Howe, Inc.	n/20	√	12,600
				63,900
				(120)/(201)

Individual amounts are posted daily to the subsidiary ledger.

Totals are posted at the end of the accounting period to the general ledger.

ACCOUNTS PAYABLE SUBSIDIARY LEDGER

Eaton and Howe, Inc.

Date	Ref.	Debit	Credit	Balance
2008				
May 10	P1		7,200	7,200
28	P1		12,600	19,800

Fabor and Son

Date	Ref.	Debit	Credit	Balance
2008				
May 14	P1		6,900	6,900
26	P1		8,700	15,600

Jasper Manufacturing Inc.

Date	Ref.	Debit	Credit	Balance
2008				
May 9	S1		11,000	11,000
17	CR1		17,500	28,500

GENERAL LEDGER

Merchandise Inventory — No. 120

Date	Ref.	Debit	Credit	Balance
2008				
May 31	S1		62,190	62,190 Cr.
31	CR1		2,930	65,120 Cr.
31	P1	63,900		1,220 Cr.

Accounts Payable — No. 201

Date	Ref.	Debit	Credit	Balance
2008				
May 30	P1		63,900	63,900

Accounts Payable is a control account.

The subsidiary ledger is separate from the general ledger.

Illustration C-6 ◀

Purchases journal—perpetual inventory system

Helpful hint When a periodic inventory system is used, this journal is still known as a purchases journal. The debit to the Merchandise Inventory account is replaced by a debit to the Purchases account.

Journalizing Credit Purchases of Merchandise

Entries in the purchases journal are made from purchase invoices. The journalizing procedure for the purchases journal is similar to that for the sales journal. In contrast to the sales journal, the purchases journal may not have an invoice number column, because invoices received from different suppliers would not be in numerical sequence.

Posting the Purchases Journal

The procedures for posting the purchases journal are similar to those for the sales journal. In this case, postings are made daily to the accounts payable subsidiary ledger accounts and monthly to the Merchandise Inventory and Accounts Payable accounts in the general ledger. In both ledgers, P1 is used in the reference column to show that the postings are from page 1 of the purchases journal.

Proof of the equality of the postings from the purchases journal to both ledgers is shown by the following:

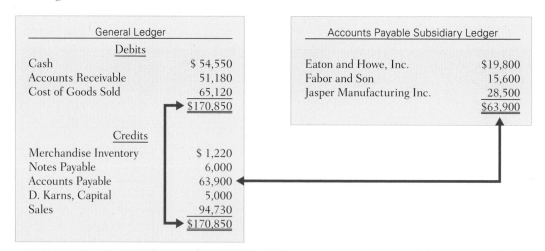

General Ledger	
Debits	
Cash	$ 54,550
Accounts Receivable	51,180
Cost of Goods Sold	65,120
	$170,850
Credits	
Merchandise Inventory	$ 1,220
Notes Payable	6,000
Accounts Payable	63,900
D. Karns, Capital	5,000
Sales	94,730
	$170,850

Accounts Payable Subsidiary Ledger	
Eaton and Howe, Inc.	$19,800
Fabor and Son	15,600
Jasper Manufacturing Inc.	28,500
	$63,900

Note that not all the general ledger accounts listed above have been included in Illustration C-6. You will have to refer to Illustration C-5 to determine the balances for the accounts Cash, Accounts Receivable, Cost of Goods Sold, Notes Payable, Capital, and Sales.

Cash Payments Journal

Alternative terminology
The cash payments journal is also called the *cash disbursements journal*.

All disbursements of cash are entered in a cash payments journal. Entries are made from prenumbered cheques. Because cash payments are made for various purposes, the cash payments journal has multiple columns. A four-column journal is shown in Illustration C-7.

Journalizing Cash Payments Transactions

The procedures for journalizing transactions in this journal are similar to those described earlier for the cash receipts journal. Each transaction is entered on one line, and for each line there must be equal debit and credit amounts. It is common practice in the cash payments journal to record the name of the company or individual receiving the cheque (the payee), so that later reference to the cheque is possible by name in addition to cheque number. The entries in the cash payments journal shown in Illustration C-7 are based on the following transactions for Karns Wholesale Supply:

May 3	Cheque No. 101 for $1,200 issued for the annual premium on a fire insurance policy from Corporate General Insurance.
3	Cheque No. 102 for $100 issued to CANPAR in payment of freight charges on goods purchased.
7	Cheque No. 103 for $4,400 issued for the cash purchase of merchandise from Zwicker Corp.
10	Cheque No. 104 for $11,000 sent to Jasper Manufacturing Inc. in full payment of the May 6 invoice.
19	Cheque No. 105 for $7,200 mailed to Eaton and Howe, Inc., in full payment of the May 10 invoice.
24	Cheque No. 106 for $6,900 sent to Fabor and Son in full payment of the May 14 invoice.
28	Cheque No. 107 for $17,500 sent to Jasper Manufacturing Inc. in full payment of the May 19 invoice.
31	Cheque No. 108 for $500 issued to D. Karns as a cash withdrawal for personal use.

Illustration C-7 ◀

Cash payments journal— perpetual inventory system

Helpful hint In a periodic inventory system, the debits to Merchandise Inventory would be recorded to the accounts Purchases and Freight In.

KARNS WHOLESALE SUPPLY
Cash Payments Journal
CP1

Date	Cheque No.	Account Credited	Cash Cr.	Mdse. Inventory Dr.	Accounts Payable Dr.	Account Debited	Ref.	Other Accounts Dr.
2008								
May 3	101	Corporate General Ins.	1,200			Prepaid insurance	130	1,200
3	102	CANPAR	100	100				
7	103	Zwicker Corp.	4,400	4,400				
10	104	Jasper Manufacturing Inc.	11,000		11,000	Jasper Manuf. Inc.	√	
19	105	Eaton & Howe, Inc.	7,200		7,200	Eaton & Howe, Inc.	√	
24	106	Fabor & Son	6,900		6,900	Fabor and Son	√	
28	107	Jasper Manufacturing Inc.	17,500		17,500	Jasper Manuf. Inc.	√	
31	108	D. Karns	500			D. Karns, Drawings	310	500
			48,800	4,500	42,600			1,700
			(101)	(120)	(201)			(X)

Individual amounts are posted daily to the subsidiary ledger.

Totals are posted at the end of the accounting period to the general ledger.

ACCOUNTS PAYABLE SUBSIDIARY LEDGER

Eatons and Howe, Inc.

Date	Ref.	Debit	Credit	Balance
2008				
May 10	P1		7,200	7,200
19	CP1	7,200		0
28	P1		12,600	12,600

Fabor and Son

Date	Ref.	Debit	Credit	Balance
2008				
May 14	P1		6,900	6,900
24	CP1	6,900		0
26	P1		8,700	8,700

Jasper Manufacturing Inc.

Date	Ref.	Debit	Credit	Balance
2008				
May 6	P1		11,000	11,000
10	CP1	11,000		0
19	P1		17,500	17,500
28	CP1	17,500		0

The subsidiary ledger is separate from the general ledger.

Accounts Payable is a control account.

GENERAL LEDGER

Cash   No. 101

Date	Ref.	Debit	Credit	Balance
2008				
May 31	CR1	54,550		54,550
31	CP1		48,800	5,750

Merchandise Inventory   No. 120

Date	Ref.	Debit	Credit	Balance
2008				
May 31	S1		62,190	62,190Cr.
31	CR1		2,930	65,120Cr.
31	P1	63,900		1,220Cr.
31	CP1	4,500		3,280

Prepaid Insurance   No. 130

Date	Ref.	Debit	Credit	Balance
2008				
May 31	P1	1,200		1,200

Accounts Payable   No. 201

Date	Ref.	Debit	Credit	Balance
2008				
May 31	C1		63,900	63,900
31	CP1	42,600		21,300

D. Karns, Drawings   No. 310

Date	Ref.	Debit	Credit	Balance
2008				
May 31	CP1	500		500

Note that whenever an amount is entered in the Other Accounts column, a specific general ledger account must be identified in the Account Debited column. The entries for cheque numbers 101 and 108 show this situation. Similarly, a subsidiary account must be identified in the Account Debited column whenever an amount is entered in the Accounts Payable column (as, for example, the entry for cheque no. 104).

After the cash payments journal has been journalized, the columns are totalled. The totals are then balanced to prove the equality of debits and credits. Debits ($4,500 + $42,600 + $1,700 = $48,800) do equal credits ($48,800) in this case.

Posting the Cash Payments Journal

Helpful hint If a company has a subsidiary ledger for merchandise inventory, amounts in the merchandise inventory column would be posted daily in the cash payments journal, as well as in the sales, cash receipts, and purchases journals.

The procedures for posting the cash payments journal are similar to those for the cash receipts journal:

1. Cash and Merchandise Inventory are posted only as a total at the end of the month.
2. The amounts recorded in the Accounts Payable column are posted individually to the subsidiary ledger and in total to the general ledger control account.
3. Transactions in the Other Accounts column are posted individually to the appropriate account(s) noted in the Account Debited column. No totals are posted for the Other Accounts column.

The posting of the cash payments journal is shown in Illustration C-7. Note that the abbreviation CP is used as the posting reference. After postings are completed, the equality of the debit and credit balances in the general ledger should be determined. The control account balance should also agree with the subsidiary ledger total balance. The agreement of these balances is shown below. Note that not all the general ledger accounts have been included in Illustration C-7. You will also have to refer to Illustration C-5 to determine the balances for the Accounts Receivable, Cost of Goods Sold, Notes Payable, Capital, and Sales accounts.

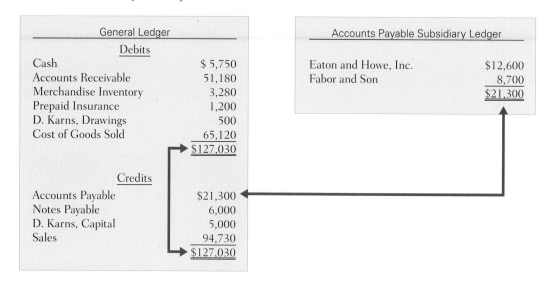

General Ledger		Accounts Payable Subsidiary Ledger	
Debits			
Cash	$ 5,750	Eaton and Howe, Inc.	$12,600
Accounts Receivable	51,180	Fabor and Son	8,700
Merchandise Inventory	3,280		$21,300
Prepaid Insurance	1,200		
D. Karns, Drawings	500		
Cost of Goods Sold	65,120		
	$127,030		
Credits			
Accounts Payable	$21,300		
Notes Payable	6,000		
D. Karns, Capital	5,000		
Sales	94,730		
	$127,030		

Effects of Special Journals on the General Journal

Special journals for sales, purchases, and cash greatly reduce the number of entries that are made in the general journal. **Only transactions that cannot be entered in a special journal are recorded in the general journal.** For example, the general journal may be used to record a transaction granting credit to a customer for a sales return or allowance. It may also be used to record the receipt of a credit from a supplier for purchases returned, the acceptance of a note receivable from a customer, and the purchase of equipment by issuing a note payable. Correcting, adjusting, and closing entries are also made in the general journal.

When control and subsidiary accounts are not used, the procedures for journalizing and posting transactions in the general journal are the same as those described in earlier chapters. When control and subsidiary accounts are used, two modifications of earlier procedures are required:

1. In journalizing, both the control and the subsidiary account must be identified.
2. In posting, there must be a dual posting: once to the control account and once to the subsidiary account.

To illustrate, assume that on May 31 Karns Wholesale Supply returns $500 of merchandise for credit to Fabor and Son. The entry in the general journal and the posting of the entry are shown in Illustration C-8. Note that if cash had been received instead of the credit granted on this return, then the transaction would have been recorded in the cash receipts journal.

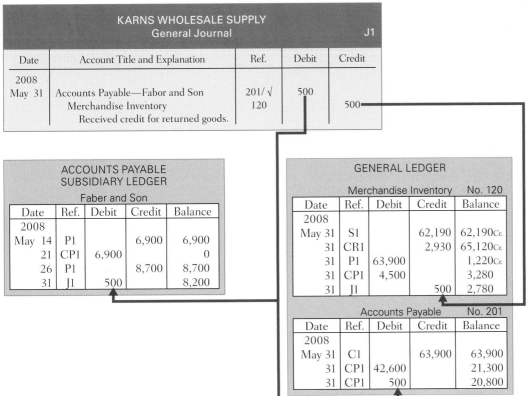

Illustration C-8 ◀

General journal

Helpful hint In a periodic inventory system, the credit would be to the Purchase Returns and Allowances account rather than to Merchandise Inventory.

Notice that in the general journal two accounts are indicated for the debit (the Accounts Payable control account and the Fabor and Son subsidiary account). Two postings (201/√) are indicated in the reference column. One amount is posted to the control account in the general ledger (no. 201) and the other to the creditor's account in the subsidiary ledger (Fabor and Son).

Special Journals in a Periodic Inventory System

Recording and posting transactions in special journals is essentially the same whether a perpetual or a periodic inventory system is used. But there are two differences. The first difference relates to the accounts Merchandise Inventory and Cost of Goods Sold in a perpetual inventory system. In this system, an additional column is required to record the cost of each sale in the sales and cash receipts journals, something which is not required in a periodic inventory system.

The second difference concerns the account titles used. In a perpetual inventory system, Merchandise Inventory and Cost of Goods Sold are used to record purchases and the cost of the merchandise sold. In a periodic inventory system, the accounts Purchases and Freight In accumulate the cost of the merchandise purchased until the end of the period. No cost of goods sold is recorded during the period. Cost of goods sold is calculated at the end of the period in a periodic inventory system.

Each of the special journals illustrated in this appendix is shown again here. Using the same transactions, we assume that Karns Wholesale Supply uses a periodic inventory system instead of a perpetual inventory system.

Illustration C-9 ▶

Sales journal—periodic inventory system

Helpful hint Compare this sales journal to the one presented in Illustration C-4.

	KARNS WHOLESALE SUPPLY			
	Sales Journal			S1
Date	Account Debited	Invoice No.	Ref.	Accts Receivable Dr. Sales Cr.
2008				
May 3	Abbot Sisters	101	√	10,600
7	Babson Co.	102	√	11,350
14	Carson Bros.	103	√	7,800
19	Deli Co.	104	√	9,300
21	Abbot Sisters	105	√	15,400
24	Deli Co.	106	√	21,210
27	Babson Co.	107	√	14,570
				90,230

Illustration C-10 ▶

Cash receipts journal—periodic inventory system

Helpful hint Compare this cash receipts journal to the one presented in Illustration C-5.

	KARNS WHOLESALE SUPPLY						
	Cash Receipts Journal						CR1
Date	Account Credited	Ref.	Cash Dr.	Accounts Receivable Cr.	Sales Cr.	Other Accounts Cr.
2008						
May 1	D. Karns, Capital	301	5,000			5,000
7			1,900		1,900	
10	Abbot Sisters	√	10,600	10,600		
12			2,600		2,600	
17	Babson Co.	√	11,350	11,350		
22	Notes Payable	200	6,000			6,000
23	Carson Bros.	√	7,800	7,800		
28	Deli Co.	√	9,300	9,300		
			54,550	39,050	4,500	11,000

Illustration C-11 ▶

Purchases journal—periodic inventory system

Helpful hint Compare this purchases journal to the one presented in Illustration C-6.

	KARNS WHOLESALE SUPPLY			
	Purchases Journal			P1
Date	Account Credited	Terms	Ref.	Purchases Dr. Accounts Payable Cr.
2008				
May 6	Jasper Manufacturing Inc.	n/20	√	11,000
10	Eaton and Howe, Inc.	n/20	√	7,200
14	Fabor and Son	n/20	√	6,900
19	Jasper Manufacturing Inc.	n/20	√	17,500
26	Fabor and Son	n/20	√	8,700
28	Eaton and Howe, Inc.	n/20	√	12,600
				63,900

Illustration C-12 ▶

Cash payments journal—periodic inventory system

Helpful hint Compare this cash payments journal to the one presented in Illustration C-7.

	KARNS WHOLESALE SUPPLY							
	Cash Payments Journal							CP1
Date	Cheque No.	Payee	Cash Cr.	Accounts Payable Dr.	Account Debited	Ref.	Other Accounts Dr.
2008							
May 3	101	Corporate General Ins.	1,200		Prepaid Insurance	130	1,200
3	102	CANPAR	100		Freight In	516	100
7	103	Zwicker Corp.	4,400		Purchases	510	4,400
10	104	Jasper Manufacturing Inc.	11,000	11,000	Jasper Manuf. Inc.	√	
19	105	Eaton & Howe, Inc.	7,200	7,200	Eaton & Howe, Inc.	√	
24	106	Fabor and Son	6.900	6,900	Fabor and Son	√	
28	107	Jasper Manufacturing Inc.	17,500	17,500	Jasper Manuf. Inc.	√	
31	108	D. Karns	500		D. Karns, Drawings	310	500
			48,800	42,600			6,200

Brief Exercises

BEC–1 Information related to Bryan Company is presented below for its first month of operations. Calculate (a) the balances that appear in the accounts receivable subsidiary ledger for each customer, and (b) the accounts receivable balance that appears in the general ledger at the end of January.

Calculate subsidiary ledger and control account balances.

Credit Sales			Cash Collections		
Jan. 7	Duffy Co.	$8,000	Jan. 17	Duffy Co.	$7,000
15	Hanson Inc.	6,000	24	Hanson Inc.	5,000
23	Lewis Co.	9,000	29	Lewis Co.	9,000

BEC–2 Identify in which ledger (general or subsidiary) each of the following accounts is shown:

Identify general and subsidiary ledger accounts.

1. Rent Expense
2. Accounts Receivable—O'Malley
3. Notes Payable
4. Accounts Payable—Kerns
5. Merchandise Inventory
6. Sales

BEC–3 Chiasson Co. uses special journals and a general journal. Identify the journal in which each of the following transactions is recorded:

Identify special journals.

1. Paid cash for equipment purchased on account.
2. Purchased merchandise on credit.
3. Paid utility expense in cash.
4. Sold merchandise on account.
5. Granted a cash refund for a sales return.
6. Received a credit on account for a purchase return.
7. Sold merchandise for cash.
8. Purchased merchandise for cash.

BEC–4 Swirsky Company uses the cash receipts and cash payments journals illustrated in this appendix for a perpetual inventory system. In April, the following selected cash transactions occurred:

Identify special journals—perpetual inventory system.

1. Made a refund to a customer for the return of damaged goods that had been purchased on credit.
2. Received payment from a customer.
3. Purchased merchandise for cash.
4. Paid a creditor.
5. Paid freight on merchandise purchased.
6. Paid cash for office equipment.
7. Received a cash refund from a supplier for merchandise returned.
8. Withdrew cash for personal use of owner.
9. Made cash sales.

Instructions

Indicate (a) the journal, and (b) the columns in the journal that should be used in recording each transaction.

BEC–5 Identify the journal and the specific column title(s) in which each of the following transactions is recorded. Assume the company uses a periodic inventory system.

Identify special journals—periodic inventory system.

1. Cash sale
2. Credit sale
3. Sales return on account
4. Cash purchase of merchandise
5. Credit purchase of merchandise
6. Payment of freight on merchandise purchased from a supplier
7. Return of merchandise purchased for cash refund
8. Payment of freight on merchandise delivered to a customer

Exercises

Identify special journals.

EC–1 Below are some transactions for Dartmouth Company:

1. Payment of creditors on account
2. Return of merchandise sold for credit
3. Collection on account from customers
4. Sale of land for cash
5. Sale of merchandise on account
6. Sale of merchandise for cash
7. Credit received for merchandise returned to a supplier
8. Payment of employee wages
9. Revenues and expenses closed to income summary
10. Amortization on building
11. Purchase of office supplies for cash
12. Purchase of merchandise on account

Instructions

For each transaction, indicate whether it would normally be recorded in a cash receipts journal, cash payments journal, sales journal, purchases journal, or general journal.

Record transactions in sales and purchases journals— perpetual inventory system.

EC–2 Sing Tao Company uses special journals and a general journal. The company uses a perpetual inventory system and had the following transactions:

Sept. 2 Sold merchandise on account to T. Meto, $520, invoice #101, terms n/30. The cost of the merchandise sold was $360.
3 Purchased office supplies on account from Berko Co., $350.
10 Purchased merchandise on account from Miramichi Co., $800, FOB shipping point, terms n/30. Paid freight of $50 to Apex Shippers.
11 Returned unsatisfactory merchandise to Miramichi Co., $200, for credit on account.
12 Purchased office equipment on account from Wells Co., $8,000.
16 Sold merchandise for cash to L. Maille, for $800. The cost of the merchandise sold was $480.
18 Purchased merchandise for cash from Miramichi Co., $450, FOB destination.
20 Accepted returned merchandise from customer L. Maille, $800 (see Sept. 16 transaction). Gave full cash refund. Restored the merchandise to inventory.
24 Paid the correct amount owing for the merchandise purchased from Miramichi earlier in the month.
25 Received payment from T. Meto for Sept. 2 sale.
26 Sold merchandise on account to M. Christie, $890, invoice #102, terms n/30, FOB destination. The cost of the merchandise was $520. The appropriate party paid $75 to Freight Co. for shipping charges.
30 Paid September salaries, $2,800.
30 Withdrew cash for owner's personal use, $600.
30 Paid for office supplies purchased on September 3.

Instructions

(a) Draw a sales journal and a purchases journal (see Illustrations C-3 and C-6). Use page 1 for each journal.
(b) Record the transaction(s) for September that should be recorded in the sales journal.
(c) Record the transaction(s) for September that should be recorded in the purchases journal.

EC–3 Refer to the information provided for Sing Tao Company in EC–2.

Instructions

(a) Draw cash receipts and cash payments journals (see Illustrations C-5 and C-7) and a general journal. Use page 1 for each journal.
(b) Record the transaction(s) provided in EC–2 that should be recorded in the cash receipts journal.
(c) Record the transaction(s) provided in EC–2 that should be recorded in the cash payments journal.
(d) Record the transaction(s) provided in EC–2 that should be recorded in the general journal.

EC–4 Argentina Company has the following selected transactions during March:

Mar. 2 Purchased equipment on account, costing $7,400, from Lifetime Inc.
     5 Received credit memorandum for $300 from Lyden Company for merchandise returned that had been damaged in shipment to Argentina.
     7 Issued a credit memorandum for $400 to Marco Presti for merchandise the customer returned. The returned merchandise has a cost of $275 and was restored to inventory.

Argentina Company uses a purchases journal, a sales journal, two cash journals (receipts and payments), and a general journal. Argentina also uses a perpetual inventory system.

Instructions

(a) Record the appropriate transactions in the general journal.
(b) In a brief memo to the president of Argentina Company, explain the postings to the control and subsidiary accounts.

EC–5 Maureen Company uses both special journals and a general journal. On June 30, after all monthly postings had been completed, the Accounts Receivable controlling account in the general ledger had a debit balance of $320,000, and the Accounts Payable controlling account had a credit balance of $87,000.

The July transactions recorded in the special journals are summarized below. Maureen Company maintains a perpetual inventory system. No entries that affected accounts receivable and accounts payable were recorded in the general journal for July.

Sales journal: total sales, $161,400; cost of goods sold, $112,800
Purchases journal: total purchases, $56,400
Cash receipts journal: accounts receivable column total, $141,000
Cash payments journal: accounts payable column total, $47,500

Instructions

(a) What is the balance of the Accounts Receivable control account after the monthly postings on July 31?
(b) What is the balance of the Accounts Payable control account after the monthly postings on July 31?
(c) To what accounts are the column totals for total sales of $161,400 and cost of goods sold of $112,800 in the sales journal posted?
(d) To what account(s) is the accounts receivable column total of $141,000 in the cash receipts journal posted?

EC–6 On September 1, the balance of the Accounts Receivable control account in the general ledger of Pirie Company was $11,960. The customers' subsidiary ledger contained account balances as follows: Jana, $2,440; Kingston, $2,640; Cavanaugh, $2,060; Bickford, $4,820. At the end of September, the various journals contained the following information:

Sales journal: Sales to Bickford, $800; to Jana, $1,260; to Iman, $1,030; to Cavanaugh, $1,100. The cost of each sale, respectively, was $480, $810, $620, and $660.
Cash receipts journal: Cash received from Cavanaugh, $1,310; from Bickford, $2,300; from Iman, $380; from Kingston, $1,800; from Jana, $1,240.
General journal: A $190 sales allowance is granted to Bickford, on September 30.

Instructions

(a) Set up control and subsidiary accounts, and enter the beginning balances.

(b) Post the various journals to the control and subsidiary accounts. Post the items as individual items or as totals, whichever would be the appropriate procedure. Use page 1 for each journal.

(c) Prepare a list of customers and prove the agreement of the control account with the subsidiary ledger at September 30.

Record transactions in sales and purchases journals—periodic inventory system.

EC–7 Refer to the information provided for Sing Tao Company in EC–2. Complete instructions (a), (b), and (c), assuming that the company uses a periodic inventory system instead of a perpetual inventory system.

Record transactions in cash receipts, cash payments, and general journals—periodic inventory system.

EC–8 Refer to the information provided for Sing Tao Company in EC–3. Complete instructions (a) to (d), assuming that the company uses a periodic inventory system instead of a perpetual inventory system.

Problems

Record transactions in special and general journals—perpetual inventory system.

PC–1 Selected accounts from the chart of accounts of Genstar Company are shown below:

101	Cash	201	Accounts payable
112	Accounts receivable	401	Sales
120	Merchandise inventory	412	Sales returns and allowances
126	Supplies	505	Cost of goods sold
157	Equipment	726	Salaries expense

The company uses a perpetual inventory system. The cost of all merchandise sold is 60% of the sales price. During January, Genstar completed the following transactions:

Jan. 3 Purchased merchandise on account from Sun Distributors, $19,800.
      4 Purchased supplies for cash, $280.
      4 Sold merchandise on account to R. Gilbertson, $6,500, invoice no. 371.
      5 Issued a debit memorandum to Sun Distributors and returned $450 of damaged goods.
      6 Made cash sales for the week totalling $4,650.
      8 Purchased merchandise on account from Irvine Co., $5,400.
      9 Sold merchandise on account to Mays Corp., $5,600, invoice no. 372.
     11 Purchased merchandise on account from Chaparal Co., $4,300.
     13 Paid Sun Distributors account in full.
     13 Made cash sales for the week totalling $2,290.
     15 Received payment from Mays Corp. for invoice no. 372.
     15 Paid semi-monthly salaries of $14,300 to employees.
     17 Received payment from R. Gilbertson for invoice no. 371.
     17 Sold merchandise on account to AMB Co., $1,500, invoice no. 373.
     19 Purchased equipment on account from Johnson Corp., $4,800.
     20 Cash sales for the week totalled $3,400.
     20 Paid Irvine Co. account in full.
     23 Purchased merchandise on account from Sun Distributors, $7,800.
     24 Purchased merchandise on account from Levine Corp., $4,690.
     27 Made cash sales for the week totalling $3,370.
     30 Received payment from AMB Co. for invoice no. 373.
     31 Paid semi-monthly salaries of $13,200 to employees.
     31 Sold merchandise on account to R. Gilbertson, $9,330, invoice no. 374.

Genstar Company uses a sales journal, a purchases journal, a cash receipts journal, a cash payments journal, and a general journal.

Instructions

(a) Record the January transactions in the appropriate journal.
(b) Foot and cross-foot all special journals.
(c) Show how postings would be made by placing ledger account numbers and check marks as needed in the journals. (Actual posting to ledger accounts is not required.)

PC–2 Selected accounts from the chart of accounts of Tigau Company are shown below:

Record transactions in special and general journals— perpetual inventory system.

101	Cash	145	Buildings
112	Accounts receivable	201	Accounts payable
120	Merchandise inventory	401	Sales
126	Supplies	505	Cost of goods sold
140	Land	610	Advertising expense

The company uses a perpetual inventory system. The cost of all merchandise sold was 65% of the sales price. During October, Tigau Company completed the following transactions:

Oct. 2 Purchased merchandise on account from Madison Co., $15,800.

 4 Sold merchandise on account to Petro Corp., $8,600, invoice no. 204.

 5 Purchased supplies for cash, $315.

 7 Made cash sales for the week that totalled $9,610.

 9 Paid the Madison Co. account in full.

 10 Purchased merchandise on account from Quinn Corp., $4,900.

 12 Received payment from Petro Corp. for invoice no. 204.

 13 Issued a debit memorandum to Quinn Corp. and returned $260 of damaged goods.

 14 Made cash sales for the week that totalled $8,810.

 16 Sold a parcel of land for $25,000 cash, the land's book value.

 17 Sold merchandise on account to Callebaut Co., $5,530, invoice no. 205.

 18 Purchased merchandise for cash, $2,215.

 21 Made cash sales for the week that totalled $8,640.

 23 Paid in full the Quinn Corp. account for the goods kept.

 25 Purchased supplies on account from Frey Co., $260.

 25 Sold merchandise on account to Golden Corp., $5,520, invoice no. 206.

 25 Received payment from Callebaut Co. for invoice no. 205.

 26 Purchased for cash a small parcel of land and a building on the land to use as a storage facility. The total cost of $35,000 was allocated $16,000 to the land and $19,000 to the building.

 27 Purchased merchandise on account from Schmid Co., $9,000.

 28 Made cash sales for the week that totalled $9,320.

 30 Purchased merchandise on account from Madison Co., $16,200.

 30 Paid advertising bill for the month from The Gazette, $600.

 30 Sold merchandise on account to Callebaut Co., $5,200, invoice no. 207.

Tigau Company uses a sales journal, purchases journal, cash receipts journal, cash payments journal, and general journal.

Instructions

(a) Record the October transactions in the appropriate journals.
(b) Foot and cross-foot all special journals.
(c) Show how postings would be made by placing ledger account numbers and check marks as needed in the journals. (Actual posting to ledger accounts is not required.)

Record transactions in special and general journals— perpetual inventory system.

PC–3 The post-closing trial balance for Gibbs Music Co. follows:

GIBBS MUSIC CO.
Post-Closing Trial Balance
December 31, 2007

	Debit	Credit
101 Cash	$ 49,500	
112 Accounts receivable	15,000	
115 Notes receivable	45,000	
120 Merchandise inventory	22,000	
140 Land	25,000	
145 Building	75,000	
146 Accumulated amortization—building		$ 18,000
157 Equipment	6,450	
158 Accumulated amortization—equipment		1,500
200 Notes payable		–
201 Accounts payable		42,000
275 Mortgage payable		82,000
301 M. Gibbs, capital		94,450
310 M. Gibbs, drawings	–	
401 Sales	–	
410 Sales returns and allowances	–	
505 Cost of goods sold	–	
725 Salaries expense	–	
920 Loss—damaged inventory	–	
	$237,950	$237,950

The subsidiary ledgers contain the following information:

1. Accounts Receivable—R. Christof, $3,000; B. Hibberd, $7,500; S. Armstrong, $4,500
2. Accounts Payable—Fieldstone Corp., $9,000; Watson & Co., $17,000; Harms Distributors, $16,000

Gibbs Music Co. uses a perpetual inventory system. The transactions for January 2008 are as follows:

Jan. 3 Sold merchandise to B. Rohl, $1,000. The cost of goods sold was $550.
    5 Purchased merchandise from Warren Parts, $2,400.
    7 Received a cheque from S. Armstrong, $3,000, in partial payment of its account.
    11 Paid freight on merchandise purchased, $350.
    13 Received payment of account in full from B. Rohl.
    14 Issued a credit memo to acknowledge receipt of $600 of damaged merchandise returned by R. Christof. The cost of the returned merchandise was $250. (*Hint*: Debit Loss—Damaged Inventory instead of Merchandise Inventory.)
    15 Sent Harms Distributors a cheque in full payment of account.
    17 Purchased merchandise from Lapeska Co., $1,900.
    18 Paid salaries of $3,700.
    20 Gave Watson & Co. a 60-day note for $17,000 in full payment of account payable.
    23 Total cash sales amounted to $8,200. The cost of goods sold was $3,840.
    24 Sold merchandise on account to B. Hibberd, $7,800. The cost of goods sold was $3,300.
    27 Sent Warren Parts a cheque for $950 in partial payment of the account.
    29 Received payment on a note of $35,000 from S. Lava.
    30 Returned merchandise costing $600 to Lapeska Co. for credit.
    31 Withdrew $800 cash for personal use.

Instructions

(a) Open general and subsidiary ledger accounts and record December 31, 2007, balances.

(b) Record the January transactions in a sales journal, a purchases journal, a cash receipts journal, a cash payments journal, and a general journal, as illustrated in this appendix.

(c) Post the appropriate amounts to the subsidiary and general ledger accounts.

(d) Prepare a trial balance at January 31, 2008.

(e) Determine whether the subsidiary ledgers agree with control accounts in the general ledger.

PC–4   The post-closing trial balance for Scholz Co. follows:

Record transactions in special and general journals, post, and prepare trial balance— perpetual inventory system.

SCHOLZ CO.
Post-Closing Trial Balance
April 30, 2008

		Debit	Credit
101	Cash	$ 36,700	
112	Accounts receivable	15,400	
115	Notes receivable—Cole Company	48,000	
120	Merchandise inventory	22,000	
157	Equipment	8,200	
158	Accumulated amortization—equipment		$ 1,800
200	Notes payable	–	
201	Accounts payable		43,400
301	C. Scholz, capital		85,100
310	C. Scholz, drawings	–	
401	Sales		–
410	Sales returns and allowances	–	
505	Cost of goods sold	–	
725	Salaries expense	–	
730	Rent expense	–	
		$130,300	$130,300

The subsidiary ledgers contain the following information:

1. Accounts Receivable—W. Karasch, $3,250; L. Cellars, $7,400; G. Parrish, $4,750
2. Accounts Payable—Winterware Corp., $10,500; Elite Sports, $15,500; Buttercup Distributors, $17,400

Scholz uses a perpetual inventory system. The transactions for May 2008 are as follows:

May   3 Sold merchandise to B. Simone, $2,400. The cost of the goods sold was $1,050.
     5 Purchased merchandise from WN Widgit, $2,600, on account.
     7 Received a cheque from G. Parrish, $2,800, in partial payment of account.
    11 Paid freight on merchandise purchased, $318.
    12 Paid rent of $1,500 for May.
    13 Received payment in full from B. Simone.
    14 Issued a credit memo to acknowledge $750 of merchandise returned by W. Karasch. The merchandise (original cost, $325) was restored to inventory.
    15 Sent Buttercup Distributors a cheque in full payment of account.
    17 Purchased merchandise from Lancio Co., $2,100, on account.
    18 Paid salaries of $4,700.
    20 Gave Elite Sports a two-month, 10% note for $15,500 in full payment of account payable.
    20 Returned merchandise costing $510 to Lancio for credit.
    23 Total cash sales amounted to $9,500. The cost of goods sold was $4,450.
    27 Sent WN Widgit a cheque for $1,000, in partial payment of account.
    29 Received payment on a note of $40,000 from Cole Company.
    31 Withdrew $1,000 cash for personal use.

Instructions

(a) Open general and subsidiary ledger accounts and record April 30, 2008, balances.
(b) Record the May transactions in a sales journal, a purchases journal, a cash receipts journal, a cash payments journal, and a general journal, as illustrated in this chapter.
(c) Post the appropriate amounts to the subsidiary and general ledger accounts.
(d) Prepare a trial balance at May 31, 2008.
(e) Determine whether the subsidiary ledgers agree with the control accounts in the general ledger.

Record transactions in special and general journals—periodic inventory system.

PC–5 Selected accounts from the chart of accounts on Weir Company are shown below:

101	Cash	401	Sales
112	Accounts receivable	412	Sales returns and allowances
126	Supplies	510	Purchases
157	Equipment	512	Purchase returns and allowances
201	Accounts payable	726	Salaries expense

During February, Weir completed the following transactions:

Feb. 3 Purchased merchandise on account from Zears Co., $9,200.
       4 Purchased supplies for cash, $290.
       4 Sold merchandise on account to Gilles Co., $7,220, invoice no. 371.
       5 Issued a debit memorandum to Zears Co. and returned $450 worth of goods.
       6 Made cash sales for the week totalling $3,950.
       8 Purchased merchandise on account from Fell Electronics, $5,200,
       9 Sold merchandise on account to Mawani Corp., $7,050, invoice no. 372.
      11 Purchased merchandise on account from Thomas Co., $3,100.
      13 Paid Zears Co. account in full.
      13 Made cash sales for the week totalling $4,850.
      15 Received payment from Mawani Corp. for invoice no. 372.
      15 Paid semi-monthly salaries of $14,700 to employees.
      17 Received payment from Gilles Co. for invoice no. 371.
      17 Sold merchandise on account to Lumber Co., $1,600, invoice no. 373.
      19 Purchased equipment on account from Brown Corp., $6,400.
      20 Cash sales for the week totalled $4,900.
      20 Paid Fell Electronics account in full.
      23 Purchased merchandise on account from Zears Co., $8,800.
      24 Purchased merchandise on account from Lewis Co., $5,130.
      27 Made cash sales for the week totalling $3,560.
      28 Received payment from Lumber Co. for invoice no. 373.
      28 Paid semi-monthly salaries of $14,900 to employees.
      28 Sold merchandise on account to Gilles Co., $9,810, invoice no. 374.

Weir Company uses a sales journal, purchases journal, cash receipts journal, cash payments journal, and general journal. Weir uses a periodic inventory system.

Instructions

(a) Record the February transactions in the appropriate journal.
(b) Foot and cross-foot all special journals.
(c) Show how postings would be made by placing ledger account numbers and check marks as needed in the journals. (Actual posting to ledger accounts is not required.)

Cumulative Coverage—
Chapters 2 to 6 and Appendix C

Kassam Company has the following opening account balances in its general and subsidiary ledgers on January 1. All accounts have normal debit and credit balances. Kassam uses a perpetual inventory system. The cost of all merchandise sold was 40% of the sales price.

GENERAL LEDGER

Account No.	Account Title	January 1 Opening Balance
101	Cash	$ 35,050
112	Accounts receivable	14,000
115	Notes receivable	39,000
120	Merchandise inventory	20,000
125	Office supplies	1,000
130	Prepaid insurance	2,000
140	Land	50,000
145	Building	100,000
146	Accumulated amortization—building	25,000
157	Equipment	6,450
158	Accumulated amortization—equipment	1,500
201	Accounts payable	36,000
275	Mortgage payable	125,000
301	A. Kassam, capital	80,000

Accounts Receivable Subsidiary Ledger		Accounts Payable Subsidiary Ledger	
Customer	January 1 Opening Balance	Creditor	January 1 Opening Balance
R. Draves	$1,500	Liazuk Co.	$10,000
B. Jacovetti	7,500	Mikush Bros.	15,000
S. Kysely	5,000	Nguyen & Son	11,000

Kassam's January transactions follow:

Jan. 3 Sold merchandise on credit to B. Sota $3,100, invoice no. 510, and J. Ebel $1,800, invoice no. 511.

5 Purchased merchandise on account from Welz Wares for $3,000 and Laux Supplies for $2,700.

7 Received cheques for $5,000 from S. Kysely and $2,000 from B. Jacovetti on accounts.

8 Paid freight on merchandise purchased, $180.

9 Sent cheques to Liazuk Co. for $10,000 and Nguyen & Son for $11,000 in full payment of accounts.

9 Issued credit memo for $400 to J. Ebel for merchandise returned. The merchandise was restored to inventory.

10 Summary cash sales totalled $16,500.

11 Sold merchandise on credit to R. Draves for $1,900, invoice no. 512, and to S. Kysely for $900, invoice no. 513.

15 Withdrew $2,000 cash for A. Kassam's personal use.

16 Purchased merchandise on account from Nguyen & Son for $15,000, from Liazuk Co. for $13,900, and from Welz Wares for $1,500.

17 Paid $400 cash for office supplies.

18 Returned $500 of merchandise to Liazuk and received credit.

20 Summary cash sales totalled $17,500.

21 Issued $15,000 note to Mikush Bros. in payment of balance due. The note bears an interest rate of 10% and is due in three months.

21 Received payment in full from S. Kysely.

Jan. 22 Sold merchandise on credit to B. Soto for $1,700, invoice no. 514, and to R. Draves for $800, invoice no. 515.

23 Sent cheques to Nguyen & Son and Liazuk Co. in full payment of accounts.

25 Sold merchandise on credit to B. Jacovetti for $3,500, invoice no. 516, and to J. Ebel for $6,100, invoice no. 517.

27 Purchased merchandise on account from Nguyen & Son for $14,500, from Laux Supplies for $1,200, and from Welz Wares for $2,800.

28 Paid $800 cash for office supplies.

31 Summary cash sales totalled $19,920.

31 Paid sales salaries of $4,300 and office salaries of $2,600.

31 Received payment in full from B. Soto and J. Ebel on account.

In addition to the accounts identified in the trial balance, the chart of accounts shows the following: No. 200 Notes Payable, No. 230 Interest Payable, No. 300 Income Summary, No. 310 A. Kassam, Drawings, No. 401 Sales, No. 410 Sales Returns and Allowances, No. 505 Cost of Goods Sold, No. 711 Amortization Expense, No. 718 Interest Expense, No. 722 Insurance Expense, No. 725 Salaries Expense, and No. 728 Office Supplies Expense.

Instructions

(a) Record the January transactions in the appropriate journal—sales, purchases, cash receipts, cash payments, and general.

(b) Post the journals to the general and subsidiary ledgers. New accounts should be added and numbered in an orderly fashion as needed.

(c) Prepare an unadjusted trial balance at January 31, 2008. Determine whether the subsidiary ledgers agree with the control accounts in the general ledger.

(d) Prepare adjusting journal entries. Prepare an adjusted trial balance, using the following additional information:

1. Office supplies at January 31 total $700.
2. Insurance coverage expires on September 30, 2008.
3. Annual amortization on the building is $6,000 and on the equipment is $1,500.
4. Interest of $45 has accrued on the note payable.
5. A physical count of merchandise inventory has found $44,850 of goods on hand.

(e) Prepare a multiple-step income statement and a statement of owner's equity for January, and a classified balance sheet at the end of January.

(f) Prepare and post the closing entries.

(g) Prepare a post-closing trial balance.

Company Index

Subject Index

A cumulative index appears at the end of each Part.